Music

IN THEORY AND PRACTICE

VOLUME II

Music

IN THEORY AND PRACTICE

VOLUME II

Seventh Edition

Bruce Benward
University of Wisconsin–Madison

Marilyn Saker
Eastern Michigan University

Boston   Burr Ridge, IL   Dubuque, IA   Madison, WI   New York   San Francisco   St. Louis
Bangkok   Bogotá   Caracas   Kuala Lumpur   Lisbon   London   Madrid   Mexico City
Milan   Montreal   New Delhi   Santiago   Seoul   Singapore   Sydney   Taipei   Toronto

McGraw-Hill Higher Education

A Division of The **McGraw-Hill** *Companies*

MUSIC IN THEORY AND PRACTICE, VOLUME II

Published by McGraw-Hill, a business unit of The McGraw-Hill Companies, Inc. 1221 Avenue of the Americas, New York, NY, 10020. Copyright © 2003, 1997 by The McGraw-Hill Companies, Inc. All rights reserved. No part of this publication may be reproduced or distributed in any form or by any means, or stored in a database or retrieval system, without the prior written consent of The McGraw-Hill Companies, Inc., including, but not limited to, in any network or other electronic storage or transmission, or broadcast for distance learning. Some ancillaries, including electronic and print components, may not be available to customers outside the United States.

This book is printed on acid-free paper.

1 2 3 4 5 6 7 8 9 0 QPD/QPD 0 9 8 7 6 5 4 3

ISBN 0-07-294261-4

Publisher: *Christopher Freitag*
Developmental editor: *Nadia Bidwell*
Senior marketing manager: *David Patterson*
Project manager: *Rebecca Nordbrock*
Production supervisor: *Susanne Riedell*
Producer, Media technology *Todd Vaccaro*
Freelance design coordinator: *Gino Cieslik*
Lead supplement producer: *Marc Mattson*
Cover design: *Jennifer McQueen*
Cover illustrator: *Wendy Grossman*
Interior design: *Karen Lafond*
Typeface: *10/12 Times Roman*
Compositor: *UG / GGS Information Services, Inc.*
Printer: *Quebecor World Dubuque Inc.*

Library of Congress Cataloging-in-Publication Data

Benward, Bruce.
   Music in theory and practice / Bruce Benward, Marilyn Saker.--7th ed.
      p. cm.
   ISBN 0-07-294262-2 (v. 1)--ISBN 0-07-294261-4 (v. II)
      1. Music theory.   I. Saker, Marilyn Nadine.   II. Title.

MT6.B34 M9 2002
781--dc21

                                                          2001032967

www.mhhe.com

Contents

Contents

Preface

To the Student

Volume 1 of *Music in Theory and Practice* was a general introduction to music theory. You spent time mastering the details of music syntax and discovering how small patterns such as scales, intervals, and triads combine to create larger units—phrases, periods, two-part form, and three-part form. This volume focuses on musical styles from the Renaissance to the present. It includes more complex chords, an emphasis on larger forms, and strategies to help you analyze the compositions you perform.

The goal of this volume is the practical application of information. The analytical techniques presented here are carefully designed to be clear, uncomplicated, and readily applicable to the repertoire you will develop during your career as a musician. The thorough understanding of the musical structure of a composition that you gain through analysis considerably reduces the time required for preparing a performance of that work.

To the Instructor

This seventh edition of *Music in Theory and Practice,* Volume 2, contains the following improvements:

1. The workbook for this edition of *Music in Theory and Practice* now includes a CD-ROM containing the *Finale Workbook*™ tool. This software tool produced in conjunction with Coda Music Technology is based on the *Finale*™ notation software and is compatible with both Windows and Macintosh computers. The *Finale Workbook*™ permits students to complete assignments while introducing them to the use of current music notation technology. Assignments can be printed, e-mailed, or posted to the Web. Self-contained and easy to use, the *Finale Workbook*™ is a valuable addition to the 7th Edition.
2. Also new to this edition of the text is the support of a website. Online resources include assignment templates for the *Finale Workbook*™, music fundamental review exercises, and additional recordings. The website can be found at www.mhhe.com/mtp7.
3. Recordings of several assignment scores have been included on the CD which accompanies this book. Instructors and students may find this set of recordings useful, not only for individual study, but also for classroom presentations and discussions. Recorded musical examples are identified throughout the text by the following graphic:

4. Every effort has been made to thoroughly edit and update this edition. The outline format has been maintained throughout the volume to ensure efficient presentation of topics, while the chapter organization makes it possible for topics to be studied in the order preferred by the instructor.
5. Many assignments have been reformatted to better accommodate student work. Assignments requiring music notation include larger-sized staves, and analysis assignments are accompanied by a more generous between-staff spacing. These changes have been made to simplify the process of completing assignments on the text pages.

The seventh edition is part of a carefully integrated package. An instructor's manual, a workbook/anthology, and a solutions manual also accompany the text.

1. The instructor's manual offers helpful suggestions for class presentations and contains answers to objective assignments in the text.
2. The workbook/anthology provides a convenient source for assignments that can be handed in for correction, as well as a representative collection of scores for analysis, making a separate anthology unnecessary.
3. The solutions manual gives suggested answers to the problems in the workbook/anthology.

Acknowledgments

The authors would like to gratefully acknowledge the following professors and reviewers, whose suggestions for the seventh edition were extremely helpful: Larry Arnold, University of North Carolina at Pembroke; Karel A. Lidral, University of Maine–Orono; Chinny Ohia, Morgan State University; David Patterson, University of Massachusetts–Boston; Jane Pyle, Miami Dade Community College; Daniel Sommerville, Wheaton College; D. Charles Truitt, Marywood University. The authors would also like to thank the many respondents who completed the *Evaluation Request* questionnaire distributed with the sixth edition of *Music in Theory and Practice*. The suggestions and comments were invaluable to the authors and deeply appreciated.

Bruce Benward
Marilyn Saker

Music

IN THEORY AND PRACTICE

VOLUME II

The Renaissance and Baroque Periods

**Renaissance
Period
(1450–1600)**

The term *Renaissance* refers to the era of the flowering of the arts and literature that followed the Middle Ages. The overriding function of music in the Renaissance period was to contribute to worship. Although greatly overshadowed by the sacred music of the period, secular works did exist and were an important part of the literature at that time.

Vocal music was far more common than instrumental music during the Renaissance. Choruses came into being shortly before the beginning of the Renaissance but did not reach full flower until well into the era. Choruses of the time were usually small groups of perhaps 12 to 15 singers. The choral group was often divided into four parts—the familiar soprano, alto, tenor, and bass. Late Renaissance music often required a fifth part, either a second soprano or a second tenor, and works for 6, 8, and even 16-part choruses were not unusual. Choruses were frequently accompanied by instrumental groups that usually doubled the voice parts. In chapels, however, the groups sang *a cappella,* or unaccompanied.

As an introduction to the music of the late Renaissance, we will study two- and three-part vocal polyphony, concentrating our attention on the works of Orlande de Lassus, Josquin Desprez, Giovanni Pierluigi da Palestrina, and Tomás Luis de Victoria.

**Baroque Period
(1600–1750)**

The *baroque* was a period of great change. Baroque composers enabled the words of sung texts to be more easily heard. They preferred new tonality systems to the modality of the Renaissance. Instrumental music began to assume more importance than vocal music for the first time in history. Improvisation of music was a common practice, particularly in the performance of accompaniments and in the performance of opera singers, who were expected to improvise embellishments at certain points in their arias. Much of the music of the baroque included a figured bass that served as a basis for improvising accompaniments.

We will examine instrumental works of the baroque period in contrapuntal texture, principally the two-part inventions and fugues of J. S. Bach.

CHAPTER 1

Late Renaissance Polyphony

Topics

Modes	Unaccented passing tone	Consonant 4th
Dorian mode	Accented passing tone	Hocket
Phrygian mode	Lower neighboring tone	Clausula vera
Lydian mode	Suspensions	Plagal cadence
Mixolydian mode	Portamento	Weak interior cadences
Ionian mode	Nota cambiata	Text setting
Aeolian mode	Six-five figure	Agogic accent
Musica ficta		Imitation

Important Concepts

Late Renaissance polyphony refers to music from approximately 1550 to 1600. The polyphony of this period is perhaps the purest ever written because it is not influenced by the functional harmony of later periods.

Modes

Sixteenth-century music is essentially modal. The following *modes* were in common use:

Mode	White Keys of Piano Beginning on
Dorian	D
Phrygian	E
Lydian	F
Mixolydian	G

The *ionian* (major scale) and *aeolian* (natural minor scale) modes were used occasionally.

Musica Ficta

Altered tones were frequently added to the pure modes. This practice became known as *musica ficta*. *Musica ficta* accidentals were not written in the original manuscripts but were sung by the performers according to performance practices of the period. In modern editions the *musica ficta* accidentals are often indicated above the staves. The melodic tritone between F and B was avoided by lowering the B to B-flat (figure 1.1).

Figure 1.1

Lassus: *Beatus homo* (Happy is the man), mm. 24–26.

Tritone avoided by *musica ficta*

ne - go - ti - a - ti - o - ne ar - gen - -

In the dorian and mixolydian modes a "leading tone" was created at cadences by raising the seventh scale degree. The phrygian and lydian modes required no alteration at cadence points (figure 1.2).

Figure 1.2

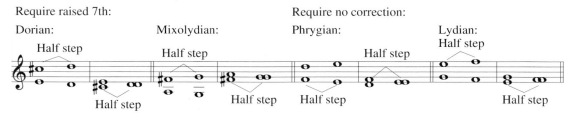

Require raised 7th:

Dorian: Mixolydian:

Require no correction:

Phrygian: Lydian:

Transposed Modes

The modes were often transposed a perfect fifth lower, creating a key signature of one flat (figure 1.3).

Figure 1.3

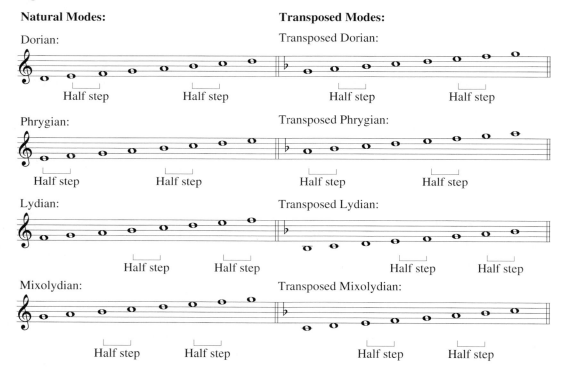

Natural Modes:

Dorian:

Phrygian:

Lydian:

Mixolydian:

Transposed Modes:

Transposed Dorian:

Transposed Phrygian:

Transposed Lydian:

Transposed Mixolydian:

Consonance

In late Renaissance polyphony vertical structures were organized according to the consonant intervals above the lowest-sounding tone (figure 1.4).

Figure 1.4

Consonant intervals in sixteenth-century style

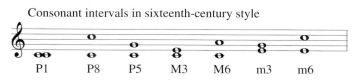

P1   P8   P5   M3   M6   m3   m6

The lowest-sounding tone may not always be the lowest voice in the score, because voice crossing was quite common (figure 1.5).

Figure 1.5

Palestrina: *Missa Inviolata,* Credo, mm. 14–15.

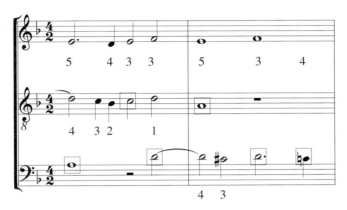

☐ = Lowest-sounding tone

The numbers between the staves in figure 1.5 refer to the interval above the lowest-sounding tone. This method of analysis is employed throughout this chapter.

The concept of tonal harmony was unknown during the Renaissance period. Composers thought only in terms of consonances and dissonances.

Dissonance

Vertical dissonance was treated with considerable care. The dissonant intervals are P4, M2, m2, M7, m7, and all diminished and augmented intervals.

Dissonance Types in Two-Voice Writing

Passing tones, lower neighboring tones, suspensions, portamentos, and cambiatas are the only dissonances found in two-voice writing.

Unaccented Passing Tone

Unaccented passing tones in half notes are found on beats 2 and 4 in $\frac{4}{2}$ meter, in quarter notes on the second half of any beat, and in eighth notes in unstressed locations. Unaccented passing tones are used in ascending and descending directions (figure 1.6).

Figure 1.6

Josquin Desprez: *Missa l'homme armé super voces musicales* (Mass based on The Armed Man), Benedictus, mm. 26–27.

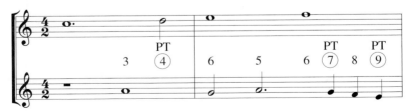

Accented Passing Tone

Accented passing tones in quarter notes occur only on beats 2 and 4 in $\frac{4}{2}$ meter and only in a descending direction. No other accented passing tones were allowed (figure 1.7).

Figure 1.7

Lower Neighboring Tone

Lower neighboring tones occur in quarter notes in unstressed locations (figure 1.8).

Figure 1.8

Josquin Desprez: *Missa Da pacem,* Credo, mm. 9–10.

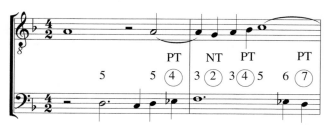

Suspensions

In two-voice writing, the only suspensions available are 7–6 and 2–3. The suspension occurs on beats 1 or 3 in $\frac{4}{2}$ meter and the resolutions on beats 2 or 4 (figure 1.9).

Figure 1.9

Lassus: *Beatus vir in sapientia* (Blessed is the man), mm. 23–24.

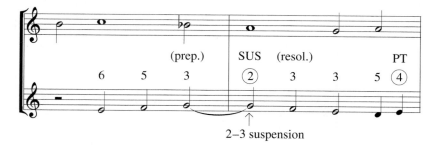

Decorated suspensions are common. The decorations usually consist of a *portamento* (discussed below) or with double eighth notes where the second eighth note is a lower neighboring tone (figure 1.10).

Figure 1.10

Lassus: *Serve bone* (Well done), mm. 5–6.

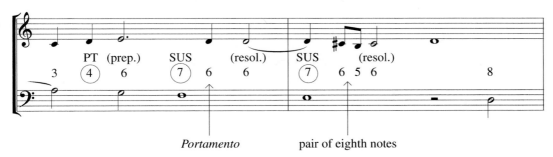

Portamento

The *portamento* is a common device of the late Renaissance that resembles the anticipation found in later periods. The *portamento* figure consists of three notes—often a dotted half note (or a half note tied to a quarter note), a quarter note, and a half or quarter note. The *portamento* tone is the second of the three (figure 1.11).

Figure 1.11

Portamento figure as suspension decoration:

Dissonant *portamento*:

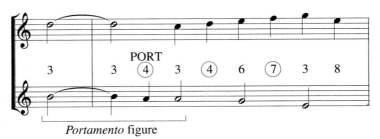

Nota Cambiata

A forerunner of the eighteenth-century changing tones, the *nota cambiata* is a four-note melodic figure. The second note of the four is the *nota cambiata* itself. The first and third notes are always consonant with the lowest-sounding tone, whereas the second and fourth may or may not be dissonant (figure 1.12).

Figure 1.12

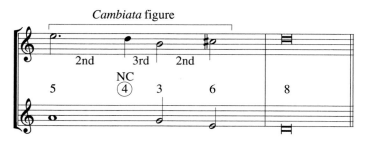

Dissonance Types in Three or More Voices

Suspensions

In polyphony with three or more voices, the 9–8 (2–1) and 4–3 suspensions occur, as well as the 7–6 and 2–3 suspensions described on page 6 (figure 1.13).

Figure 1.13

Palestrina: *Missa Inviolata,* Credo, mm. 20–21.

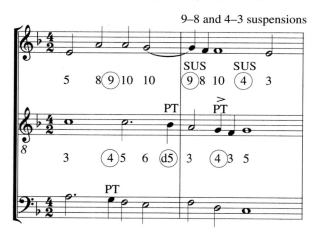

The Six–Five Figure

Occasionally one voice will sing a 5th above the lowest-sounding tone at the same time that another voice sings a 6th. Although both of these intervals are consonances, there is a dissonance between them that requires resolution. The 5th resolves downward as a suspension, whereas the lowest-sounding voice moves upward, creating a 3rd (figure 1.14).

Figure 1.14

Palestrina: *Missa Jam Christus astra ascenderat*, Credo, m. 24.

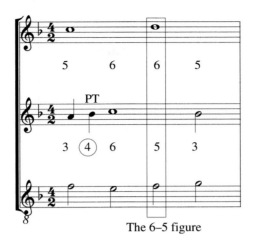

The 6–5 figure

The Consonant 4th

The 4th is normally considered to be a dissonance, but at cadence points a figure similar to the cadential six-four chord in tonal music sometimes occurs. The 4th in this case is considered to be consonant (figure 1.15).

Figure 1.15

Victoria: *Magnificat Septimi Toni: De posuit potentes,* mm. 11–12.

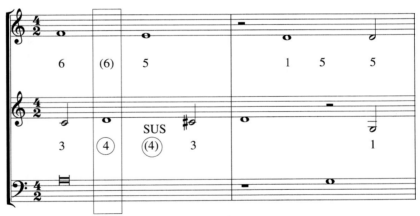

The consonant 4th

Melody

The melodic lines in sixteenth-century choral music have the following characteristics:

1. Melodic movement is predominantly stepwise.
2. Although skips occur, the following intervals are avoided:

   Ascending M6ths

   All descending 6ths

   All 7ths

   All diminished and augmented intervals

   Skips greater than an octave

3. Triads are sometimes outlined in the melody.

4. Two or more successive skips in the same direction (other than skips that outline a triad) are rare.

5. A skip greater than a 3rd is preceded and followed by an interval that is in the opposite direction to the skip and most often stepwise. For example, the approach to, and departure from, an ascending skip is by a descending interval (usually a step) (figure 1.16).

Figure 1.16

6. Melodic sequences, so common in the eighteenth century, are infrequent in this style.

Rhythm and Meter

The two common meters in late Renaissance polyphony were quadruple meter and triple meter. This chapter deals only with quadruple meter. The rhythms in quadruple meter were limited to the following note values:

Breve (double whole note)

Half note

Dotted half note

Eighth note (used sparingly and in pairs)

Whole note

Dotted whole note

Quarter note

1. Note values were tied only to a succeeding note of equal or next shorter value (figure 1.17).

Figure 1.17

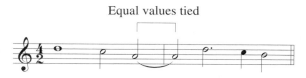

2. Quarter rests were not used at all, and half rests are found only on beats 1 and 3 (figure 1.18).

Figure 1.18

Unstylistic   Unstylistic

Quarter rests not found   Half rest on beats 1 and 3 only

3. Eighth notes occur only on the second half of a beat and always in pairs (figure 1.19).

Figure 1.19

Unstylistic

Eighth notes not found on
accented portion of the beat

4. Compositions generally begin with a note of at least dotted half-note value. More often the beginning note is a whole note or breve.
5. The final note is at least a whole-note value and most often a breve.
6. There was considerable rhythmic variety in late Renaissance polyphony. Two simultaneous voices never have the same rhythm and rhythmic figures were not repeated in successive measures (figure 1.20).

Figure 1.20

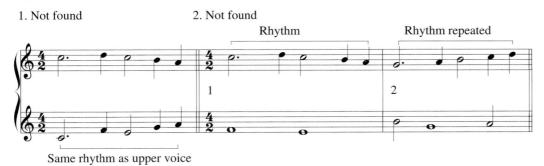

1. Not found   2. Not found

Rhythm   Rhythm repeated

1   2

Same rhythm as upper voice

7. To keep the rhythmic flow from being interrupted at interior cadence points, one voice usually rests and then begins the next phrase immediately. This staggering of rests is referred to as *hocket* (figure 1.21).

Figure 1.21

Lassus: *Beatus homo* (Happy is the man), mm. 23–24.

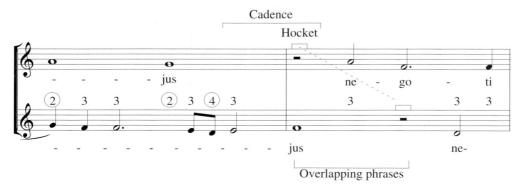

8. Original manuscripts of the period did not contain bar lines. However, for the sake of twentieth-century musicians, most modern editions include bar lines.
9. The rhythms in individual voices sometimes suggest meters other than the meter signature. Most modern editions place the bar lines according to the prevailing meter, regardless of the meter suggested in individual voices, to avoid notational complexity (figure 1.22).

Figure 1.22

Cadences
Clausula Vera

Most final cadences in two-voice writing are of the *clausula vera* type, in which the two voices approach an octave or a unison through stepwise motion (figure 1.23).

Figure 1.23

Lassus: *Beatus homo* (Happy is the man), mm. 34–35.

In three-voice writing the third voice often adds falling 5th motion to the *clausula vera*, creating a cadence similar to the authentic cadence in tonal music (figure 1.24).

Figure 1.24

Palestrina: *Magnificat Secundi Toni: De posuit potentes,* mm. 27–28.

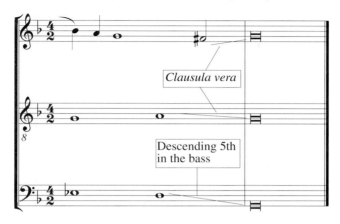

Plagal Cadence

A *plagal cadence* is occasionally found at interior cadence points. In a two-voice plagal cadence the lower voice moves up a P5th or down a P4th (figure 1.25).

Figure 1.25

Plagal cadences:

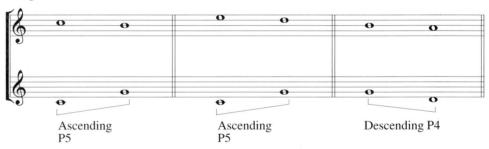

Weak Interior Cadences

Pauses often occur in individual melodic lines in compositions of this period. These momentary breaks in rhythmic activity sometimes have the effect of cadences (figure 1.26).

Figure 1.26

Lassus: *Qui vult venir post me* (He who would follow me . . .), mm. 3–5.

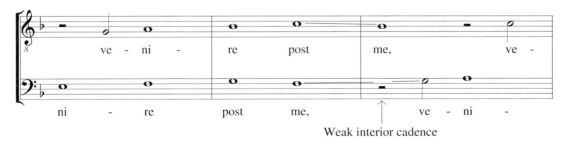

Parallel Motion

As in eighteenth-century style, parallel P8ths, P5ths, and P1s were prohibited during this period (figure 1.27).

Figure 1.27

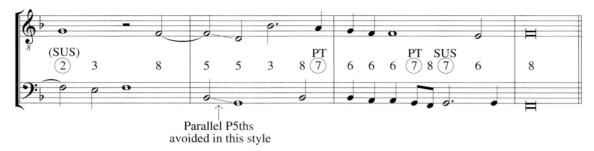

Parallel P5ths
avoided in this style

Parallel M3rds, m3rds, M6ths, and m6th intervals were common, though these were usually limited to four or five notes in succession (figure 1.28).

Figure 1.28

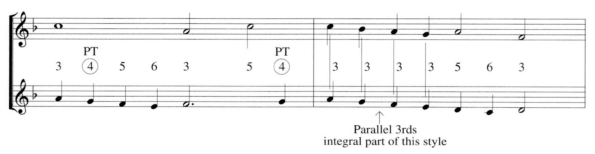

Parallel 3rds
integral part of this style

Text Setting

In late Renaissance polyphony there were a number of conventions for the setting of texts, including the following:

1. Syllables are assigned only to half-note (or larger) values. A single quarter note may carry a syllable only when preceded by a dotted half note and followed by a half or whole note.
2. After a series of quarter notes, a syllable is not changed until after a white note value occurs (figure 1.29).

Figure 1.29

Palestrina: *Alleluja tulerunt* (Hallelujah, they had borne), mm. 1–3.

1st white note   2nd white note

Al   -   le   -   lu   -   -   -   ja

Syllable changes on 2nd white note

3. The rhythms follow the accents of the words quite closely. Accented syllables are often given *agogic* (durational) stress (figure 1.30).

Figure 1.30

Palestrina: *Alleluja tulerunt* (Hallelujah, they had borne), mm. 1–3.

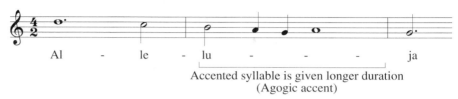

Accented syllable is given longer duration
(Agogic accent)

Form

Late Renaissance vocal compositions have a formal design that parallels the text.

1. Each phrase of text is considered a section and is set musically so that a cadence or at least a pause will occur at the end of the line.
2. Each section of music begins with imitation that is usually abandoned before the end of the section.
3. After each interior cadence a new imitation begins.

History

The four composers—Josquin Desprez (ca.1440–1521), Giovanni Pierluigi da Palestrina (ca. 1525–1594), Orlande Lassus (ca. 1530–1594), and Tomás Luis de Victoria (1548–1611)—whose music is presented in the examples in this chapter are the best-known composers of sacred music in the Renaissance. The works of these composers are remarkable for their stylistic consistency and musical value. They continue to appear in concerts of choral music today.

Josquin Desprez (ca. 1440–1521)

Josquin Desprez was born in the north of France, performed as a singer in the papal chapel choir in Rome, and returned to France to serve in the court of Louis XII. He perfected the technique of pervasive imitation (imitation at the beginning of each section) during his stay in Rome. His works were known throughout Europe and influenced many later composers, including Palestrina, Lassus, and Victoria. In addition to sacred music, Josquin composed a number of secular chansons.

Giovanni Pierluigi da Palestrina (ca. 1525–1594)

Born in Palestrina, Italy, Giovanni Pierluigi da Palestrina became the master of the chapel choir in several of Rome's greatest churches. His reputation as a composer of sacred music was so great that he was asked to rewrite the church's plainchant books to bring them in line with the reforms instituted by the Council of Trent. (The Council of Trent required that the text of the Mass always be understandable by a congregation.) In the twentieth century Palestrina's music has been studied extensively. The stylistic norms described in this chapter are based on Knud Jeppesen's monumental work *The Style of Palestrina and the Dissonance.*

Orlande Lassus (ca. 1530–1594)

Orlande Lassus was a Franco-Flemish composer who also learned his craft as a composer in the churches in Rome. Returning to his native Mons (now a part of Belgium), he began publishing works that became known throughout Europe. In 1556 he joined the court of Duke Albrecht V of Bavaria, where he spent the remainder of his life. In addition to sacred music, Lassus composed over four hundred secular works, including madrigals, villanellas, chansons, and lieder.

Tomás Luis de Victoria (1548–1611)   Born in Avila, Spain, where he became a choirboy at the Avila Cathedral, Tomás Luis de Victoria moved to Rome in 1565 and studied composition with Palestrina. Victoria became a priest and returned to Spain as chaplain to Philip II's sister in Madrid, where he spent the remainder of his life. He is considered to be the greatest Spanish composer of the Renaissance. Victoria composed only sacred music, which is known for its dramatic and emotional interpretation of the texts.

Applications

Beatus homo, which is analyzed in figure 1.31, is from a group of two-voiced motets by Orlande Lassus. The text for this motet is taken from Proverbs 3:13–14.

Figure 1.31

Lassus: *Beatus homo* (Happy is the man).

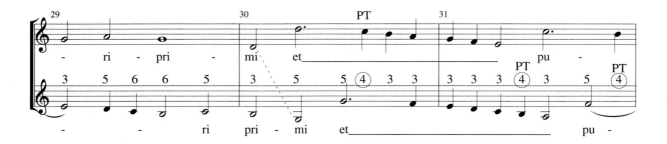

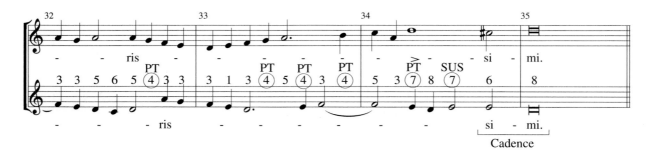

Cadence

Mode

Beatus homo is in the dorian mode. Four of the five cadences are on D. The few accidentals that appear are C♯ (three times) and B♭ (six times). Their purpose is clear: the former provides a leading tone at cadence points, and the latter corrects for tritones (figure 1.32).

Figure 1.32

Dorian mode with *musica ficta* tones:

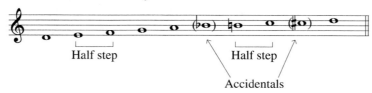

Half step   Half step

Accidentals

Melody

Eighty-eight percent of the melodic intervals in *Beatus homo* are seconds. Triad outlines appear in measures 6, 7, 8, 11, and 20 (figure 1.33).

Figure 1.33

Measure 7:

Outlined triad

There are no sequences or repetitions in the melodic lines. However, the opening part of each phrase is treated in *imitation.* Much of the imitation is strict, but sometimes there are modifications of intervals (figure 1.34).

Figure 1.34

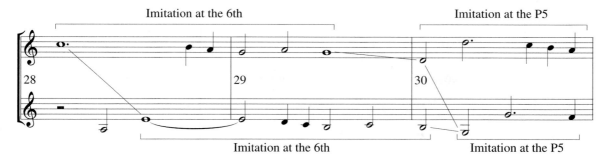

Imitation at the 6th   Imitation at the P5

Imitation at the 6th   Imitation at the P5

Vertical Intervals
Consonance
Dissonance

Vertical intervals are primarily the consonances, which account for the vast majority of the vertical intervals in the composition.

The composition contains 24 dissonant intervals. The following frequency chart shows the dissonant types represented in the composition:

Unaccented passing tones	18
Accented passing tones	1
7–6 suspensions	1
2–3 suspensions	3
Lower neighbor tone	1

Cadences

Beatus homo contains three *clausula vera* and two plagal cadences as shown below:

Measure(s)	Ending On	Cadence Type
5	D	Plagal
11–12	D	*Clausula vera* (with hocket)
16–17	D	Plagal (with hocket)
23–24	F	*Clausula vera* (with hocket)
34–35	D	*Clausula vera*

Text Setting

Both melismatic (one syllable of text to two or more notes of music) and syllabic (one syllable of text to one note of music) treatments are found in *Beatus homo,* although melismatic style predominates (figure 1.35).

Figure 1.35

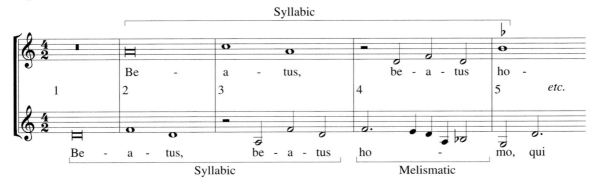

Syllabic

Be - a - tus,   be - a - tus   ho -

Be - a - tus,   be - a - tus   ho -   mo, qui

Syllabic   Melismatic

Form

The five phrases of the text create the form of the composition:

Phrase	Text	Measures
1	*Beatus homo* Happy is the man	1–5
2	*Qui invenit sapientiam* Who finds wisdom	5–12
3	*Et qui affluit prudentia* And who is rich in understanding	12–17
4	*Melior est acquisitio ejus* The acquiring of it	17–24
5	*Negotiatione argenti et auri primi et purissimi* Is better than the purchase of silver and the finest and purest gold	24–35

The *clausulae vera* cadences divide the composition into three equal parts: measures 1 to 12, 12 to 24, and 24 to 35. Such symmetry is typical of the Renaissance.

Assignment 1.1

Analyze the following two-voice, sixteenth-century motet in the same way as the specimen analysis in this chapter (page 16). Label each dissonance with a circle and name it. The tenor voice contains two treble clefs, meaning that the pitches are an octave lower than printed.

Lassus: *Benedictus* from *Missa ad imitationem moduli Iager (Jäger)*. CD Track 1

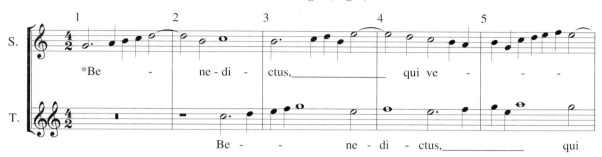

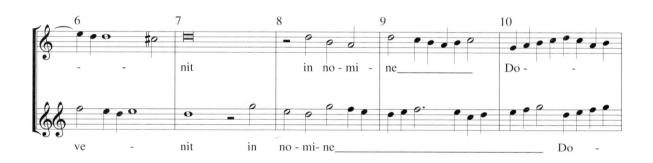

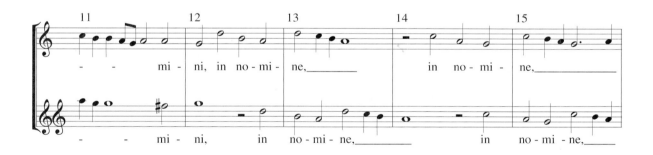

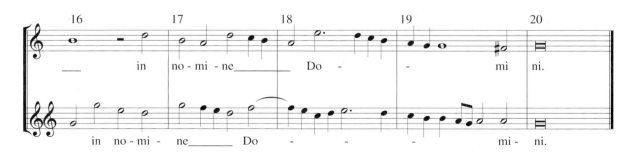

*Translation: Blessed is he that cometh in the name of the Lord.

Assignment 1.2   In each exercise that follows, there is at least one error in style. Circle the note or notes that create the error and pencil-in a correction.

Suggested Procedure

1. Analyze the vertical intervals in each exercise and check for parallel 5ths, octaves, and unisons. Parallel 5ths, octaves, and unisons can be easily located by observing repetitions of the numbers 5, 8, and 1 in your analysis. For example, if a "5" is immediately followed by another "5," parallel 5ths may have occurred.
2. Identify the dissonant numbers in your interval analysis and check to see if the dissonance types are appropriate to the style. If a dissonance cannot be identified as a passing tone, lower neighboring tone, suspension, portamento, or cambiata true to the sixteenth-century style, an error has occurred. If the dissonance has been placed on the wrong beat, a stylistic error has occurred.
3. Analyze the melodic intervals and melodic shape of each individual voice. Be sure the melodies are constructed using intervals appropriate to the style. For example, the skip of a melodic tritone, as well as the outline of a tritone in a melody, are considered errors in this style.
4. Examine the ties in the exercises. The sixteenth-century style limits the use of ties to specific duration pairings. Watch out for notes tied to notes of inappropriate values.

Assignment 1.3

Analyze the following example of three-voice polyphony. Note that the interval between the lowest-sounding tone and each of the upper two voices should be named. Label each dissonance with a circle and name it. The small "8" below the clef in the tenor voice means that the pitches are an octave lower than printed.

Palestrina: *Missa Jam Christus astra ascenderat,* Credo. CD Track 2

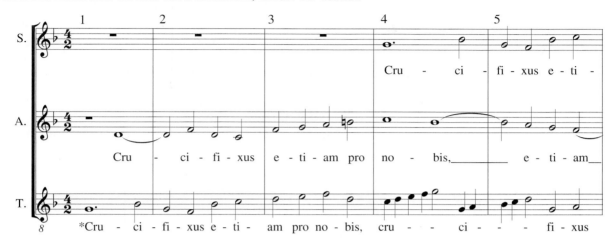

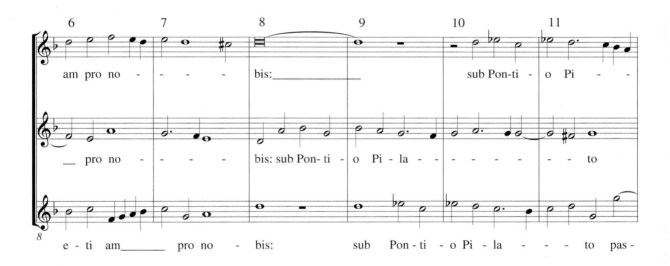

*Translation: He was crucified also for us, suffered under Pontius Pilate, and was buried. And the third day He rose again according to the Scriptures; and ascended into heaven. He sitteth at the right hand of the Father; and He shall come again with glory to judge the living and the dead; and His kingdom shall have no end.

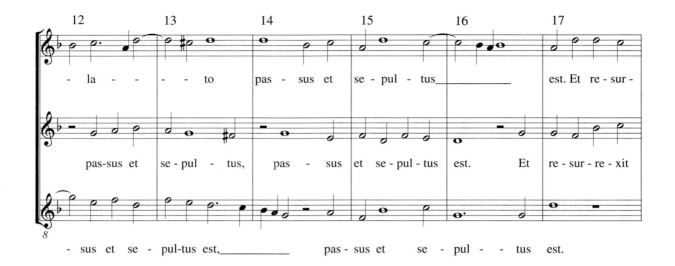

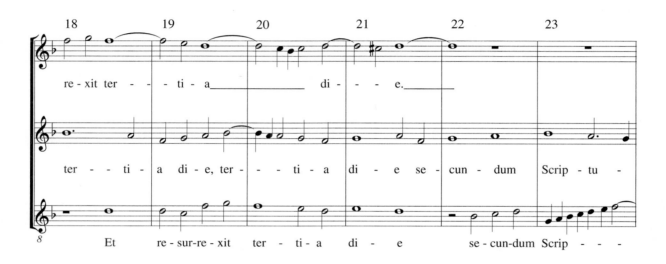

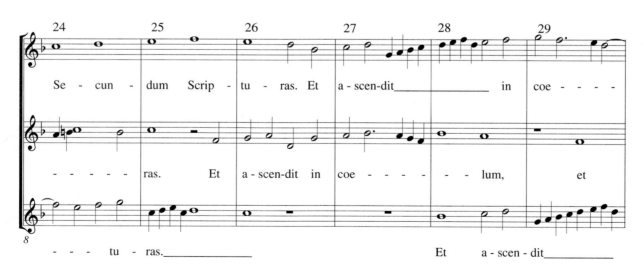

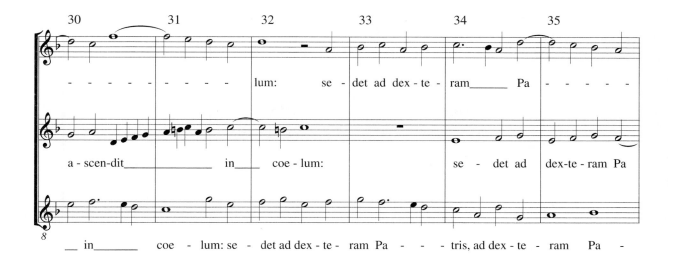

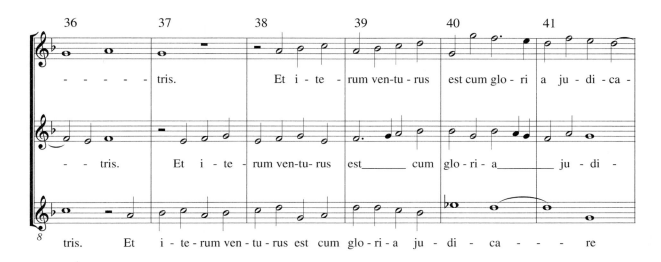

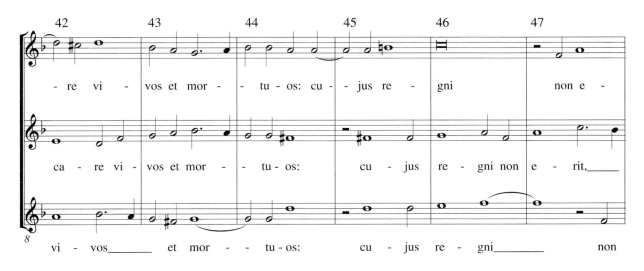

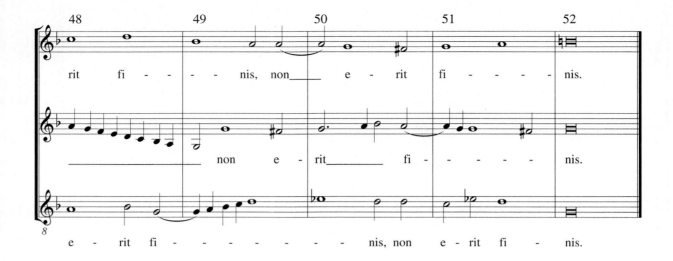

The Renaissance and Baroque Periods

Two-Voice Eighteenth-Century Counterpoint

Topics	Counterpoint	Countermotive	Harmonic rhythm
	Polyphony	Sequence	Hidden 5ths
	Two-part invention	Sectional form	Hidden octaves
	Motive		

Important Concepts

This chapter covers approximately the years 1675 to 1750. Although the time span is somewhat at odds with this chapter's title, the label is traditional and probably due to the overpowering influence of J. S. Bach (1685–1750).

Counterpoint

Counterpoint literally means "point-against-point," but the term has come to mean the combination of two or more melodic lines. Both terms *polyphony* and *counterpoint* refer to textures that consist of more than one melodic line. The term counterpoint is generally associated with the eighteenth century and polyphony with the sixteenth.

Two-Part Invention

This chapter is devoted to the study of two-voice counterpoint, especially that of J. S. Bach. A *two-part invention* is a two-voice composition in which a short musical idea, called the *motive*, and its counterpoint, called the *countermotive*, form the basis for the entire work (figure 2.1). By far the best-known two-part inventions are the fifteen inventions of J. S. Bach.

Figure 2.1

Bach: Invention no. 4, BWV 775 in D Minor from *Fifteen Two-Part Inventions*, mm. 1–6.

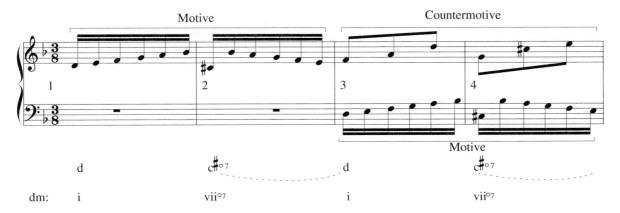

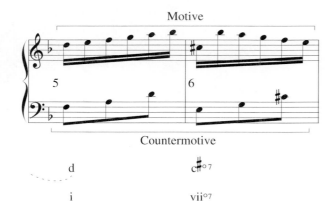

Bach Inventions

The distinguishing features of two-part inventions by Bach are as follows:

1. Contrapuntal texture is employed throughout.
2. A single motive, unaccompanied, usually occurs first in the composition. See figure 2.1, Bach: Invention no. 4, measures 1 and 2 (p. 27).
3. After the unaccompanied statement of the motive, it is imitated in the other voice along with the countermotive. This may be seen in figure 2.1, Bach: Invention no. 4, measures 3 and 4 (p. 27). In this particular invention the motive and countermotive occur again, this time with the voices switched in mm. 5 and 6 (p. 28).
4. Both the motive and countermotive are based on distinctive melodic, rhythmic, and/or harmonic ideas, and recur repeatedly throughout the composition in both straightforward and developed presentations. Invention motives and countermotives are typically short—from a half measure to two measures long—and may be identified as the primary opening melodic ideas.
5. After the motive has appeared in both voices (the second statement accompanied by the countermotive), most inventions continue with one or more *sequences*. A sequence is the immediate restatement of a melodic motive or figure at a higher or lower pitch. In Invention no. 4 (figure 2.2), a sequence occurs in measures 7 to 10. The upper voice is derived from the motive, whereas the lower voice comes from the countermotive. The purpose of sequences is to facilitate a modulation to the key of the next section, usually the dominant or the relative major.

Figure 2.2

Bach: Invention no. 4, BWV 775 in D Minor from *Fifteen Two-Part Inventions*, mm. 7–10.

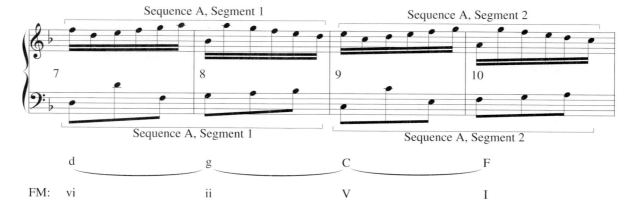

The Renaissance and Baroque Periods

6. On completion of the sequence or sequences, the new key is most often established and a short passage prepares for the cadence. Measures 15 and 16 of Invention no. 4 (figure 2.3) introduce derived material in the upper voice while sequence B is coming to completion in the lower voice. The cadence in the relative major (F major) is reached in measures 17 to 18. This completes section 1.

Figure 2.3

Bach: Invention no. 4, BWV 775 in D Minor from *Fifteen Two-Part Inventions*, mm. 15–18.

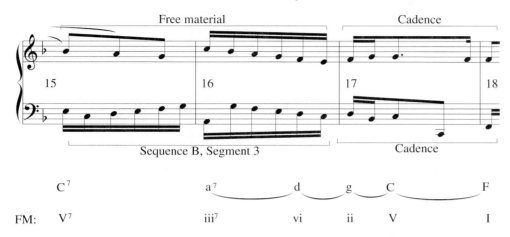

Most inventions are partitioned into subdivisions known as *sections*. Each section concludes with an authentic cadence, thereby making the *sectional form* evident. Bach's inventions are in either two or three sections, and Invention no. 4 (figure 2.4) contains three sections. For inventions with three sections, the following keys typically occur:

Section	Key(s)
1	Tonic modulating to dominant or relative major
2	Begins in dominant or relative major but features other closely related keys
3	Begins in a closely related key but quickly modulates to reestablish a tonic key

The first sections of inventions are generally more rigidly organized than those that follow. In Invention no. 4, section 2 begins (in F major) with an accompanied motive that is immediately sequenced (sequence C). Note that in sequence C only the lower voice is sequenced. Section 2 has no fewer than three sets of sequences and very little free material. The perfect authentic cadence in measures 37 to 38 signals the end of section 2.

Not all inventions have three sections. However, Invention no. 4 employs section 3 to return the invention to the tonic key (m. 44) and to prepare for the final cadence. This section is organized in a similar manner to that of section 2 but contains only one sequence. Note that the motive and countermotive in measures 44 to 45 are an exact duplicate of measures 5 to 6. The key scheme is an important factor in determining the form of Bach's two-part inventions.

Figure 2.4

Bach: Invention no. 4, BWV 775 in D Minor from *Fifteen Two-Part Inventions.*

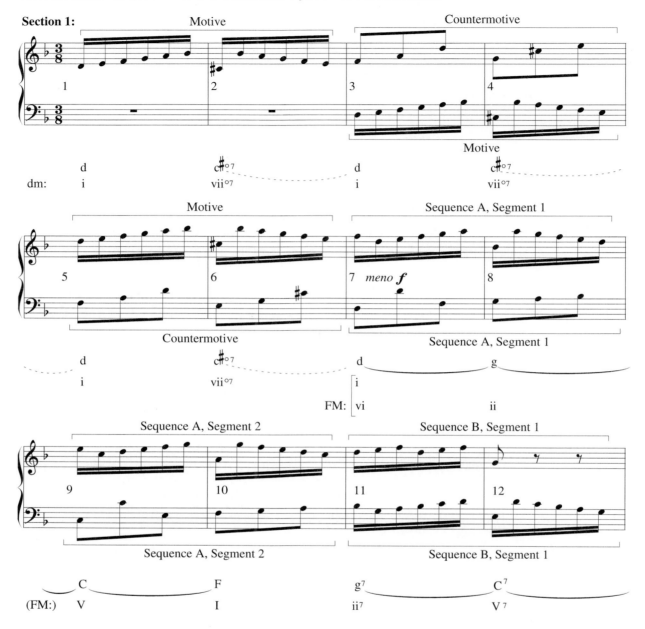

The Renaissance and Baroque Periods

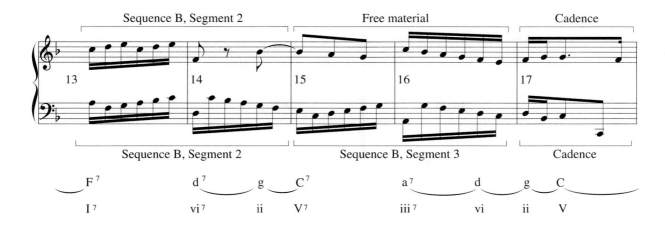

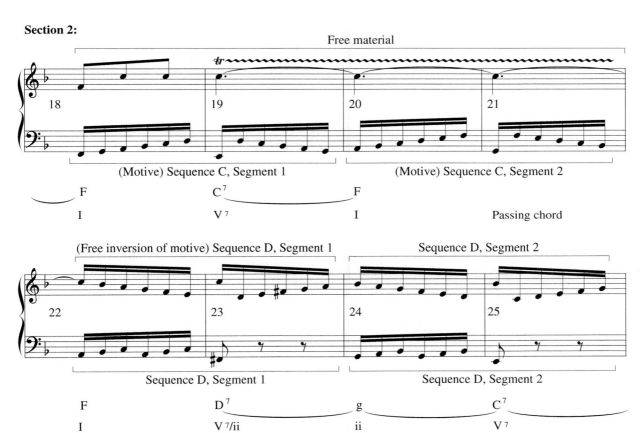

Section 2:

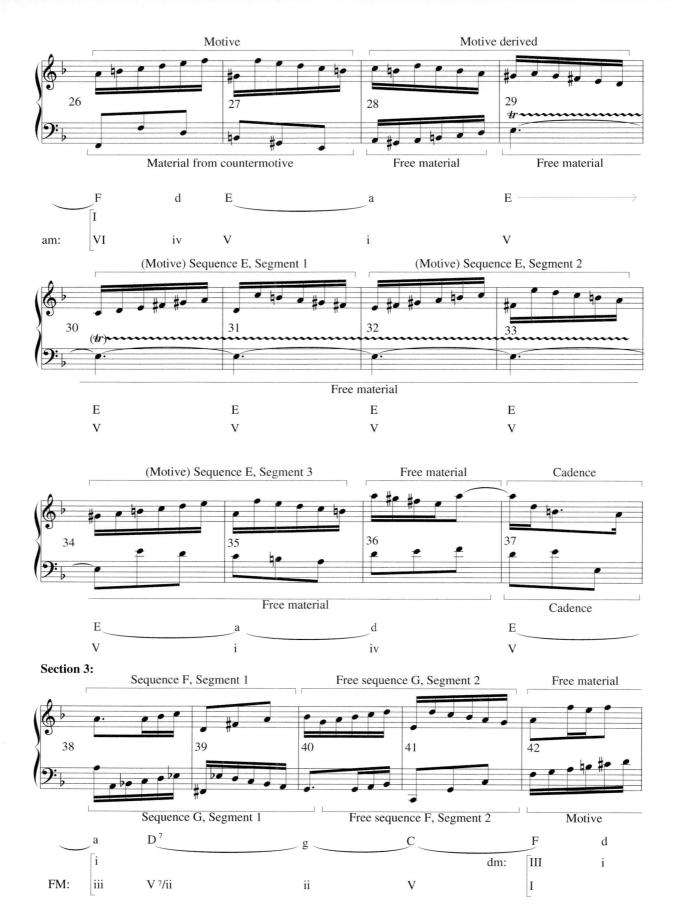

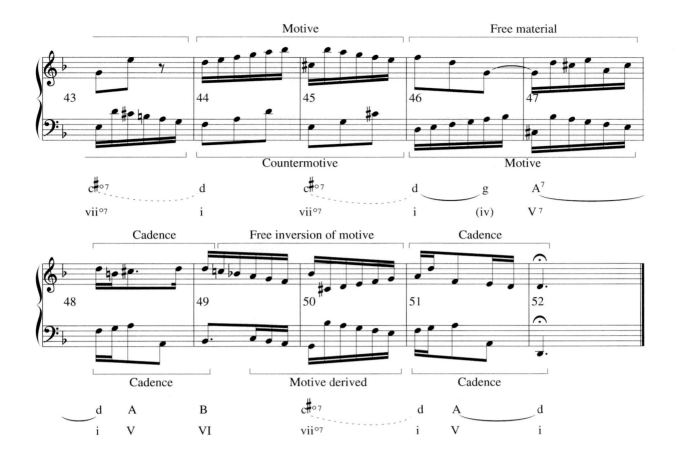

History

Both eighteenth-century counterpoint and sixteenth-century polyphony are considered by many musicians to be among the most distinctively pure and noble of all musical styles. The seeds for the development of eighteenth-century counterpoint reside in sixteenth-century polyphony, and although the two are quite different in many ways, a number of similarities exist. The following chart enumerates the analogous and disparate elements of two-voice writing in both sixteenth- and eighteenth-century writing.

Two-Voice Sixteenth-Century Polyphony	Two-Voice Eighteenth-Century Counterpoint
Similarities	
Successive parallel 5ths, octaves, and unisons are avoided.	Same as in sixteenth century.
Consonances consist of P8ths, P5ths, P1s, M3rds, m3rds, M6ths, and m6ths.	Same consonances as in sixteenth century.
Dissonances are M2nds, m2nds, P4ths, M7ths, m7ths, as well as all diminished and augmented intervals.	Same dissonances as in sixteenth century.
	(continued)

Two-Voice Sixteenth-Century Polyphony	Two-Voice Eighteenth-Century Counterpoint
Differences	
Modal (church modes).	Tonal (key oriented).
Vertical sonority based on intervals above the lowest-sounding voice; not constituted as functional harmony.	Based on functional harmony.
Dissonance regulated metrically according to beats and portions thereof.	Dissonance still regulated but not as strictly organized metrically.
Dissonant tones restricted to passing tone, suspension, portamento, nota cambiata, and an occasional neighboring tone.	Nonharmonic devices extend to passing tone, neighboring tone, suspension, anticipation, appoggiatura, escape tone, changing tone, and pedal tone.
Melodic sequences rare.	Melodic sequences an intrinsic part of the style.
Rhythmic figures seldom repeated immediately in the same voice.	Rhythms frequently repeated in the same voice.
No bar lines in original manuscripts.	Bar lines used in original manuscripts.

Applications

Writing Two-Voice Counterpoint

The soprano and bass voices of a four-voice chorale provide a good example of two-voice counterpoint, so you will find the general style quite familiar. However, from the analysis of Invention no. 4, you will remember that the harmony does not change every beat, as so often occurs in chorales. Also, in the chorales, which are most often in quadruple or triple meter, the beat is rarely divided any further than two eighth notes. Instrumental two-voice writing of this period tends to be more florid and less predictable in regard to *harmonic rhythm*. Invention no. 4 maintains a fairly steady harmonic rhythm of one chord per measure, but in no. 10 the harmonic rhythm is quite variable.

To ensure a smooth transition from chorales to instrumental two-voice writing, some guidance is offered to help you avoid common pitfalls.

Harmonic Progression

No instrumental two-voice writing will be successful without a clearly defined basis in functional harmony. Before you begin to write counterpoint, plan the cadences and other chord progressions carefully, making sure they include a sufficient number of circle progressions to provide the necessary forward motion.

Acceptable						Unacceptable—No Circle Progressions and No Cadence					
I	V^6	I^6	ii^6	V	I	I	ii^6	vi	iii^6	vi	I

Parallel Perfect Intervals

As in chorale writing, parallel perfect, as well as unequal 5ths, octaves, and unisons, are to be avoided. In two-voice writing you must be even more vigilant concerning these parallels because both voices are exposed (no inner voices). In harmony that sometimes changes only once per measure, it is very easy to overlook such parallels. Some situations to avoid regarding parallels are the following:

1. Direct parallel perfect intervals are not acceptable (figure 2.5a).
2. Strong accents with intervening counterpoint often suggest parallel perfect intervals and should be avoided (figure 2.5b).
3. Nonharmonic tones cannot be used to avoid parallel perfect intervals (figure 2.5c).
4. Even perfect-to-diminished or diminished-to-perfect 5ths are prohibited in two-voice writing (figure 2.5d).

Figure 2.5

a.

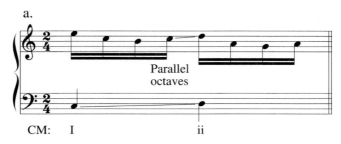

b.

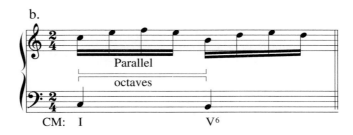

c.

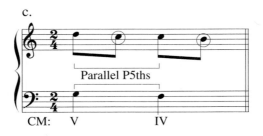

d.

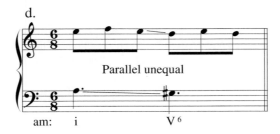

Hidden 5ths and Octaves

Hidden 5ths and *hidden octaves* (also known as direct 5ths and octaves) occur when the two voices move in similar motion to form a P5th or P8th. Hidden 5ths and octaves are to be avoided when both voices skip to the perfect interval but are permissible if the upper voice moves by step (see figure 2.6).

Figure 2.6

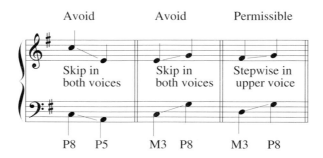

Nonharmonic Tones

With a few exceptions, the nonharmonic tones available in chorale harmonizations are also found in two-voice counterpoint.

Nonharmonic Tones to Be Used

Unaccented passing tones

Unaccented neighboring tones

Anticipations (at cadences)

Changing tones

Retardations (sparingly)

Accented passing tones

Accented neighboring tones

7–6, 4–3, and 2–3 suspension

Pedal tones (sparingly)

Nonharmonic Tones to Avoid

The 2–1 and 9–8 suspensions

The appoggiatura

Doublings

As in chorale harmonizations, avoid doubling the 7th scale degree and altered tones.

Harmonic Intervals

Of the harmonic intervals available in two-voice writing, 3rds and 6ths (both major and minor) occur with great frequency. Perfect octaves, 5ths, and unisons, on the other hand, are used sparingly because of their lack of sonority. In the Bach Invention no. 4 (figure 2.4), harmonic 3rds and 6ths outnumber perfect intervals by nearly 10 to 1. Except for cadence points, try to relegate P8ths, P5ths, and P1s to weak beats or weak portions of beats.

Restrictions on Parallel 3rds and 6ths

Too many successive 3rds or 6ths tend to negate independence of line. For assignments in this chapter, avoid writing more than four successive 3rds or 6ths. Figure 2.7 shows an upper-voice melody with two different bass lines.

Figure 2.7

Avoid too many successive 3rds:

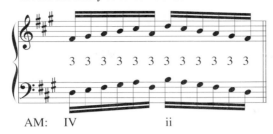

AM: IV   ii

Same passage by Bach:

Bach: English Suite no. 1, BWV 806 in A Major (Gigue), m. 38.

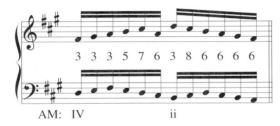

AM: IV   ii

Melodic Intervals to Avoid

Avoid melodic augmented 4ths, diminished 5ths, and augmented 2nds, unless the intervals outline the prevailing harmony.

General Suggestions

Melodic Contour

Although not strict rules, the following are some considerations you should keep in mind while writing.

When you are writing, think of the melodic line (especially the upper voice) that extends for an entire section. Try to give your line a definite shape (often a single ascent and descent) that leads logically to the cadence.

Rhythm

There are no specific rules concerning rhythm, but it is not good practice to introduce sudden changes in both voices at the same time. Writing a two-voice counterpoint with sixteenth-note motion in all measures and then suddenly changing to half- and quarter-note values in both voices is a blatant example of what not to do. Usually the two melodic lines exchange rhythmic activity.

Analysis

When you finish a two-voice counterpoint assignment, analyze it immediately. Circle and name nonharmonic tones, indicate the harmonic rhythm, and provide a Roman numeral analysis. If you find your counterpoint impossible to analyze, you will know there are problems with it.

Play Your Assignment

Either play your assignment or get another class member to play it for you. Otherwise, unless you have unusually good tonal memory, you will not know what you have written. Playing your assignment as you write it will provide insights enabling you to improve its quality. Computer notation programs with MIDI output can be a great help if your keyboard skills are not well developed.

Fresh Ideas

If you get stuck and are unable to proceed, listen to or play parts of either of the two-part inventions presented in this chapter. Often, playing two-voice counterpoint by Bach will bring forth ideas.

Assignment 2.1

Below is two-part Invention no. 8 in F Major by J. S. Bach. Using the model analysis of Invention no. 4 (figure 2.4) as a guide, prepare the same kind of analysis for Invention no. 8.

Bach: Invention no. 8, BWV 779 in F Major from *Fifteen Two-Part Inventions.* CD Track 3

Assignment 2.2
The following composition contains errors, all of which are violations of guidelines given in this chapter. Find each error and enter it in the table below.

Suggested Procedure

1. Analyze the vertical intervals in each exercise.
   a. Check for parallel fifths, octaves, and unisons. Parallel 5ths, octaves, and unisons can be easily located by observing repetitions of the numbers 1, 5, and 8 in your analysis.
   b. Look for hidden 5ths and hidden octaves. Study each "5" and "8" and determine whether or not hidden fifths and octaves occur.
   c. Observe the intervals that occur on beat 1. Be sure that the intervals occurring on beat 1 are typical of this composition style.
   d. Check for excessive use of same intervals and perfect intervals in succession.
2. Examine the dissonant intervals in your analysis to see if they correspond with the nonharmonic tone types appropriate to the composition style.
3. Determine the leading tone of the composition. Scrutinize each presentation of the leading tone to see if it has been vertically doubled in an unstylistic manner.
4. Analyze the melodic intervals in each individual voice. Melodic augmented 2nds, 4ths, and diminished 5ths should not occur in the melodies of this compositional type.

Error at Letter(s)   **Describe Error**

_____   _____

_____   _____

_____   _____

_____   _____

_____   _____

_____   _____

_____   _____

Assignment 2.3

Each of the examples is the lower voice of a two-voice contrapuntal composition. Copy the given bass line on a separate sheet of score paper and compose an upper voice for each.

In number 1 the harmonic rhythm and chord symbols are given, but in numbers 2, 3, and 4 you must figure out the harmony and harmonic rhythm yourself.

Do not change the given bass line.

Numbers 1 and 2:
a. Write a melody composed mostly of quarter-note values.
b. Write a melody composed mostly of eighth-note values.
c. Write a melody composed of whatever note values you consider appropriate.

Number 3:
a. Write a melody composed mostly of dotted quarter notes.
b. Write a melody containing a mixture of quarter- and eighth-note values.
c. Write a melody containing whatever note values you consider appropriate.

Number 4:
a. Write a melody containing a mixture of half and whole notes.
b. Write a melody containing whatever note values you consider to be appropriate for this particular bass line.

The Renaissance and Baroque Periods

4.

D.C.

Assignment 2.4   Each of the examples is the upper voice of a two-voice counterpoint composition. Copy the given upper line on a separate sheet of score paper and compose a lower voice for each.

   Before you start writing, determine the harmony and harmonic rhythm you intend to follow. Do not change the given notes.

Numbers 1 and 2:
a. Compose a bass line made up of half-, quarter-, and eighth-note values.
b. Compose a bass line using whatever values you consider appropriate.

Numbers 3 and 4:
a. Compose a bass line made up of quarter- and eighth-note values.
b. Compose a bass line using whatever values you consider appropriate.

1.

2.

3.

4.

Assignment 2.5

Write a two-part invention.

1. Your instructor will tell you whether to write an entire two-part invention or only a section or two.
2. Use one of the motives provided or make up your own.

3. Before you start to put your invention together, test out several countermotives. Make sure your countermotive is different enough from the motive to be easily identified yet simple enough to avoid problems later. Also, try out your countermotive both above and below the motive, because there will be many times in the invention when the voices may be reversed. Any P5ths (consonant) in the original counterpoint will become P4ths (dissonant) in the inverted version. If you treat P5ths in the original counterpoint as if they were dissonant, the inversion will not be a problem.
4. Use the following form, one of the two-part inventions printed in this text, or another invention supplied by your instructor as a model.

No. of Measures	Content
	First Section:
2	Motive alone in upper voice
2	Motive in lower voice with countermotive above
2–3	Sequence (derived from motive or countermotive) of two or three segments that do not modulate
2–3	Sequence (derived from motive or countermotive) that modulates to the dominant or relative major (if in a minor key)
1	Dominant preparation of the new key

Second Section:

2	Motive alone in lower voice and in the new key
2	Motive in upper voice accompanied by countermotive in the lower voice (new key)
2	Sequence (derived from motive or countermotive) of two or three segments leading to a third key (closely related)
2	Motive in third key accompanied by countermotive
2–3	Sequence (derived from motive or countermotive) of two or three segments leading back to original key
1	Dominant preparation of the original key

Third Section:

2	Motive accompanied by countermotive in original key
2–4	Material derived from either motive or countermotive ending in a deceptive cadence in the original key
2–4	Material derived from either motive or countermotive ending in an authentic cadence in the original key

_____

26–33 total measures

5. Arrange the invention for two instruments and perform it in class.
6. For all the inventions performed in class, determine the following through listening only:
   a. The relationship of new keys to the original
   b. The cadence points
   c. The sequences
   d. Motive- and countermotive-derived material

CHAPTER 3

The Fugue

Topics		
Subject	*Countersubject*	*Entry*
Exposition	*Invertible counterpoint*	*Stretto*
Answer	*Inversion at the octave*	*Augmentation*
Real answer	*Link*	*Diminution*
Tonal answer	*Bridge*	*Retrograde*
Modulating subject	*Episode*	*Melodic inversion*
		Coda

Important Concepts

A *fugue* is a contrapuntal composition in two or more voices built on a *subject* (short melody) that is stated in all voices and repeated throughout the composition.

Exposition

The first section is called the *exposition,* which is the most fully structured part of the fugue.

Subject

The basis of the entire fugue is the subject. *Subjects* are short melodies ranging from two notes to eight measures. The fugue opens with the subject alone.

Answer

When the subject is completed, it is imitated in another voice, usually at the P5th above or P4th below. This imitation is known as the *answer.*

If the answer is a literal (exact) imitation of the subject, it is called a *real answer.* If the answer is slightly modified, it is a *tonal answer.* Tonal answers occur for a variety of reasons, but two basic reasons are to create a strong tonic–dominant relationship in the exposition and to take care of situations where the subject modulates. A strong tonic–dominant relationship at the beginning of the subject is often answered as dominant–tonic in the answer (figure 3.1).

Figure 3.1

Bach: Fugue no. 8, BWV 853 in D-sharp Minor from *The Well-Tempered Clavier,* Book I, mm. 1–3.

47

A subject that modulates usually takes a tonal answer to prevent the fugue from spiraling out of the closely related key range. Figure 3.2a shows a *modulating subject.* If a real answer were used it would modulate to a key that is outside the orbit of closely related keys (figure 3.2b). Instead, Bach modifies the end of the answer to return to the tonic key (figure 3.2c).

Figure 3.2

Bach: Organ Fugue in C Minor, BWV 574, mm. 1–4.

a. Subject: Begins in C Minor   Ends in G Minor

b. Real answer: Begins in G Minor   Ends in D Minor
                                              (not a closely related key to C Minor)

c. Tonal answer (as Bach wrote it):

Transposed a step lower to end in C Minor

Countersubject

A *countersubject* is the continuation of counterpoint in the voice that began with the subject (figure 3.10, mm. 3–4). The countersubject occurs as counterpoint against the answer, not the subject. This is a typical beginning of a fugue:

Tenor voice:		Answer
Bass voice:	Subject	**Countersubject**

Occasionally a second countersubject is introduced, usually in the exposition.

Invertible Counterpoint

Because a countersubject might be used both above and below an answer, composers of the period constructed countersubjects that are *invertible.* In *inversion at the octave,* all harmonic P5ths require special treatment because when inverted, the P5th becomes a P4th—a dissonance in this style. To find out if a countersubject is invertible, play the first entrance of the answer and countersubject but place the upper voice an octave or two lower. If the P4ths produced by the inversion are properly treated as dissonances, then the countersubject is invertible. Figure 3.3 shows an example of a countersubject that is in invertible counterpoint.

Figure 3.3

Bach: Fugue no. 2, BWV 847 in C Minor from *The Well-Tempered Clavier,* Book I, mm. 7–8.

Bach: Fugue no. 2, BWV 847 in C Minor from *The Well-Tempered Clavier,* Book I, mm. 20–21.

Link

Sometimes a fugue subject ends on a pitch that does not connect conveniently to the countersubject. To make the junction smooth, composers added some extra notes known as a *link*. Links are quite short, occasionally only a few notes. Not all fugues contain a link.

Tenor voice:			Answer
Bass voice:	Subject	**Link**	Countersubject

Bridge

A *bridge* is a short passage at the end of the first entrance of the answer and the beginning of the second entrance of the subject. Its purpose is to modulate back to the tonic key (subject) from the answer (which is in the dominant key). Not all fugues include a bridge.

Soprano:				Subject
Alto:		Answer	**Bridge**	Countersubject
Bass:	Subject	Countersubject	**Bridge**	Free material

Exposition Design

Although the design of the exposition differs from fugue to fugue, one simple pattern is shown here:

Soprano	Subject	Countersubject	Free material	Free material
Alto		Answer	Countersubject	Free material
Tenor			Subject	Countersubject
Bass				Answer

Exposition Alternatives

Possible alternative designs are as follows:

1. The order of entrances may be subject-answer-answer-subject.
2. Voices may be introduced in almost any order, such as tenor-alto-soprano-bass, and the number of voices in a fugue varies. A large number contain only three voices.

3. The countersubject does not always appear three times as shown in the chart, and some fugues contain more than one countersubject.
4. Both links and bridges have been omitted from the chart in the interest of simplicity.

Episodes and Entries

The second section of the fugue consists of a series of *episodes* and *entries*.

Characteristics of an Episode

1. There are no complete statements of subject or answer in any voice during an episode.
2. Episodes frequently contain sequences.
3. Episodes are usually short (a few beats to four measures).

Characteristics of an Entry

1. There are one or more complete statements of subject and/or answer in an entry.
2. If there are multiple statements, they are linked together, occurring more or less continuously, sometimes looking very much like complete expositions.

As you can see from this description, the most important distinction between an episode and an entry is the presence of the subject or answer in entries.

Purpose of Episodes

1. To lead smoothly from one entry of the subject to another.
2. To effect modulations to new keys. A typical second section of a fugue might appear as follows:

End of Exposition:	Episode	Subject/Answer	Episode	Subject/Answer (etc.)
Keys: FM	Modulation	dm	Modulation	gm (etc.)

The introduction of keys beyond tonic and dominant occurs in almost all second sections. Almost any of the closely related keys is likely to appear. Measures 17 and 18 of Fugue no. 2 in C Minor, printed in its entirety in figure 3.10, contain a typical episode (figure 3.4).

Figure 3.4

Bach: Fugue no. 2, BWV 847 in C Minor from *The Well-Tempered Clavier,* Book I, mm. 17–20.

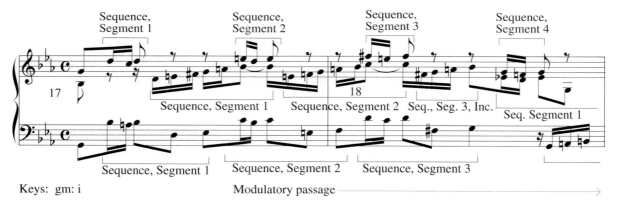

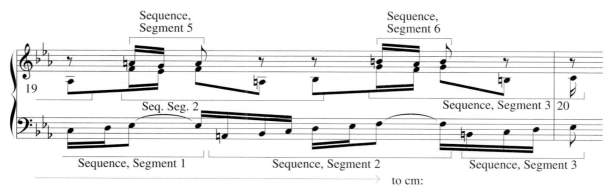

Variants of Subjects and Answers in an Entry

Stretto

Subjects and answers are treated in a less structured manner after the exposition, as can be seen in the following discussion of variants.

Stretto is the overlapping of subjects or answers. That is, a subject enters in one voice and, before it is completed, another subject enters in a different voice (figure 3.5).

Figure 3.5

Bach: Fugue no. 1, BWV 846 in C Major from *The Well-Tempered Clavier,* Book I, mm. 21–23.

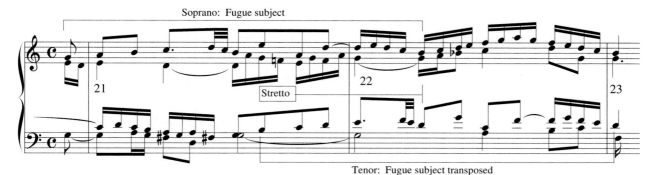

Augmentation

Augmentation in eighteenth-century fugal writing refers to the doubling or tripling of note values. If a certain subject consisted entirely of quarter-note values, that subject might occur later with half-note values. Figure 3.6 shows the fugue subject (alto voice) and its augmentation (bass voice).

Figure 3.6

Bach: Fugue no. 8, BWV 853 in D-sharp Minor from *The Well-Tempered Clavier,* Book I, mm. 62–66.

The Fugue

Diminution

Diminution is the reverse of augmentation—note values are reduced. Figure 3.7 shows a fugue subject in diminution. Notice the two examples of stretto, one in measure 27 and one in measures 28 to 29.

Figure 3.7

Bach: Fugue no. 9, BWV 878 in E Major from *The Well-Tempered Clavier,* Book II, mm. 1–2.

Bach: Fugue no. 9, BWV 878 in E Major from *The Well-Tempered Clavier,* Book II, mm. 27–29.

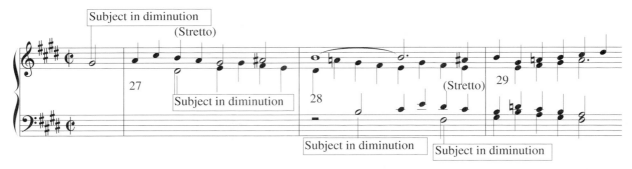

Retrograde

If a melody is played backward, it is called a *retrograde* (also *cancrizan*—from "crab"). This contrapuntal device is more often found in canons than in fugues. Figure 3.8, an example of a retrograde canon (a melody played forward and backward at the same time), is from Bach's *Musical Offering.* The first four measures of the solution are included.

Figure 3.8

Bach: Retrograde canon from *Musikalisches Opfer* (Musical Offering), BWV 1079.

Solution (first four measures only):

Melodic Inversion

This is a device, occurring more often in canons than in fugues, that reverses the direction of the melody. Thus upward motion becomes downward, and downward becomes upward. Figure 3.9, an excerpt from the *Clavier-Übüng,* illustrates *melodic inversion.* The interval-by-interval change of direction (upper voice) produces a change of mode (F major to F minor).

Figure 3.9

Bach: Duet no. 2 in F Major from *Clavier-Übüng,* Part III, BWV 803, mm. 1–4, 74–77.

Theme:

Same theme in inversion (treble clef)

Final Part of a Fugue

Near the end of the fugue there is a return to the tonic key and usually a restatement of the subject. A fugue often closes with a short section called a *coda,* which emphasizes the tonic key.

History

Unquestionably, the most famous of Bach's works for the clavier is the set of preludes and fugues entitled *The Well-Tempered Clavier* (completed circa 1742). *Clavier* is a broad term meaning "keyboard," so these compositions were written to be played on any keyboard instrument, except the organ. At the time of Bach (1685–1750), such instruments included the *clavichord,* the popular *harpsichord,* and possibly an occasional *pianoforte* (piano), invented in 1709. Today, because of large concert halls and the ubiquitous piano, *The Well-Tempered Clavier* is most often performed on that instrument. Both the harpsichord and the clavichord can muster only a fraction of the volume possible on a piano.

The complete work is divided into two sections: Book I and Book II. Each book contains a prelude and fugue in each of the 12 possible major and minor keys—a total of 24 preludes and fugues in each book.

Bach's purpose in preparing the work was, in part, to demonstrate the flexibility of a tuning system approaching equal temperament, which at the time was considered experimental. Gradually, the new system gained a measure of acceptance over the more limited mean-tone system (see Volume l), although universal endorsement did not take place until the nineteenth century.

The following fugue from *The Well-Tempered Clavier* is analyzed according to the descriptions made earlier in this chapter (figure 3.10).

Figure 3.10

Bach: Fugue no. 2, BWV 847 in C Minor from *The Well-Tempered Clavier,* Book I.

Exposition:

Subject

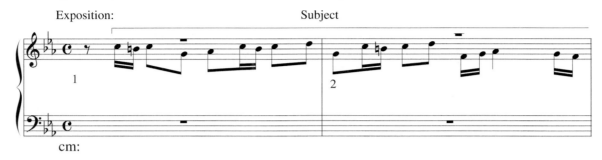

cm:

Answer

Countersubject A

(gm:)

Bridge between answer and next entrance of the subject

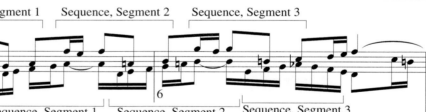

Sequence, Segment 1   Sequence, Segment 2   Sequence, Segment 3

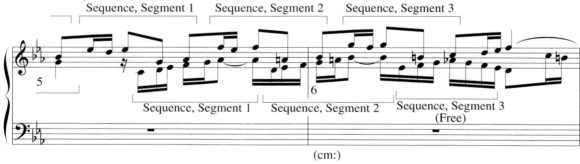

Sequence, Segment 1   Sequence, Segment 2   Sequence, Segment 3 (Free)

(cm:)

Countersubject A

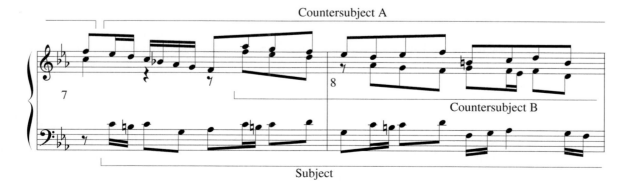

Countersubject B

Subject

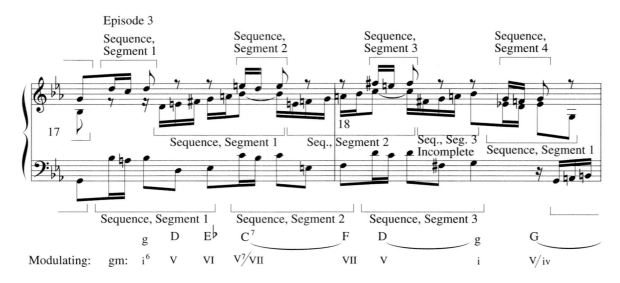

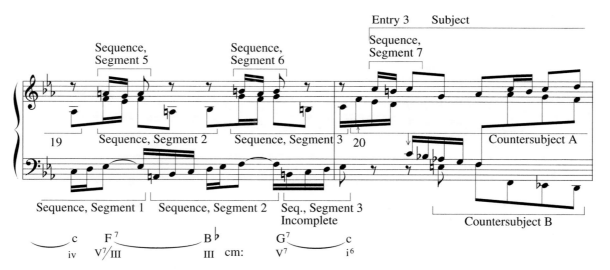

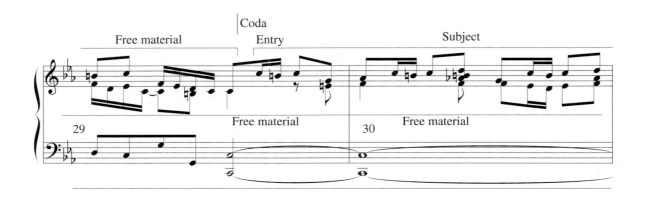

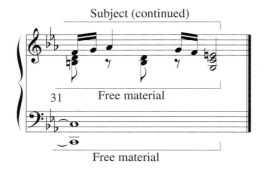

Form

Exposition--|

			(Bridge)	
Upper voice:		Answer in gm	Sequence (sub.)	Countersubject A
		─────────────	─────────────	─────────────
Middle voice:	Subject in cm	Countersubject A	Sequence (CS A inv.)	Countersubject B
	─────────────	─────────────	─────────────	─────────────
Lower voice:				Subject in cm
				─────────────
Meas.	1 2	3 4	5 6	7 8

Episodes and entries--

	(Episode 1)	**(Entry 1)**	**(Episode 2)**	**(Entry 2)**
Upper voice:	Sequence (sub.)	Sub. in E-flat Major	Seq. (B, mm.10–11 inv.)	Countersubject A
	─────────────	─────────────	─────────────	─────────────
Middle voice:	Sequence (sub.)	Countersubject B	Sequence (CS B)	Answer in gm
	─────────────	─────────────	─────────────	─────────────
Lower voice:	Sequence (free)	Countersubject A	Sequence (CS B)	Countersubject B
	─────────────	─────────────	─────────────	─────────────
Meas.	9 10	11 12	13 14	15 16

	(Episode 3)	(Entry 3)	(Episode 4)
Upper voice:	Sequence (sub.)	Subject in cm	Sequence (sub.)
Middle voice:	Sequence (from sub.)	Countersubject A	Sequence (sub.)
Lower voice:	Sequence (sub.)	Countersubject B	Sequence (see mm. 9–10)
Meas.	17　18　19	20　21	22　23　24

| | | (Entry 4) | Coda---------------------------------\| | |
			(Eps. 5)	(Entry 5)
Upper voice:		Countersubject A	Free mat.	Subject in cm
Middle voice:		Countersubject B	Free mat.	Chordal expansion
Lower voice:		Subject in cm	Free mat.	Tonic pedal point
Meas.	25　26	27　28	29	30　31

Subject

The subject, stated in the first two measures, is the basis of the entire composition (figure 3.11).

Figure 3.11

The subject:

Answer

The answer, derived from the subject, is tonal rather than real. The subject and answer are placed together in figure 3.12 to show the slight alteration of the answer.

Figure 3.12

Tonal answer:

Change made here

Subject: P5---------P4　P5---------

Countersubject

This fugue has two countersubjects that play principal roles, accompanying either the subject or the answer throughout (figure 3.13).

Figure 3.13

Countersubject A:

Countersubject B:

Episodes

The fugue includes five episodes. The episodes contain no complete subjects or answers, but all are based on fragments or motives therefrom. Sequences abound in episodes:

Episode Measures	Sequences	Modulating
9–11	Yes	cm to E♭M
13–14	Yes	E♭M to cm
17–20	Yes	gm to cm
22–26	Yes	No
28–29	No	No

Melodic Inversion

The melody in the lowest voice (mm. 9–10) appears again in the upper voice (mm. 13–14) in melodic inversion (figure 3.14).

Figure 3.14

This bass voice appears in measures 9 and 10

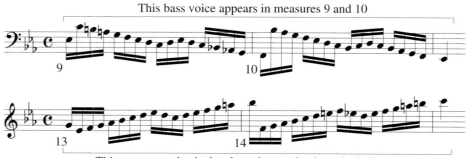

This soprano voice is the above bass voice in melodic inversion

Miscellaneous Imitation

In addition to the imitation that is a part of the formal design of the fugue are a number of imitations in the episodes. One example is in measures 9 and 10, where the imitation is in sequences (figure 3.15).

Figure 3.15

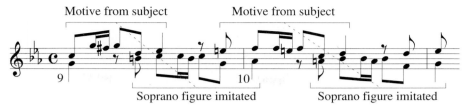

Assignment 3.1

Ten fugue subjects follow. Determine whether each should have a real or a tonal answer, and write the type of answer in the blank provided above the music. Remember that tonal answers are usually given to subjects that:

a. begin on the dominant tone,
b. begin on the tonic and move to the dominant immediately, and/or
c. modulate.

1. Select one of the subjects that takes a real answer and write a countersubject. Remember that the countersubject accompanies the answer, not the subject.
2. With this same subject, write a fugue exposition. Use the Bach fugue analyzed in this chapter as a general guide. Remember, however, that different subjects require different treatment, so do not expect to handle your exposition exactly as Bach did.
3. When the exposition is completed, write the remainder of the fugue.
4. Perform the fugue in class. Ask the class members to identify the subject and countersubject, the type of answer, the episodes and entries of the fugue, and other compositional devices that might be present.

Assignment 3.2

This is the sixteenth fugue in the first book of *The Well-Tempered Clavier* by J. S. Bach.

1. Make a complete analysis of the fugue following the same procedures as applied to Fugue no. 2 earlier in this chapter.
2. Arrange the fugue for four instruments and perform it in class.

Bach: Fugue no. 16, BWV 861 in G Minor from *The Well-Tempered Clavier,* Book I. CD Track 4

The Renaissance and Baroque Periods

Chromatic Harmony

This section continues the investigation of chromatic harmony, including harmony that borrows chords from both major and minor modes as well as chords of more distant origin (the Neapolitan 6th and the augmented 6th chords). These harmonic materials were developed during the baroque period and become more common in the classical and romantic periods.

Macro Analysis

Macro analysis is, in many respects, no different from the harmonic analysis found in most music theory textbooks. All tonal music from the beginning of the baroque to the middle of the romantic period contains a preponderance of circle progressions. An example of the circle flow is shown on the next page (circle progressions are shown by the use of slurs). Macro analysis emphasizes the forward movement of a composition by studying and diagnosing the circle patterns. In this example, as is typical of music of this period, every chord is either the beginning or the ending of a circle progression.

To prepare a macro analysis, do the following:

1. Extract the roots of chords and place the chord symbol below the staves.
2. Place slurs wherever a circle progression is found. A circle progression occurs between chords whose roots are in a descending 5th or an ascending 4th relationship. In the example on the next page, the first circle progression occurs between $E\flat$ and $A\flat$; $A\flat$ to $E\flat^7$ (mm. 8–9) is not a circle progression because the roots of these two chords are an ascending 5th or a descending 4th apart.
3. Place dotted slurs between diminished triads or diminished 7th chords whose roots resolve up a half step. Examples: $b°$ to C, $b°^7$ to c, $g°$ to $A\flat$, or $g°^7$ to $A\flat$. Remember that $vii°$ or $vii°^7$ are considered weaker dominants, thus the dotted slur.
4. Sometimes you can show circle relationships (with a slur) where the chords are not adjacent. The $E\flat$ (m. 13) and the $A\flat^7$ (m. 16) are connected by a slur to indicate that a strong (although not adjacent) relationship exists and helps push the musical direction toward the target chord in measure 17. A target chord occurs at the end of a circle series. Often, a longer, uninterrupted circle series creates greater tension and produces a stronger target than a single circle series simply by virtue of its length. However, circle series that complete a phrase or are otherwise in prominent positions within the phrase also create strong targets whether the circle series is long or short.
5. Ignore second inversion triads, especially I_4^6, that usually occur inside the circle progression ii^6 (I_4^6) V. Triads in second inversion seldom take part in functional harmony.

Schubert: *Moment Musical*, op. 94, no. 2, D. 780. mm. 8–17.

What important information was discovered from this macro analysis?

The entire excerpt moves from the first chord, E♭ in measure 8, toward the strongest target (m. 17), D♭. The macro analysis shows how the E♭ to A♭ circle continues from measure 8 to 13, then moves quickly in measure 15 to 17 to the target, D♭. The same chord (D♭) occurs in measure 15 but is approached by a diminished 7th chord.

Basic forward movement for measures 8–17:

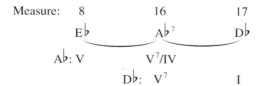

By studying the intricacies of circle patterns, compositional types are more easily recognized. This will become more apparent in future chapters. For a more complete discussion of macro analysis, see Appendix A.

CHAPTER 4

Borrowed Chords

Topics

In major keys: ii°⁶, ii°⁷,   *In minor keys: I*   *Modal mixture*
iv, ♭VI, vii°⁷   *(picardy 3rd)*

Important Concepts

Borrowed chords are chords borrowed from a parallel major or minor key. Another term often used is *modal mixture*.

Borrowed Chords in Major Keys

Because the parallel minor key with its three scale forms provides a rich variety of triad and 7th chord colors, selections from this assortment are often borrowed for use in major keys. Although a large number of chords in the minor keys are available, the five borrowed chords in figure 4.1 have received by far the greatest utilization by composers.

Figure 4.1

Five diatonic chords in D Major:

DM: ii   ii⁷   IV   vi   vii°⁷

Same chords borrowed from parallel minor:

DM: ii°   ii°⁷   iv   ♭VI   vii°⁷

The chords in figure 4.1 are borrowed from the parallel minor, which accounts for the alterations. Notice that B, the sixth scale degree in D major, is lowered to B♭ in each of the borrowed chords. This lowered sixth scale degree is a distinctive characteristic of borrowed chords in major keys and may be used to identify chords from the parallel mode.

Although borrowed chords may occur in any position, certain positions are most commonly associated with each of the chords.

Chord	Most Common	Fairly Common
ii°	ii°⁶	—
ii⁰⁷	ii⁰⁶₅	ii⁰⁷, ii⁰⁴₃
iv	iv	iv⁶
♭VI	♭VI	—
vii°⁷	vii°⁶₅	vii°⁴₃ vii°⁴₂

Progression

All borrowed chords progress in the same manner as the diatonic chords they replace, except for the ♭VI, which progresses to V or V⁷.

Purpose

Borrowed chords are almost universally used as color chords: that is, they are employed to provide variety through the use of contrasting scale forms. Figure 4.2 from the song cycle *Die Winterreise* (Winter's Journey), in F minor, contains a borrowed ii°⁶ and a iv.

Figure 4.2

Schubert: *Das Wirtshaus* (The Inn) from *Die Winterreise* (Winter's Journey), op. 89, no. 21, D. 911, mm. 8–9.

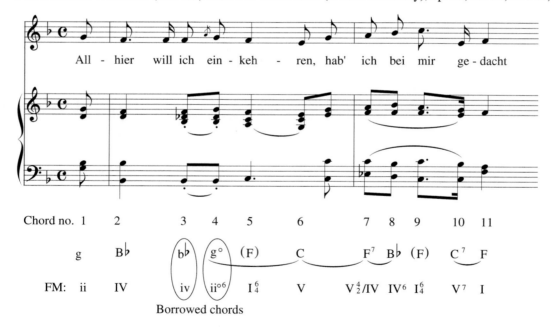

In figure 4.2 borrowed chords occur at chord numbers 3 and 4. Play the piano part (the two lower staves) of the example twice, once as written and once ignoring the D-flats in both chords 3 and 4. Although the composition would sound acceptable without the accidentals, the addition of the borrowed chords gives the example a unique effect. The effects generated by borrowed chords are often referred to as "color" effects. Can you name at least two chords in figure 4.2 that are not parts of circle progressions (neither the beginning nor the ending of a circle progression)? In performing this work, would it be proper to emphasize (play louder) the D-flats in chords 3 and 4? Does your answer agree with that of your instructor?

Chromatic Harmony

Figure 4.3, *Nachtlied,* illustrates a vii°$^4_3$ and a ii°$^6_5$ borrowed from B♭ minor.

Figure 4.3

Schubert: *Wanderers Nachtlied* (Wanderers' Night Song), op. 96, no. 3, II, D. 768, mm. 4–6.

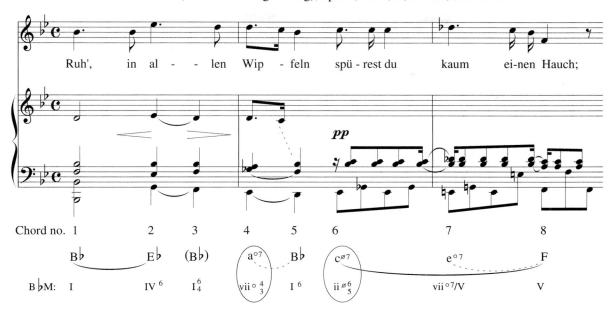

As with other examples of borrowed chords, the borrowed vii°^{7} and borrowed ii°^{7} in figure 4.3 have no influence on the circle progressions (B♭ to E♭, a°^{7} to B♭, and e°^{7} to F). They are maintained throughout, but the delicate changes in mode generate interesting musical effects not available in major or minor systems alone. Play this example, first with the G-flats (as written) and a second time with G-naturals. Do you like Schubert's choice of borrowed chord? Note that the leading-tone 7th chord (vii°$^4_3$) still resolves to the tonic and that the borrowed ii°$^6_5$ still moves to the dominant at the end of the excerpt.

Figure 4.4, an excerpt from Bach's *Vater Unser im Himmelreich,* contains a ♭VI borrowed from F minor.

Figure 4.4

Bach: *Vater unser im Himmelreich* (Our Father in Heaven), BWV 416, m. 10.

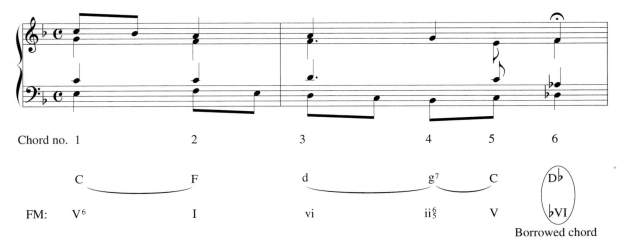

Borrowed Chords

The final chord (no. 6) in figure 4.4 is a cadence ending with a borrowed chord. Can you name the cadence type at numbers 5 and 6? Notice also that circle progressions dominate the example and are missing only at the very last progression (C to D♭). Play the example first as written, then with an F major triad substituting for the D♭ chord at the cadence (thus creating an authentic cadence).

Figure 4.5 ilustrates the tonic chord (I) borrowed from the parallel major.

Figure 4.5

Picardy 3rd:

em: I

Bach: *Jesu, meine Freude* (Jesus, My Joy), BWV 358, mm. 1–2 (Modified).

The *picardy 3rd* (chord no. 7) that ends figure 4.5 is a pattern that dates back to the Renaissance period, where cadences ending with minor triads were not considered strong enough and had to be changed to major.

The final chord, the picardy 3rd of this excerpt, is by no means a requirement. Play the example, first as written and then without the G-sharp (play G-natural). Most students agree that using the picardy 3rd is indeed an interesting artistic gesture, but it is by no means a necessity.

Chord no. 5 (F♯⁷) is a secondary dominant. How would you change the fifth chord from a secondary dominant to a diatonic 7th chord?

History

Baroque Period (1600–1750)

Mixing of major and minor modes developed in the baroque period and was considered a part of the general style.

Classical Period (1750–1825)

Composers in the classical period also used borrowed chords. Their frequency and use is little changed from that of the baroque.

Romantic and Post-Romantic Period (1825–1920)

The romantic and post-romantic period saw a freer use of borrowed chords, including a chromatic approach and departure. The excerpt in figure 4.6, by Hugo Wolf (1860–1903), shows the typical vi ii V (I) circle progression but also includes two examples of the borrowed chord, ii°⁷.

Figure 4.6

Wolf: *Wiegenlied* (Cradlesong).

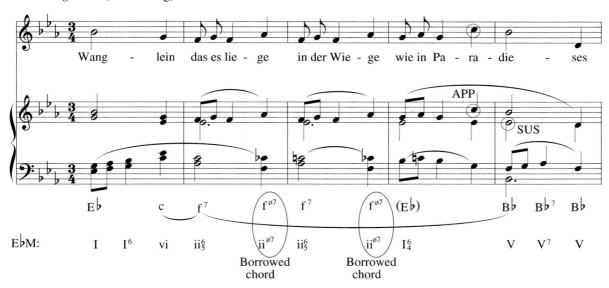

Doubling and Voice Leading

A few guidelines, which you already know, will make doubling of borrowed chords easy. Don't double either of the notes that create a tritone. It is generally best not to double an altered note. Usually the best note to double in any situation is the first, fourth, or fifth scale degree.

The ii°6 Chord

The ii°6 chord is usually found in first inversion because it is a diminished triad. See figures 4.2 and 4.7a and b for examples.

The ii∅6/5 Chord

In the ii∅7 chord all four factors (root, 3rd, 5th, and 7th) are usually present. Otherwise, the recommendations for ii° apply for ii∅6/5 as well. See figures 4.3 and 4.7c and d.

The iv Chord

The iv chord follows the general principles above. See figure 4.2 for an example. This chord contains no tritone. Another example can be found in figure 4.7e.

The ♭VI Chord

Double the tonic (3rd of triad and first scale degree). See figure 4.4 on page 71 for an example. As usual, parallel unisons, 3rds, 5ths, and octaves are avoided. Other examples are shown in figures 4.7f and g.

The vii°7 Chord

The diminished 7th chord appears with all four factors. The chord is usually in root position, but other positions may appear from time to time. The diminished 7th chord contains two tritones, but often only one can be resolved. See figure 4.3.

Borrowed Chords

The Picardy 3rd

This is the major tonic (I) in a minor key. The picardy 3rd chord is customarily in root position at the ending of a composition or a large musical section (figure 4.5).

Applications

Figure 4.7 shows standard voice-leading patterns for borrowed chords.

Figure 4.7

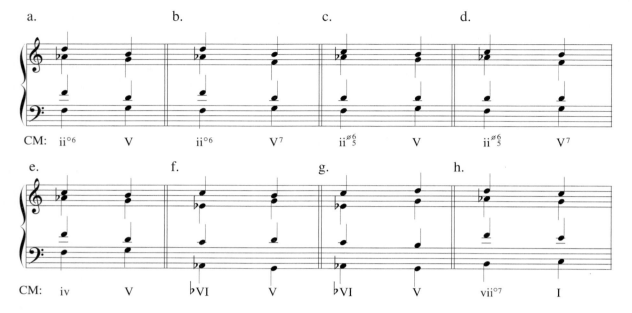

Chromatic Harmony

Assignment 4.1

1. Write each requested chord in four-part harmony on the staves provided.
2. Write the chord that most conventionally follows the chord you wrote in step 1.
3. Analyze both chords.
4. The example illustrates the correct procedure.

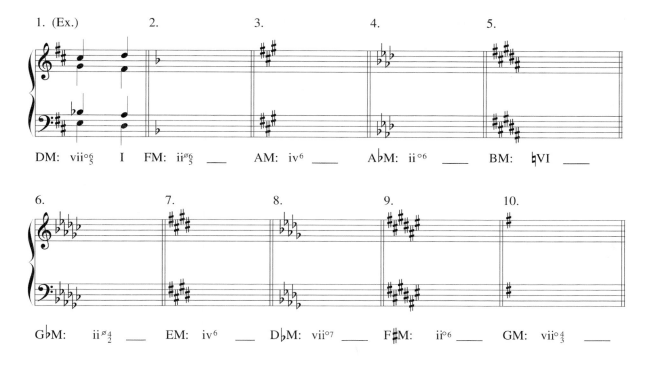

1. (Ex.)   2.   3.   4.   5.

DM: vii°⁶₅   I   FM: ii°⁶₅ ___   AM: iv⁶ ___   A♭M: ii°⁶ ___   BM: ♮VI ___

6.   7.   8.   9.   10.

G♭M: ii°₄₂ ___   EM: iv⁶ ___   D♭M: vii°⁷ ___   F♯M: ii°⁶ ___   GM: vii°₄₃ ___

Assignment 4.2

Below are four-part phrases with alto and tenor voices omitted.

Keyboard Assignment

If your instructor requests you to do so, play each chorale phrase on the piano, adding the alto and tenor voices according to the figured bass symbols. If you have difficulty with this assignment, try the following suggestions:

1. Play each chord in simple position (all voices within one octave and with the left hand). Listen to the sound and try to remember the particular quality of each chord.
2. When you have the sounds well in mind, play the two outer voices alone.
3. Start adding the alto and tenor (soprano, alto, and tenor with the right hand). Put your fifth finger (RH) on the key representing the soprano voice.
4. Place your third finger on the next factor down and your thumb on the lowest right-hand factor. Do not leave out any factors in the right hand.
5. Check to see if this position causes a voice-leading error. If not, then proceed to the next chord and repeat the procedure.

Written Assignment

1. Add alto and tenor voices according to the figured bass symbols.
2. Provide a complete harmonic analysis.

Borrowed Chords

76   Chromatic Harmony

Assignment 4.3

Each exercise is a figured bass voice.

Keyboard Assignment

1. Play each exercise, adding the soprano, alto, and tenor voices.
2. Become familiar with the chords first, then work to obtain an interesting soprano voice line, perhaps with an ascent and a descent.
3. Look at the soprano melody lines in assignment 4.2 for ideas.
4. If you have other difficulties with this assignment, use the procedures described in assignment 4.2 and adapt them.

Written Assignment

1. On a separate sheet of paper write out each figured bass line, leaving a staff above for the soprano and alto.
2. If you have difficulty with this assignment, write the letter names of each chord factor under the figured bass symbols. This will help you fashion a better soprano melody line.
3. When you have decided on a suitable soprano melody line, write it on the staff and fill in the alto and tenor accordingly.
4. To help in writing the soprano melody, observe the soprano voices in assignment 4.2. Each is a traditional chorale melody and will give you an idea of the style.

Assignment 4.4

Below is a complete chorale melody.

Bach: *Wo Gott zum Haus nicht gibt sein Gunst* (If God Does Not Give His Blessings), BWV 438.

1. Harmonize the melody on a separate sheet of score paper.
2. Use a harmonic rhythm of one chord per quarter note.
3. Write out all possible harmonies as described in previous chapters, then select a suitable harmonization and write the block chords beneath the melody tones. Be sure to include at least two or three borrowed chords.
4. Convert the block chords to four-part harmony with special emphasis on an interesting bass line.
5. Add appropriate nonharmonic tones.
6. Perform the compositions in class using a student quartet, each singing one of the four parts (soprano, alto, tenor, and bass).

Assignment 4.5

Write a composition of approximately sixteen to twenty-four measures in length.

1. Plan the composition in three-part form.
2. Use four-measure phrases.
3. Plot the harmonic progressions first in block chords.
4. Add an appropriate melody.
5. Convert the block chords to the idiomatic style of the medium you choose. As an example, if you write for a group of stringed instruments, arrange the harmony to accommodate the peculiarities of the instruments involved.
6. Be sure to include at least three or four borrowed chords. Remember that borrowed chords can generally substitute for their diatonic counterparts.

CHAPTER 5

Neapolitan 6th Chords

Topic	*Neapolitan 6th: N6*
Important Concepts	The *Neapolitan 6th* chord is a major triad on the lowered second scale degree of a major or minor scale (figure 5.1).

Figure 5.1

Major key: Minor key:

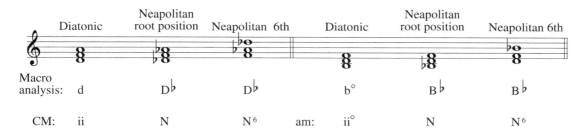

Macro analysis:	d	D♭	D♭	b°	B♭	B♭
CM:	ii	N	N⁶	am: ii°	N	N⁶

Position	The Neapolitan usually appears in first inversion—thus the name Neapolitan "sixth."
Name	The meaning of the name Neapolitan is unknown, but some believe that it is a reference to the "Neapolitan" school of eighteenth-century opera composers.
Mode	The Neapolitan is found far more often in minor than in major keys.

Figure 5.2 shows a typical use of the Neapolitan. The Neapolitan is an altered ii chord, so the N⁶ V I is a circle progression (A♭ D g). Perform figure 5.2 if you have a pianist and singer, or play the chords in the accompaniment. Then play the same example again, changing the A♭ in chord number 3 to an A-natural. You can then get the full effect of the Neapolitan chord. No doubt you have heard many Neapolitan chords without realizing it.

Figure 5.2

Schubert: *Der Müller und der Bach* (The Miller and the Brook) from *Die schöne Müllerin* (The Beautiful Miller's Daughter), op. 25, no. 19, D. 795, mm. 22–27.

Figure 5.3 is an excerpt from the familiar *Moonlight* Sonata of Beethoven. First play the excerpt as written, then change the D-naturals in chord 3 to D-sharps. Notice the similar effect to that of figure 5.2.

Figure 5.3

Beethoven: Piano Sonata (*Moonlight*) in C♯ Minor, op. 27, no. 2, I (Adagio Sostenuto), mm. 49–50.

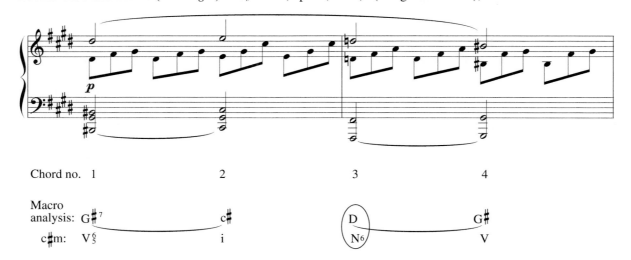

In figure 5.4 you will see how several chords can each point toward the dominant chord (chord 3). Play the example as printed, then play only chords 1 and 3 (leaving out g#°7). Because both chords (1 and 2) resolve naturally to the dominant (V), they are called *pre-dominant effects*. Later you will see larger and more complex pre-dominant sections.

Figure 5.4

Mozart: Fantasia, K. 397 in D Minor, mm. 8–9.

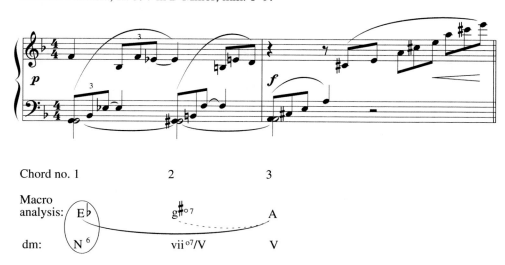

Chord no. 1   2   3

Macro analysis: Eb   g#°7   A

dm: N^6 vii°7/V   V

Some Exceptional Uses of the Neapolitan

Although the Neapolitan is usually found in minor keys and in first inversion, there are a number of other places where it sometimes appears.

1. A Neapolitan may, on occasion, be included in a passage consisting of nonfunctional harmony. During the classical period the nonfunctional harmony often contained a series of first-inversion triads in parallel motion (figure 5.6).
2. The Neapolitan may sometimes be found in root position (figures 5.7 and 5.8).
3. The Neapolitan, especially in the romantic period, may be preceded by V^7/N or vii°^{6}/N, thus the N becomes a tonicized chord (figure 5.8).
4. The Neapolitan is occasionally found in the major mode (figure 5.9).
5. Somewhat rare is a Neapolitan chord that also contains a 7th factor.

History

Baroque Period (1600–1750)

The Neapolitan 6th first appeared in the baroque period and was treated very conservatively. Most often the N^6 was placed near a cadence point and was considered a substitute for the diatonic ii or ii° (figure 5.5).

Neapolitan 6th Chords   **81**

Figure 5.5

Bach: Evangelist's recitativo from *St. Matthew's Passion*, BWV 244, no. 68, mm. 1–3.

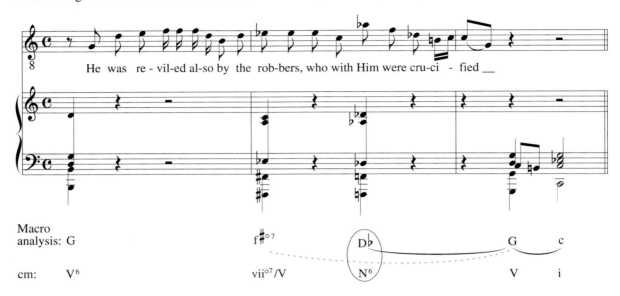

Classical Period (1750–1825)

In the classical period nontraditional examples surface occasionally. Figure 5.6, from a piano sonata by Haydn, shows a series of nonfunctional first-inversion triads that descend in parallel motion. The N^6 is one of the chords in the series and takes part in the stepwise downward movement.

Figure 5.6

Haydn: Sonata in E Minor, Hob. XVI:34, I (Presto), mm. 114–117.

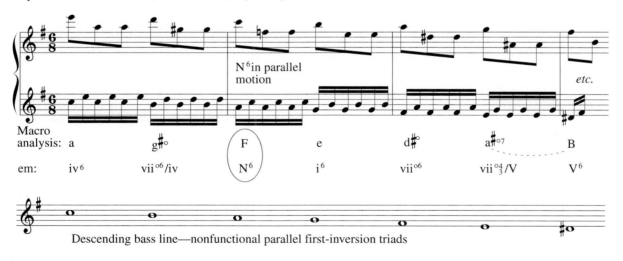

Romantic Period (1825–1900)

The use of the N^6 continued throughout the romantic period and treatment broadened considerably. In figure 5.7 most listeners hear the N as a passing chord: i^6 N V^7/iv.

Figure 5.7

Schubert: *Der Doppelgänger* (The Double) from *Schwanengesang* (Swan Song), D. 957, no. 13, mm. 56–62.

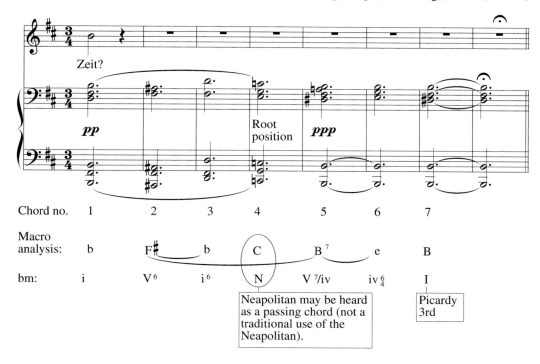

Figure 5.7 shows the Neapolitan in root position, considerable parallel voicing, and a final tonic chord (chord no. 7) that leaves some doubt about its actual function as a tonic.

Figure 5.8 illustrates the Neapolitan tonicized by a secondary leading tone. The tonicized chord appears in first inversion following an earlier presentation of the Neapolitan in root position.

Figure 5.8

Chopin: Prelude, op. 28, no. 12, mm. 70–73.

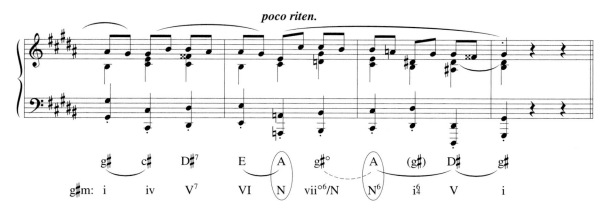

Post-Romantic and Impressionistic Period (1875–1920)

Because the N⁶ is primarily a device of the baroque, classical, and romantic periods, its presence in the post-romantic and impressionistic period is rare. However, the composers of this transitional period occasionally returned to the idiom of the romantic period. The example in figure 5.9, by Prokofiev, written circa 1910, reveals a Neapolitan sixth with nearly traditional treatment.

Figure 5.9

Prokofiev: "The Moon Strolls in the Meadows" from *Music for Children,* op. 65, no. 12, mm. 77–82.

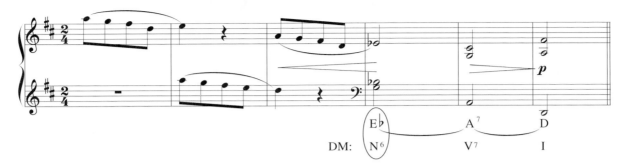

| | | **Doubling and Voice Leading** | The following guidelines are provided to assist you with writing the N⁶ chord and its resolution. |

Doubling and Voice Leading

The following guidelines are provided to assist you with writing the N^6 chord and its resolution.

Doubled Note

Double the bass note (third of the chord) whenever possible. Note the unique melodic d3rd in the soprano voice, considered a desirable trait by composers.

Motion to V

When moving from N^6 to V, you can usually move the upper voices (soprano, alto, and tenor) down in contrary motion to the bass to the nearest chord tones of V.

Motion to V⁷

In the progression N^6 to V^7 you can also move two voices down, but the remaining voice may be kept as a common tone.

Chromatic Voice Leading

Avoid chromatic voice leading (D♭ to D, for example) in any voice when leaving N^6.

Caution

When the N^6 proceeds to I_4^6 or i_4^6, watch out for parallel 5ths. Turn them upside down—into parallel 4ths.

Applications

Figure 5.10 shows standard voice-leading patterns for the Neapolitan.

Figure 5.10

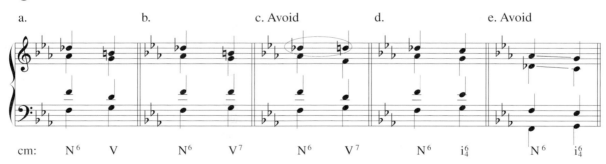

Figure 5.10a: Best voice leading: melodic skip (diminished 3rd) in highest voice

Figure 5.10b: N^6 to V^7 virtually the same as N^6 to V

Figure 5.10c: Avoid chromatic voice leading—D-flat to D-natural

Figure 5.10d: N^6 progresses smoothly to i_4^6

Figure 5.10e: Unacceptable parallel 5ths

Assignment 5.1

Each triad in four-part harmony given below is the V chord in a minor key.

1. Determine the key and write it in the blank beneath the staves.
2. Write the key signature, on the grand staff, at the beginning of each exercise.
3. Determine the Neapolitan 6th chord in this key and write it in four-part harmony so that it leads smoothly to the V triad.
4. Place the analysis in the blanks beneath each chord.

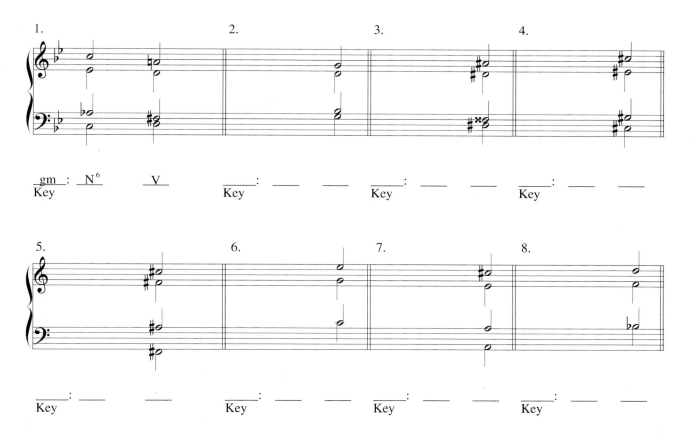

1.

gm   :   N⁶   V
Key

2.

____ : ____   ____
Key

3.

____ : ____   ____
Key

4.

____ : ____   ____
Key

5.

____ : ____   ____
Key

6.

____ : ____   ____
Key

7.

____ : ____   ____
Key

8.

____ : ____   ____
Key

Assignment 5.2

On the following pages are four four-part chorale phrases.

Keyboard Assignment

1. If your instructor requests you to do so, play each chorale phrase on the piano, adding the alto and tenor voices according to the figured bass symbols.
2. If this proves too difficult, play each chord in simple position (all voices within one octave and with the left hand).
3. When you are familiar with the sound of each, then begin working with both hands, fitting the upper voices into their range.

Written Assignment

1. Add the tenor and alto voices according to the figured bass symbols.
2. Provide a complete harmonic analysis.

Chromatic Harmony

Assignment 5.3

Each exercise consists of a figured bass voice.

Keyboard Assignment

1. Play each exercise, adding soprano, alto, and tenor voices.
2. Become familiar with the chords first, then work to obtain an interesting voice line, perhaps with an ascent and a descent.
3. If your instructor concurs, use keyboard voicing—three upper voices with the right hand and the bass with the left.

Written Assignment

1. On a separate sheet of paper write out each figured bass, leaving a staff above for the soprano and alto.
2. Complete the remaining three upper voices according to the figuration supplied.
3. Observe part-writing practices cited in this chapter.
4. To help in writing the soprano melody, observe the soprano voices in assignment 5.2. Each is a traditional chorale melody and will give you an idea of the style.

Assignment 5.4

Each exercise is similar to a music illustration in this chapter.

1. Add the macro analysis and Roman numerals using the illustrations as a guide.
2. Write a short excerpt (25 to 100 words) for each exercise summarizing the analysis or explaining a portion of the analysis that cannot be explained otherwise. Use the analyzed illustrations in this chapter as a guide.

1. Chopin: Valse, op. 64, no. 2, mm. 142–145. CD Track 5

Macro
analysis:

bm:

2. Chopin: Scherzo, op. 39, mm. 634–637. CD Track 6

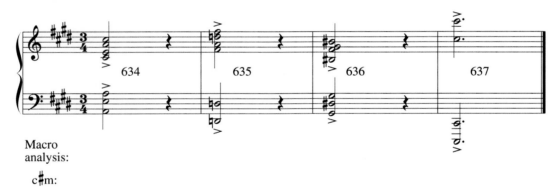

Macro
analysis:

c♯m:

3. Chopin: Valse, op. 64, no. 2, mm. 187–190. CD Track 7

Macro
analysis:

c♯m:

4. Beethoven: Bagatelle, op. 119, no. 9, mm. 17–20. CD Track 8

Macro
analysis:

  am:

5. Chopin: Mazurka, op. 7, no. 2, mm. 11–16. CD Track 9

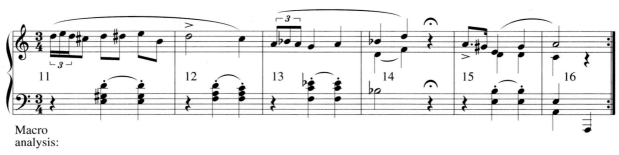

Macro
analysis:

  am:

Assignment 5.5

For the following composition:

1. Make a complete analysis (macro or traditional).
2. Discuss the following:
   a. The use of Neapolitan 6th chords.
   b. The overall form of the composition.
   c. Cadence formulae.
   d. Harmonic rhythm.
   e. The use of melodic structural tones.

Maria Theresia von Paradis: *Sicilienne.* CD Track 10

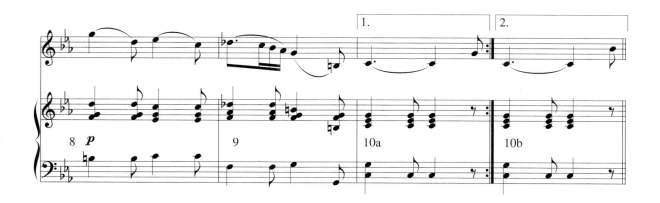

Chromatic Harmony

Neapolitan 6th Chords

CHAPTER 6

Augmented 6th Chords

<table>
<tr><td>**Topics**</td><td>*Italian 6th: It⁶*</td><td>*French 6th: Fr⁶*</td><td>*German 6th: Gr⁶*</td></tr>
</table>

Topics   *Italian 6th: It^6*   *French 6th: Fr^6*   *German 6th: Gr^6*

Important Concepts

Augmented 6th chords are chords that have been altered to include the interval of an augmented 6th. Their sound is unique and so different from the diatonic chords that they are given special analysis symbols: It^6, Fr^6, and Gr^6.

Three Types

Figure 6.1 shows the three types of augmented 6th chords. The geographic names are traditional and their origin is unknown.

Italian 6th: M3rd + Aug. 6th (total of three notes).

French 6th: M3rd + Aug. 4th + Aug. 6th (total of four notes).

German 6th: M3rd + Perf. 5th + Aug. 6th (total of four notes).

Figure 6.1

am: It^6 Fr^6 Gr^6 cm: It^6 Fr^6 Gr^6

The augmented 6th chords have three notes in common (figure 6.2).

Figure 6.2

White notes = notes in common

am: It^6 Gr^6 Fr^6

Bass Note Location

The bass note (or lowest-sounding tone) is usually a major 3rd below the tonic in both major or minor keys (figure 6.2).

Fourth Scale Degree	The fourth scale degree is raised in all three types of augmented 6th chords (figure 6.3).

Figure 6.3

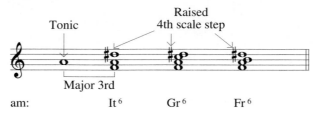

Progression	The most common progressions from an augmented 6th chord are shown in figure 6.4.

The Italian 6th resolves to V directly or through i_4^6.

The French 6th resolves to V directly or through i_4^6.

The German 6th must resolve to V through i_4^6.

Figure 6.4

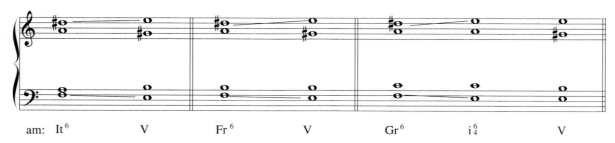

Note that the German 6th is often followed by i_4^6 in order to avoid parallell fifths. The augmented 6th expands out to an octave in all three chord types.

Examples from Literature

Figure 6.5 shows the German 6th chord in a musical context.

Figure 6.5

Schumann: *Ich kann nicht fassen* (I Cannot Comprehend) from *Frauenlieben und Leben* (A Woman's Life and Loves), op. 42, no. 3, mm. 48–52.

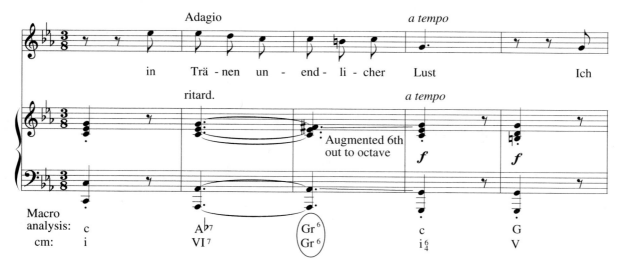

Notice the standard voice leading in figure 6.5:

1. The augmented 6th (A♭–F♯) resolves to an octave.
2. The Gr⁶ resolves to the dominant (through the i_4^6 in this case).
3. The bass note (A♭) in the Gr⁶ is a major 3rd below the tonic (C).

(The parallel octaves in the bass are not intended as independent voices but are merely a way to make the bass voice more prominent.)

Figure 6.6 shows a French 6th chord in a march by John Phillip Sousa.

Figure 6.6

Sousa: *The Free Lance*, mm. 28–31.

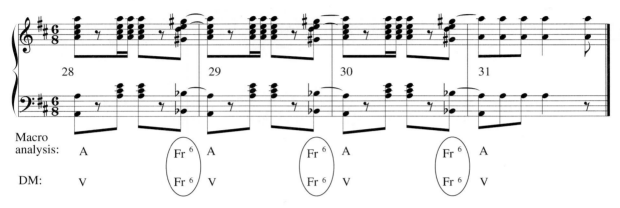

The Fr⁶ is repeated three times in this short excerpt. Notice how the three principles of resolution described above are observed each time.

Figure 6.7 shows an Italian 6th chord in another march by Sousa.

Figure 6.7

Sousa: *The Liberty Bell*, mm. 98–100.

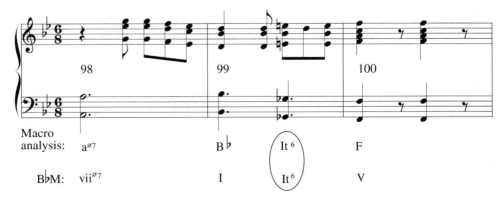

Again, notice how the three principles are observed in the resolution of the It⁶ in figure 6.7. It should be obvious from these examples that the three types of augmented 6th chords are treated in much the same way.

Figure 6.8 is a highly chromatic example from a Haydn symphony. Functional harmony is suspended through measures 81 and 82 and the music is organized around a

Augmented 6th Chords **95**

descending chromatic bass line (G, G♭, F, E, E♭, D, D♭). Nevertheless, when the German 6th chord is reached at the end of the passage, it resolves in the normal way.

Figure 6.8

Haydn: Symphony no. 97, Movement II, mm. 80–84.

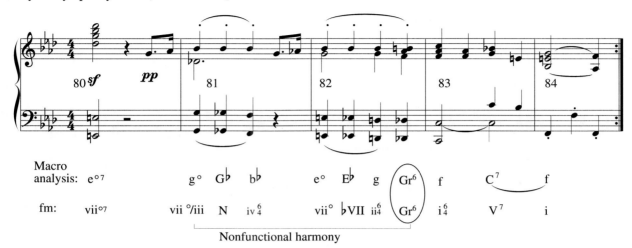

The harmonic thrust of the passage above is to prepare for the dominant. Such passages are often called pre-dominant sections.

Exceptions

Although by far the largest number of augmented 6th chords occur as described, some exceptions should be noted, as follows:

Different Position

Occasionally, augmented 6th chords occur in positions other than those listed. Traditionally the chord maintains its name (augmented 6th) even when the augmented 6th is inverted to a diminished 3rd.

Bass Note on Other Scale Degrees

In rare instances the bass note of any augmented 6th chord may be a scale degree other than the customary major 3rd below tonic.

Augmented 6th Interval Inverted

Sometimes the augmented 6th interval is inverted, thus creating a diminished 3rd (figure 6.11).

Added Notes

In some cases an augmented 6th chord may include added notes.

History

Baroque Period (1600–1750)

Treatment of the augmented 6th chords in the baroque period was conservative. Figure 6.9 is from a toccata by Domenico Zipoli (1688–1726), a contemporary of Bach. Notice how the i⁶₄ is used to avoid parallel 5ths.

Figure 6.9

Zipoli: Toccata.

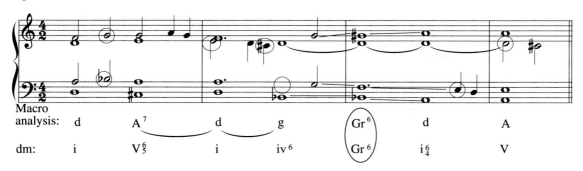

Macro
analysis: d   A⁷   d   g   (Gr⁶)   d   A

dm: i   V⁶₅   i   iv⁶   (Gr⁶)   i⁶₄   V

**Classical Period
(1750–1825)**

In the classical period the augmented 6th chords were used much more frequently. Figure 6.10 shows the Fr⁶ used in the standard way.

Figure 6.10

Mozart: *Das Veilchen* (The Violet), K. 476, mm. 39–42.

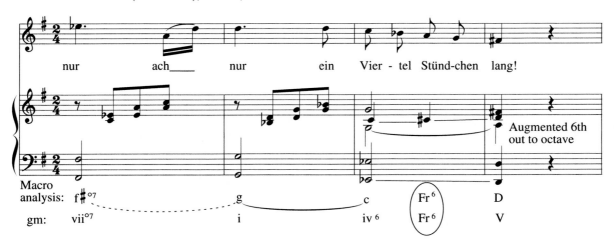

Macro
analysis: f♯°⁷   g   c   (Fr⁶)   D

gm: vii°⁷   i   iv⁶   (Fr⁶)   V

**Romantic Period
(1825–1900)**

The use of augmented 6th chords reached their zenith during the romantic period, and handling of the chords became freer and more unpredictable. Figure 6.11 contains an augmented 6th chord in a different position, with the augmented 6th interval inverted into a diminished 3rd.

Figure 6.11

Chopin: Prelude, op. 28, no. 22, mm. 39–41.

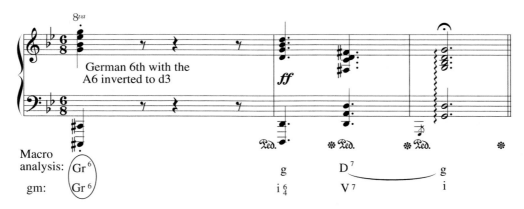

Post-Romantic and Impressionistic Period (1875–1920)

Although a number of examples of chords bear the augmented sound in this period, few would be considered true augmented 6th chords. In figure 6.12, a German 6th chord progresses directly to the tonic, destroying the characteristic sound of the augmented 6th resolution to an octave.

Figure 6.12

Ravel: *Sonatine*, I, mm. 84–87.

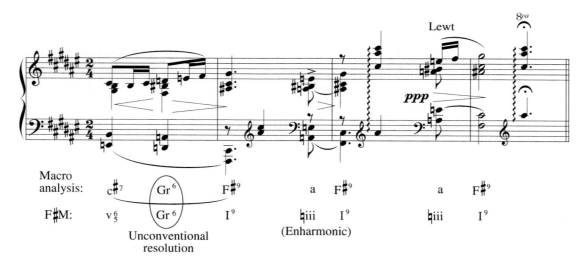

Jazz and Popular Music (1900-Present)

Augmented 6th chords occur throughout popular music, but especially in ragtime. Scott Joplin, one of the better-known composers of ragtime, often used these chords in his compositions (figure 6.13). Note again the string of pre-dominant chords—ii⁶, Gr⁶, and I⁶₄.

Figure 6.13

Joplin: "Bink's Waltz," mm. 95–99.

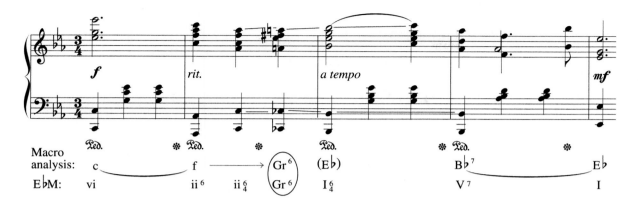

Macro analysis:						
	c	f	→ Gr^6	(E♭)	B♭^{7}	E♭
E♭M:	vi	ii^6	ii$^6_4$ Gr^6	I$^6_4$	V^7	I

Doubling and Voice Leading

Doubling
Neither of the two notes forming the augmented 6th interval is ever doubled. In the Italian 6th, double the tonic scale degree (the 3rd above the bass note).

Resolution
The bass note of the augmented 6th chord resolves down a half step—either to the root of V, or the fifth of i$^6_4$.

Tonic $^6_4$
The progression from augmented 6th chords to to i$^6_4$ is only a partial resolution. The final resolution occurs when V is reached.

Parallel 5ths
To avoid parallel 5ths, the Gr^6 proceeds i$^6_4$ or I$^6_4$ instead of V.

Gr^6 Spellings
The Gr^6 chord has two spellings. In major keys, the pitch a P5 above the bass note is sometimes respelled as an AA4:

Spelling of Gr^6 in C minor: A♭ C E♭ F♯.

Spelling of Gr^6 in C major: A♭ C D♯ F♯.

Applications
The augmented 6th chords are normally resolved using the three principles outlined on page 94 (figure 6.4). Figure 6.14 shows some problems to be avoided in resolving the Gr^6. Figure 6.14a shows the parallel 5ths that result if the Gr^6 is resolved directly to the dominant. The preferred resolution through the i$^6_4$ is shown in figure 6.14b. In major keys the normal spelling of the Gr^6 (figure 6.14c) results in an undesirable chromaticism (E♭–E♮). In these cases composers spelled the Gr^6 enharmonically to achieve a more normal voice leading (D♯–E), as shown in figure 6.14d.

Figure 6.14

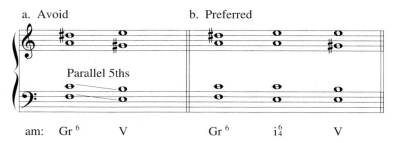

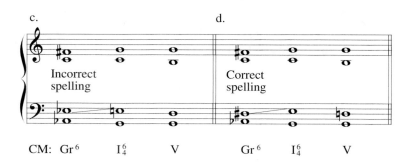

Assignment 6.1
1. Write the requested chord in simple position on the staff.
2. Name the key. Each given tone is the bass note of the augmented 6th chord and is a major 3rd below the tonic of a minor key.
3. The example illustrates the correct procedure.

1. (Ex.) Gr⁶   2. Fr⁶   3. Gr⁶   4. Fr⁶   5. Gr⁶   6. It⁶   7. Gr⁶   8. Fr⁶   9. Gr⁶   10. Fr⁶

Key: am   _____ _____ _____ _____ _____ _____ _____ _____ _____

Assignment 6.2
In each exercise, an augmented 6th chord in four-part harmony is given.

1. Write the most conventional resolution in four-part harmony.
2. In the blank provided, name the key. The bass tone of each given augmented 6th chord is a major 3rd below the tonic of the key.
3. Analyze both chords (the given chord and its resolution).
4. The example illustrates correct procedure.

1. (Ex.) g♯m   2. _____   3. _____   4. _____   5. _____   6. _____   7. _____

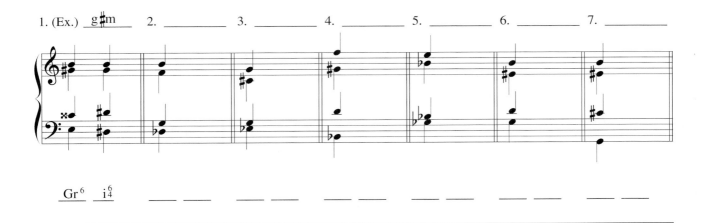

Gr⁶ i⁶₄   ____ ____   ____ ____   ____ ____   ____ ____   ____ ____   ____ ____

Assignment 6.3
The following examples are taken from four-part chorale phrases.

Keyboard Assignment
1. Play each chorale phrase on the piano, adding the alto and tenor voice according to the figured bass symbols.
2. If you have difficulty with this assignment, play each chord in simple position (all voices within one octave and with the left hand).
3. When you are familiar with the sound of each example, begin working with both hands, fitting the upper voices into their proper range.

Augmented 6th Chords

Written Assignment

1. Add the alto and tenor voices according to the figured bass symbols.
2. Provide a complete harmonic analysis.

1.

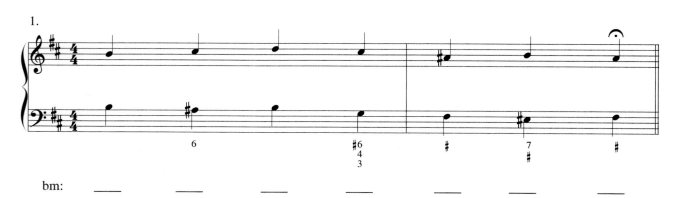

bm: ____ ____ ____ ____ ____ ____ ____

2.

em: ____ ____ ____ ____ ____ ____ ____

3.

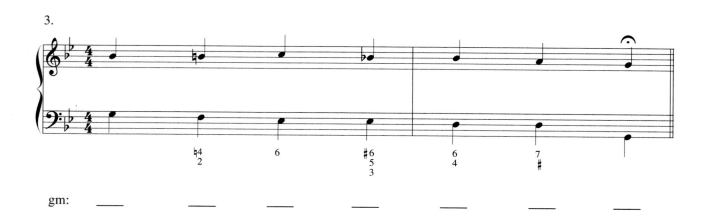

gm: ____ ____ ____ ____ ____ ____ ____

Chromatic Harmony

Assignment 6.4   The following examples are three figured bass lines.

Keyboard Assignment

1. Play each figured bass, adding soprano, alto, and tenor according to the figured bass symbols.
2. If you have difficulty, become familiar with the chords first, then work on a good soprano melody.
3. Look at the melodies in assignment 6.3 for ideas.

Written Assignment

1. On a separate sheet of paper, copy out the bass notes and figuration.
2. Be sure to include an additional staff for the soprano and alto voices.
3. If you have difficulty with this assignment, write out the pitches in simple position (one above the other without regard for voicing). With this procedure you will be better able to fashion a desirable melody.
4. When you think you have an acceptable soprano melody, fill in the inner voices (alto and tenor).
5. When you are finished, provide a complete analysis.

Assignment 6.5

Each excerpt is similar to the music analyzed in this chapter.

1. Add a macro analysis and a Roman numeral analysis using the illustrations as a guide.
2. Write a short essay (50 to 100 words) for each excerpt summarizing the analysis. Use the descriptions in the chapter as a guide.

1. Scott Joplin: "The Cascades," mm. 40–43. CD Track 11

Macro
analysis:

B♭M:

2. Tom Turpin: "The St. Louis Rag," mm. 66–68. CD Track 12

Macro
analysis:

FM:

3. Scott Joplin: "The Chrysanthemum," mm. 17–20. CD Track 13

Macro
analysis:

B♭M:

4. Mozart: Sonata in F Major, K. 332, III, mm. 61–65. CD Track 14

Macro
analysis:

CM:

5. Mozart: Sonata in D Major, K. 284, III, Variation VII, mm. 2–5. CD Track 15

Macro
analysis:

dm:

Assignment 6.6

The excerpts which follow contain augmented 6th chords. Provide a complete harmonic analysis of each excerpt and discuss the following:

1. How many instances of augmented 6th chords did you find in the excerpts?
2. How many chords in the excerpts are part (either beginning or end) of a circle progression?
3. Name all chords (other than augmented 6th chords and triads in second inversion) that are NOT part of a circle progression.

1. Beethoven: Sonata in F Minor, op. 2, no. 1, I, mm. 139–152. CD Track 16

2. Beethoven: Thirty-two Variations, WoO 80, Variation XXX. CD Track 17

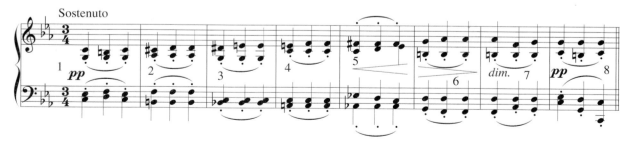

3. Beethoven: Sonata in C Minor (*Pathétique*), op. 13, no. 8, III, mm. 41–47. CD Track 18

4. Tchaikovsky: Piano Concerto no. 1 in B-flat Minor, op. 23, II, mm. 13–20. CD Track 19

Augmented 6th Chords

The Classical Period (1750–1825)

Many of our best-known composers lived during the classical period. Haydn, Mozart, and Beethoven all lived in this artistically rich period. The balance shifted even more than in the baroque period in favor of instrumental music, although operas continued to be written. Chamber music, orchestral music, and other instrumental works gained the ascendancy. The sonata and the symphony developed during the classical period, and the string quartet took the place of the older trio sonata. The pianoforte (our modern piano), invented in 1709 by Christofori, became a popular household instrument. In the classical period the orchestral literature grew in size and importance, and the orchestra itself acquired more color and flexibility. Clarinets became permanent fixtures in the orchestra, along with flutes, oboes, and bassoons.

In the following section we will examine representative movements from classical sonatas. Most of these movements are in one of three forms: theme and variation, sonata, and rondo. The classical theme and variation developed out of instrumental variations by sixteenth- and seventeenth-century composers such as Antonio de Cabezón, William Byrd, and Girolamo Frescobaldi, whereas the sonata form has historical precedents in the rounded binary forms of the baroque dance suite. The classical rondo developed from the French rondeau of Jean-Baptiste Lully, Jean-Philippe Rameau, and François Couperin. These forms, which were perfected in the classical period, became the most prominent forms of the romantic period and have persisted into the twentieth century.

CHAPTER 7

Variation Technique

Topics

Variation
Continuous variation
Ground bass
Basso ostinato
Chaconne
Passacaglia

Theme and variation
Embellished melodic line
Unique rhythmic figure
Change of meter
Change of mode
Alberti bass figure

Change of harmony
Change of tempo
Extended pitch range
Harmonic motive
Repeated motive
Change of voice

Important Concepts

Variation is a musical technique for modifying a musical idea, usually after its first appearance. In figure 7.1 the musical idea is a melody that is then decorated with neighboring tones.

Figure 7.1

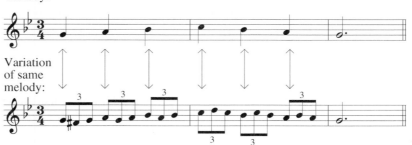

Continuous Variation

Continuous variation is a type of variation technique where there is a repeated bass line, repeated harmonic progression, repeated rhythmic pattern, or various combinations of the three. The composer weaves new musical materials around the repeated pattern. One of the most common types of continuous variation employs a *ground bass*—also called *basso ostinato*. The ground usually consists of a short melody of four to eight measures that is generally maintained in the lowest voice and is repeated throughout the composition. The terms *chaconne* or *passacaglia* refer to specific types of continuous variation compositions. The composition by André Raison (1654–1719) in figure 7.2 predates the better-known passacaglia by Bach.

Figure 7.2

Raison: Passacaille in G Minor from *Messe du Deuxieme Ton* (Mass of the Second Tone), mm. 1–16.

1st statement of ground (basso ostinato)

2nd statement of ground (basso ostinato)

3rd statement of ground (basso ostinato)

4th statement of ground (basso ostinato)

The ground bass in figure 7.2 is four measures long. The composer has created a two-voiced contrapuntal texture above the ground bass. Notice that the upper lines are different for each statement of the ground bass. Beginning with the third statement, the ground bass is decorated. As is typical with most ground bass compositions, there is little if any pause between the statements of the ground.

Theme and Variation

The *theme and variation* is a composition where a theme is stated first and then followed by a series of variations. Each variation is complete within itself and is usually followed by a short pause.

Figures 7.3 to 7.10 illustrate some of the more frequent techniques of variation. The theme chosen is the first phrase of "God Save the King," better known in the United States as "America." Most of the illustrations are excerpted from Beethoven's set of variations (1803). Of course, Beethoven employed the entire melody, but for purposes of space conservation only the first phrase is shown here. Figure 7.3 is the first phrase of the theme.

Figure 7.3

Beethoven: Seven Variations on "God Save the King," WoO 78, Theme, mm. 1–6.

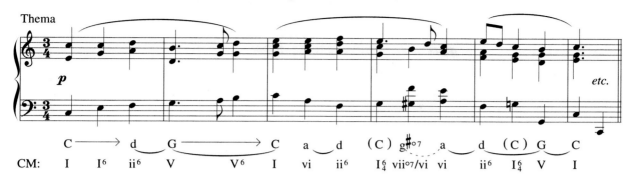

Embellished Melodic Line

One of the most common techniques is to decorate the theme with additional notes. In figure 7.4 the original melody notes are present but highly embellished. A change of meter also occurs.

Figure 7.4

Beethoven: Seven Variations on "God Save the King," WoO 78, Variation VII, mm. 1–6.

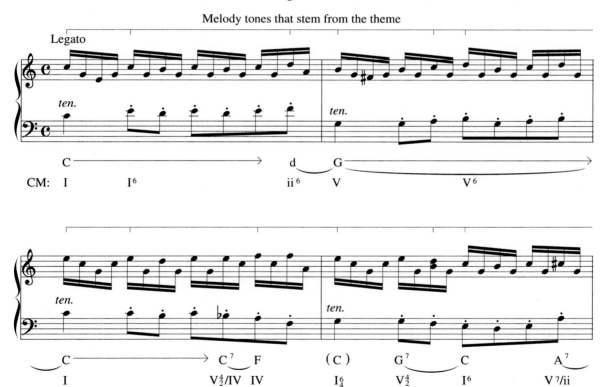

d d⁷ (C) f♯°⁷ G⁷ C

ii ii⁶ ii⁶₅ I⁶₄ vii°⁷/V V⁷ I

Introduction of a Unique Rhythmic Figure	In Variation VI (figure 7.5) Beethoven introduces a short rhythmic figure (dotted 8th–16th) not present in the original. The figure is heard 14 times in this short excerpt.
Change of Meter	Whereas the original theme ("America") is in $\frac{3}{4}$ meter, variation VI is in $\frac{4}{4}$.
Embellished Melodic Line	As in Variation VII (figure 7.4), the melody in Variation VI is also embellished.

Figure 7.5

Beethoven: Seven Variations on "God Save the King," WoO 78, Variation VI, mm. 1–6.

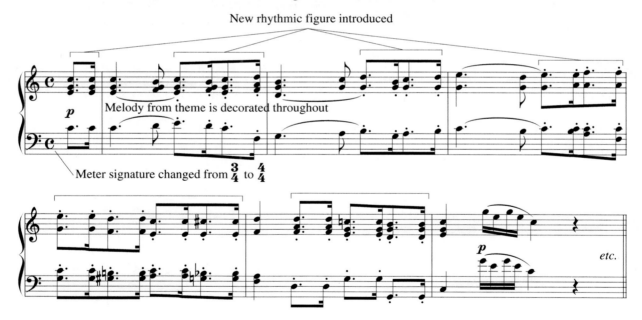

Change of Mode	In Variation V (figure 7.6) there is a change of mode to parallel minor (C major to C minor).
Alberti Bass Figure	In Variation V (figure 7.6) an Alberti bass has been added. Although the original theme is in block chords, the chords of Variation V are arpeggiated in an ascending Alberti bass pattern. As with many of the variations in this set, an embellished melodic line is also included.

Figure 7.6

Beethoven: Seven Variations on "God Save the King," WoO 78, Variation V, mm. 1–6.

Change of Harmony	In Variation VII (figure 7.7) the variation begins in a different key (D minor), and the harmony is considerably more complex. The melody itself is couched in the key of F major, but the harmonization in D minor establishes an added variation dimension.
Change of Tempo	Variation VII also demonstrates another variation technique—change of tempo. The new tempo, *Adagio*, contributes to contrast between this variation and the theme.

Figure 7.7

Beethoven: Seven Variations on "God Save the King," WoO 78, Variation VII (transition to coda), mm. 26–31.

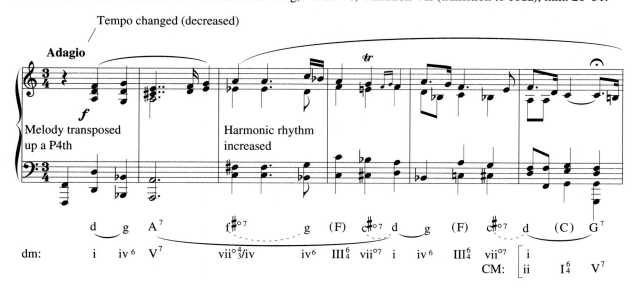

Extended Pitch Range	In Variation IV (figure 7.8) the range of the melody is extended to cover three octaves, whereas the original melody occupies the range of a diminished 5th.

Harmonic Motive	A repeated harmonic motive (dominant to tonic function) also occurs in Variation IV. The motive is harmonic since the emphasis centers on the dominant-seventh chord and its resolution.

Figure 7.8

Beethoven: Seven Variations on "God Save the King," WoO 78, Variation IV, mm. 1–6.

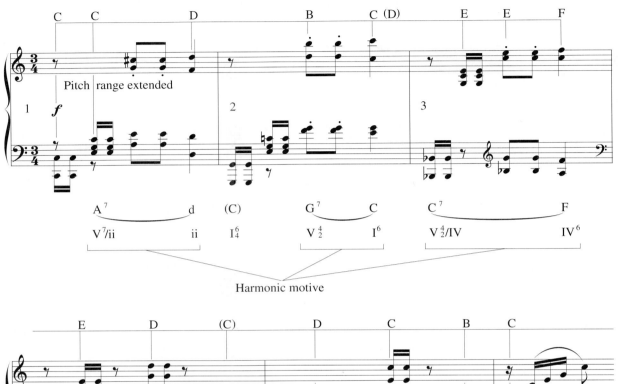

Repeated Motive	In figure 7.9 (not by Beethoven), a motive from the original melody is used as the basis for a variation. Note the imitation between the two melodic lines.

Figure 7.9

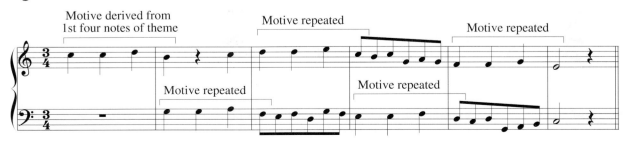

Change of Voice

In figure 7.10 (also not by Beethoven), the melody is found in the lower voice instead of the upper voice.

Figure 7.10

Theme placed in another voice:

Melody placed in bass clef:

History

Both continuous variations and theme and variations find their immediate roots in the sixteenth century. Continuous variations (also known as *basso ostinato*) were employed in English music of the late sixteenth century, and the formal aspects were maintained through the baroque, classical, and romantic periods nearly intact. The *Fitzwilliam Virginal Book* (about 1619) contains a number of continuous variations by William Byrd, John Bull, and Giles Farnaby.

The technique of theme and variations has its roots in sixteenth-century Italy and Spain, originating in dance forms such as the *passamezzo* and the *romanesca*. Almost all important composers of the baroque, classical, and romantic periods wrote compositions using theme and variation techniques.

Summary

The variation techniques listed below have been illustrated in this chapter. These are, of course, only a few of the many techniques available to composers, but they represent the more common procedures.

Embellished melodic line	Introduction of a unique rhythmic figure
Change of meter	Change of mode
Change of key	Change of harmony
Use of an Alberti bass figure	Extended pitch range
Change of tempo	Use of a repeated melodic motive
Use of harmonic motive	Change of voice

Assignment 7.1

This theme is the basis for a composition in theme-and-variation form.

1. Using the theme, write a set of five variations using the following techniques:
    a. Embellished melodic line.
    b. Introduction of an Alberti bass figure.
    c. Theme placed in another voice.
    d. Change of meter.
    e. Change of mode.
2. Write your composition for any medium you wish so long as it can be performed in class.

Russian Folk Song. CD Track 20

Assignment 7.2   Write a composition in continuous variation form.

1. Select an ostinato of four measures.
2. Plan the composition so that the ostinato is repeated eight times.
3. Sketch ideas for each new ostinato repetition.
4. Plan a perfect authentic cadence at the end of the eighth repetition.
5. Make the earlier variations on the ostinato simpler and of thinner texture.
6. Plan a gradual crescendo from the third or fourth repetition of the ostinato to the final (eighth) repetition, creating a climax with thick texture and increased dynamics.
7. If you have difficulty composing an ostinato theme of your own, you may use one of these:

Assignment 7.3

This assignment includes the complete theme and 14 excerpts from Beethoven's twenty-four variations on Righini's theme *Venni Amore*.

On a separate sheet, indicate in detail the technique or techniques used in each variation. Some variations contain more than one technique and, in addition, may include types not listed in this chapter. Describe in your own words any different or combined techniques you find that are interesting.

Beethoven: Twenty-four Variations on Righini's air *Venni Amore*, WoO 65. CD Track 21

Thema

Allegretto

Var. I, mm. 1–8.

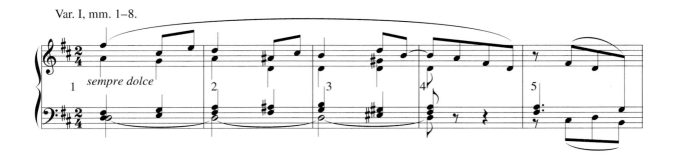

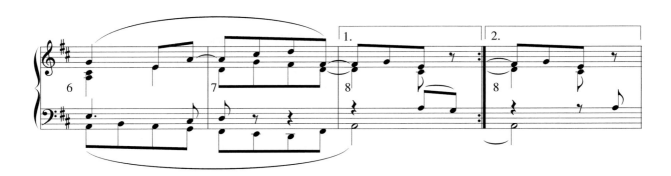

Var. II, mm. 1–4.

Var. IV, mm. 1–7.

Var. V, mm. 1–4.

Var. VI, mm. 1–8.

Var. VII, mm. 1–5.

Var. VIII, mm. 1–8.

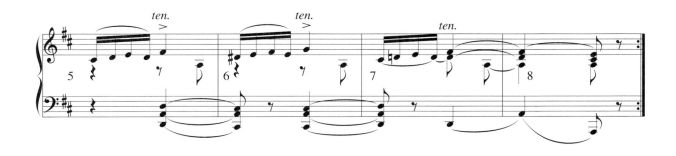

Var. XI, mm. 1–8.

Var. XII, mm. 1–8.

Var. XIII, mm. 1–5.

Var. XVI, mm. 1–5.

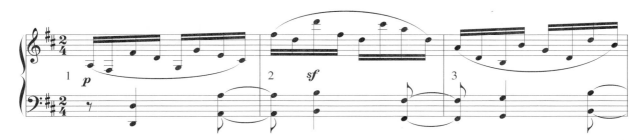

Var. XIX, mm. 1–5.

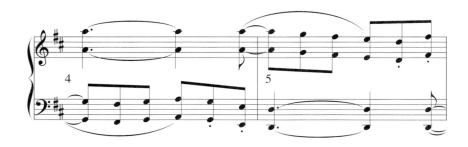

Var. XX, mm. 1–8.

Var. XXI, mm. 1–8.

Assignment 7.4   Compose a set of five variations on a theme of your choosing. You may select a well-known theme (like "Pop Goes the Weasel") or the theme from a popular song, or you may make up your own theme.

As a diversion, play only the variations (omit the statement of the theme) in class and let class members guess the theme title.

Assignment 7.5   If the *Fitzwilliam Virginal Book* is available in your music library, look over the compositions, noting all works in continuous variation form. Report the number to your class and show an example.

Assignment 7.6   Look in your school library for examples of theme-and-variation form. These are usually identified either in the title of the work or in the title of the movement in the case of multi-movement works. Sonatas from the classical period are a good place to begin your search. Report on one example of theme and variation in class, noting the variation techniques employed.

Sonata Form

Important Concepts

Sonata form is a large three-part form. The three major sections are *exposition, development,* and *recapitulation.* The term *sonata form* distinguishes the form of a single movement from the term *sonata,* which generally refers to all movements of a multimovement composition.

General Pattern

An idealized outline of the form is shown in the following chart. Few actual examples follow this structure completely.

Section	Key
Exposition	
Theme 1 or theme group 1	Tonic
Transition	Tonic to dominant, or tonic to relative major (in minor)
Theme 2 or theme group 2	Dominant, or relative major (in minor keys)
Theme 3 (optional)	Dominant, or relative major (in minor keys)
Codetta (optional)	Dominant, or relative major (in minor keys)
Development	
No standard design, but one or more themes are developed	Various keys—usually more than one
Recapitulation	
Theme 1 or theme group 1	Tonic
Transition	Tonic (no modulation or return to tonic)
Theme 2 or theme group 2	Tonic
Theme 3 or theme group 3	Tonic
Coda (optional)	Tonic

- *Exposition*
- *First Theme*
- *Theme Group*

The following movement from the Haydn piano sonata no. 4 (figure 8.1) will be analyzed and discussed.

The *exposition* states the material on which the entire movement is based. In this example the exposition is the first 28 measures of the work. The *first theme* of the sonata, in the key of G major, is stated in the first 12 measures. (Sometimes in larger sonatas, there are several melodies in this section. In such cases, they are referred to as a *theme group*.)

Figure 8.1

Haydn: Sonata in G Major, Hob. XVI:G1, I.

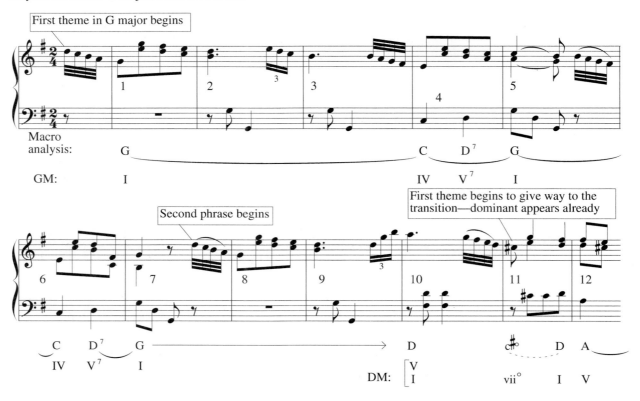

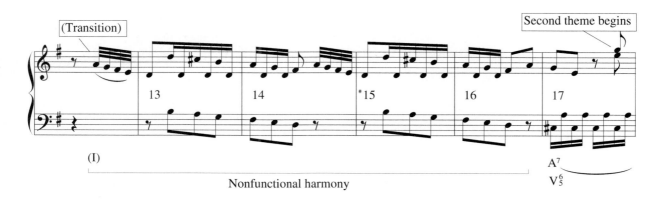

Transition

The *transition* (mm. 13–17) creates a smooth connection between the first and second themes.

- *Second Theme*
- *Third Theme (Closing Theme)*
- *Codetta*

The *second theme* (mm. 18–28) contrasts with the first theme and is in the dominant key. In movements in minor keys the second theme is often in the relative major key. In some early sonatas the second theme is a restatement of the first theme in the dominant key. Some sonatas have a *third theme* in the key of the second theme, which is often called a *closing theme*. A *codetta* often completes the exposition. In this case, we the authors feel that there is no codetta.

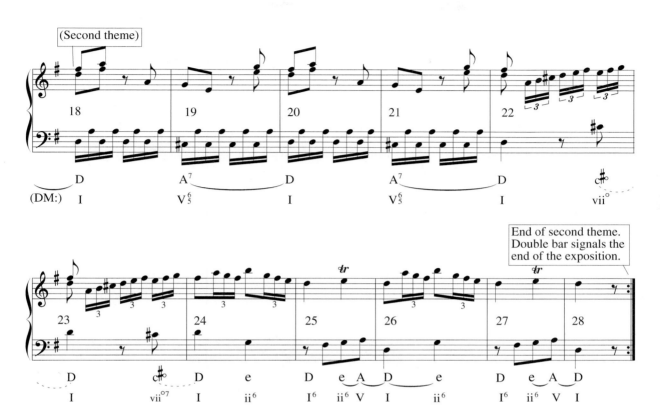

Development

The *development* consists of measures 29 to 53. Developments usually include motivic development of the themes from the exposition. Several keys not found in the exposition appear. In the Haydn sonata the development contains the first and second themes from the exposition, and the keys of C major, D major, and E minor are visited briefly. No standardized organization exists for developments, but most divide into identifiable subsections, distinguished by the thematic material.

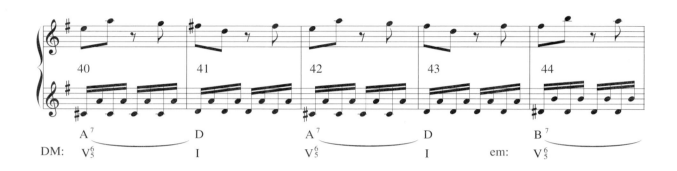

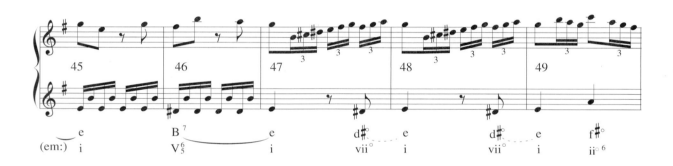

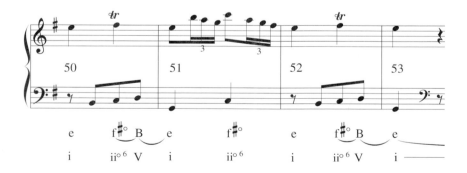

Retransition

The *retransition* is a passage at the end of the development that anticipates the recapitulation by combining fragments of the first theme and by modulating to the tonic key. In the Haydn sonata the retransition consists of measures 54 to 57.

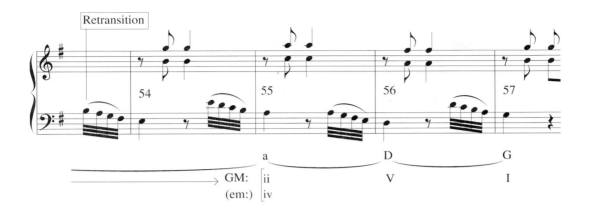

- **Recapitulation**
- **Coda**

The *recapitulation* is the balance of the sonata form. In some ways the recapitulation is quite similar to the exposition, but the original key of the composition is used for all themes. Transitions are often shorter than in the exposition because there is no need to modulate. In the Haydn sonata, the recapitulation occurs from measure 57 to the end. A *coda*, if present, is similar to, but larger than, the codetta that ended the exposition. In the present case, we the authors feel that there is no coda.

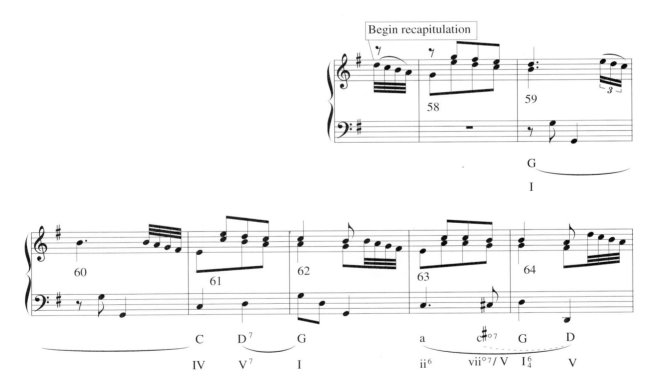

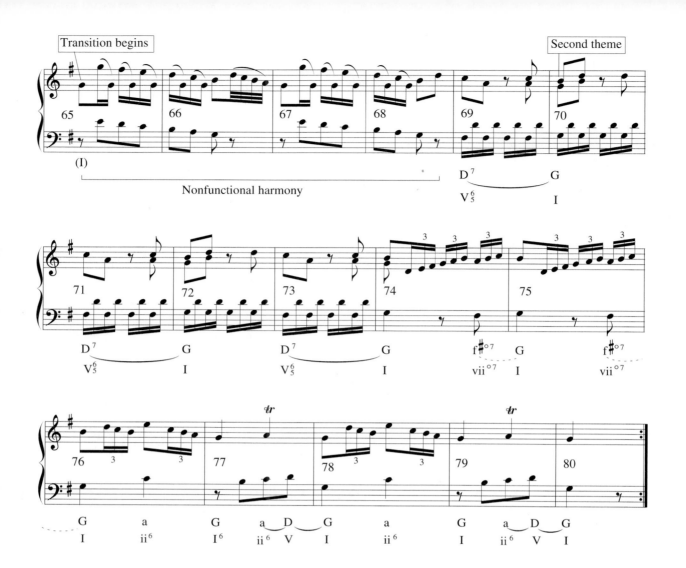

History

Although the term *sonata* was used in a variety of ways prior to 1750, this chapter addresses the form as it emerged in the mid-eighteenth century.

Sonata form developed from rounded binary form, in which the exposition was part 1 and the development–recapitulation was part 2. The process of maturation was slow, and although the binary form of the baroque period (1600–1750) contained all the necessary ingredients for sonata form, the actual culmination did not take place until the mid-eighteenth century. The form was perfected and received wide acceptance during the classical period, which saw its most concentrated application.

Applications

The Mozart sonata movement in Figure 8.2 is given a complete analysis for purposes of illustration. A harmonic analysis (both macro analysis and traditional analysis) and a sectional analysis are placed directly on the score. Phrases are indicated by circled numbers and their endings shown by two vertical lines (‖). A discussion of important features of the work and a summary can be found on pages 145 to 147.

Figure 8.2

Mozart: Sonata in C Major, K. 309, I (Allegro).

Exposition: Theme 1, group A

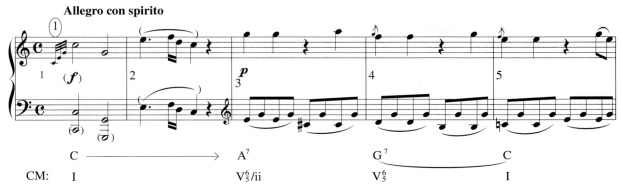

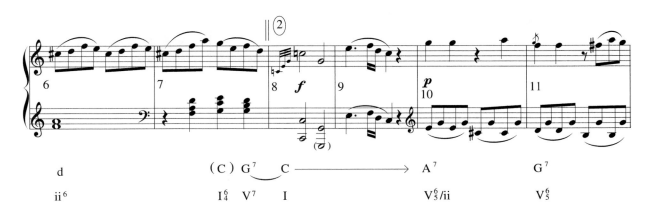

Theme 1, group B

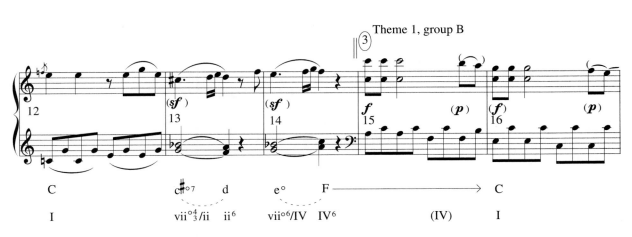

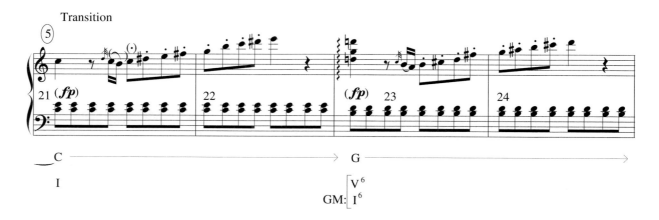

Transition

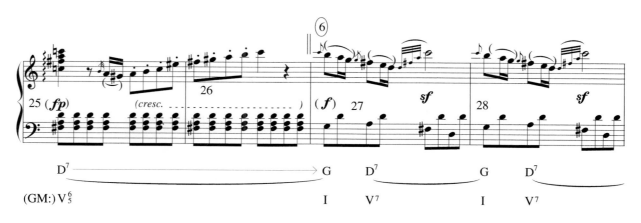

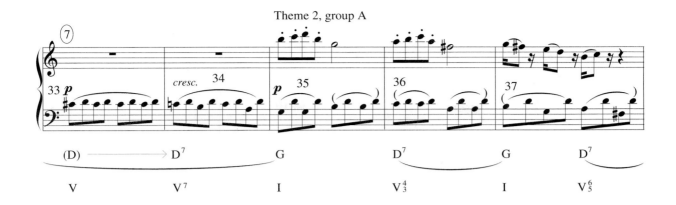

Theme 2, group A

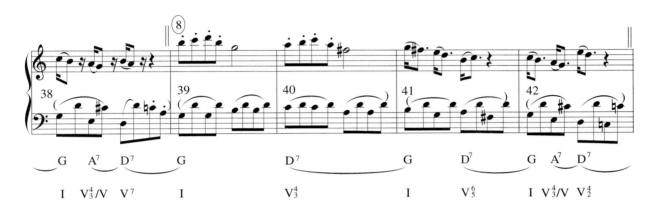

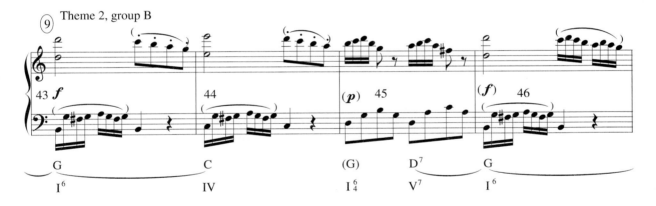

Theme 2, group B

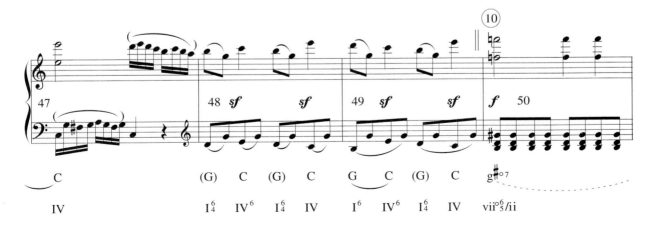

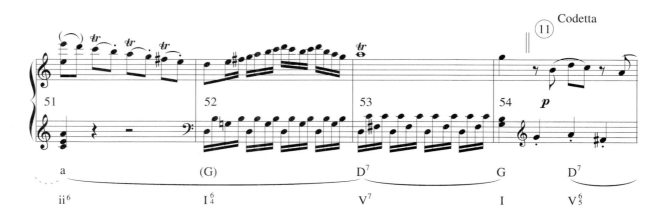

Development: (From theme 1, group A)

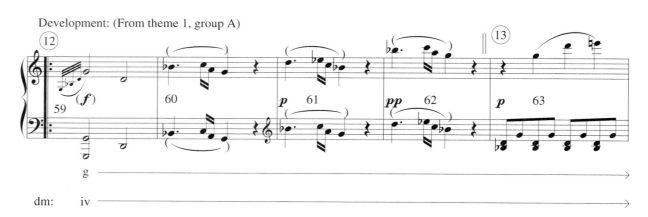

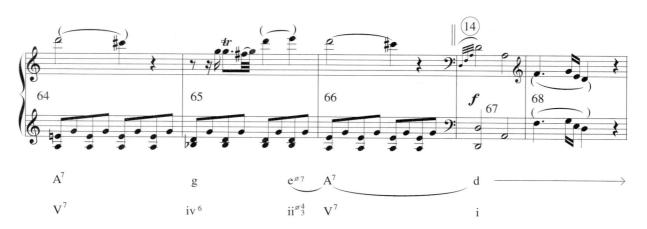

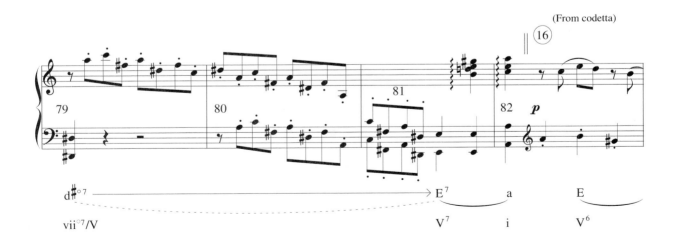

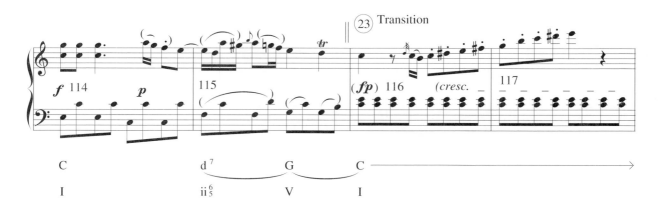

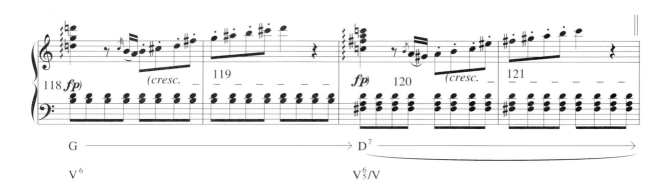

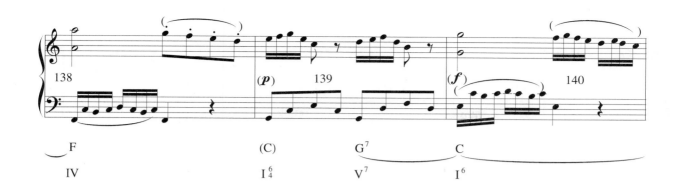

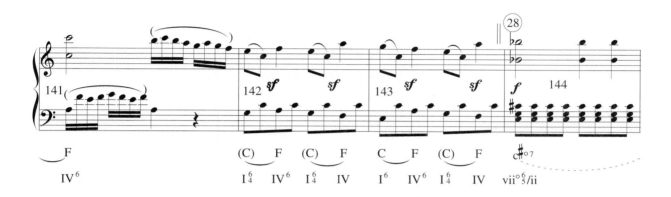

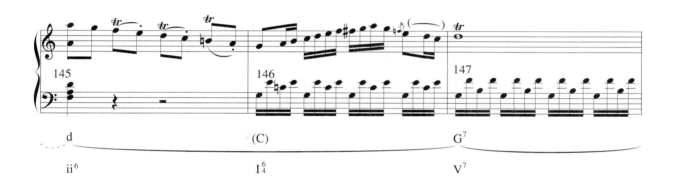

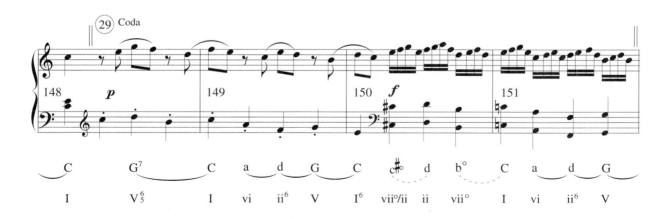

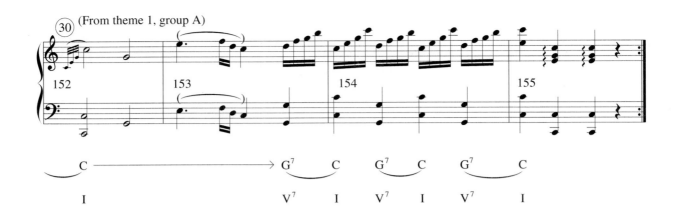

	C	G⁷	C	G⁷ C G⁷ C
	I	V⁷	I	V⁷ I V⁷ I

FIRST MOVEMENT STRUCTURE

	Phrase	Measures	Key(s)	Remarks
Exposition	1	1–7	CM	First theme, group A
	2	8–14	CM	First theme, group A, continued
	3	15–17	CM	First theme, group B
	4	18–20	CM	First theme, group B, continued
	5	21–26	CM–GM	Transition
	6	27–32	GM	Transition, second phrase
	7	33–38	GM	Second theme, group A (2 meas. extension)
	8	39–42	GM	Second theme, group A, continued
	9	43–49	GM	Second theme, group B
	10	50–54	GM	Second theme, group B, continued
	11	54–58	GM	Codetta
Development	12	59–62	Dm	Derived from first theme, group A
	13	63–66	Dm	Derived from first theme, group A
	14	67–72	Dm–Am	Derived from first theme, group A
	15	73–82	Am	Derived from first theme, group A
	16	82–85	Am	Derived from codetta
	17	86–89	Am	Derived from first theme, group A
	18	90–93	Am–CM	Derived from first theme, group A
Recapitulation	19	94–100	CM	First theme, group A
	20	101–109	CM	First theme, group A (change of mode)
	21	110–112	CM	First theme, group B
	22	113–115	CM	First theme, group B, continued
	23	116–121	CM	Transition
	24	122–126	CM	Transition, second phrase
	25	127–132	CM	Second theme, group A
	26	133–136	CM	Second theme, group A, continued
	27	137–143	CM	Second theme, group B
	28	144–148	CM	Second theme, group B, continued
	29	148–151	CM	Coda
	30	152–155	CM	Coda

<table>
<tr><td>General Comments</td><td>This sonata movement is a textbook example of sonata form. The larger sections (exposition, development, recapitulation) are easily discernible. The characteristics that make this movement unique and distinguish it from others are found in the phrase and period relationships.</td></tr>
</table>

Phrases

Phrases are frequently of odd length in comparison with the conventional four-measure phrase.

Phrase	Length (m.)	Phrase	Length (m.)
1	7	5	6
2	7	6	6
3	3	7	6
4	3	8	4

Period Construction

Parallel periods (where the phrases are related one to the other) tend to be of similar if unconventional length.

Parallel Periods	No. of Measures in Each
1 and 2	7
3 and 4	3
5 and 6	6
7 and 8	6

Phrase Members

A number of phrases are composed of dissimilar phrase members, such as those shown in figure 8.3, taken from the first phrase.

Figure 8.3

Phrase member 1   Phrase member 2   Phrase member 3

Phrase Overlap (Elision)

Some phrases in this work overlap with the subsequent phrase (figure 8.4). As an example, phrase 2 begins in measure 8, but the logical conclusion (resolution of the V^7) of phrase 1 is the first beat of phrase 2 (m. 8). For purposes of simplicity, the elision of phrases is not shown in the analysis. Because 16 of the 30 phrases contain elisions, it becomes one of the distinctive features of the work.

Figure 8.4

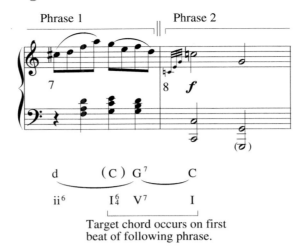

Target chord occurs on first
beat of following phrase.

Nonoverlapping Phrases

Only five phrases come to full closure within the four-measure unit. A perfect authentic cadence is reached in each of these phrases:

Phrase	Measures	Remarks
10	50–54	Signals codetta of exposition to follow
11	54–58	End of codetta (and exposition)
15	73–82	Development section
28	144–148	Signals codetta of recapitulation
30	152–155	End of movement

Delayed Resolution

In three instances, the flow of circle progressions is interrupted at the end of the phrase, and completion (tonic) is withheld—seven measures in one instance.

Circle in Phrase	Measures	Tonic Reached in Measure	Tonic Triad Delayed
3	15–17	21	4 measures
20	101–109	116	7 measures
21	110–112	116	4 measures

Phrases 12 and 17 have no harmonic movement and therefore lack a strong harmonic cadence.

Harmony

The basic understructure of the composition, as revealed by the analysis, is uncomplicated. Circle progressions dominate the movement as expected and shape the overall harmonic scheme.

Harmonic Structure	Excluding progressions that depart from tonic (I to vi, I to ii, I to V, etc.), most progressions are part of circle progressions.
Secondary Dominants and Leading-Tone Chords	Most secondary dominants and leading-tone chords resolve as expected. The exception is a V^7/ii in measure 3, where its resolution is elided (omitted from the string of circle progressions—V^7/ii [ii] V^7 I). The progression is repeated again in the recapitulation.
Absence of Altered Chords	Aside from the numerous secondary dominant and secondary leading-tone chords, the movement is free of altered chords (N^6, It^6, Gr^6, and Fr^6).
Closely Related Keys	All modulations (to GM, dm, and am) are closely related to the tonic.

Summary

A significant feature of this movement is the elision of phrases. Ending one phrase and beginning another at the same moment gives a listener little time to savor the achieved goal and prepare for the next. Elision gives the movement a dynamic forward motion throughout.

Theme groups are clearly stated, transitions are traditionally constructed, and the harmonic schemes are typical of the period.

1. Make a complete analysis of this movement using the approach illustrated in this chapter.
2. Invite a student to perform the work in class.
3. Discuss the movement in class, and compare its form with that of the first movement of the Mozart sonata analyzed in this chapter.
4. Invite a member of the piano faculty to the class and ask him or her to discuss performance practices for this particular work.

Beethoven: Sonata no. 1 in F Minor, op. 2, no. 1, I. CD Track 22

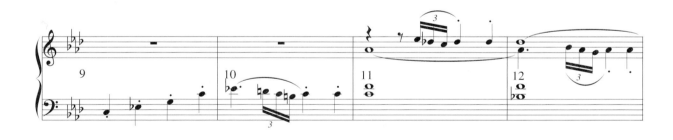

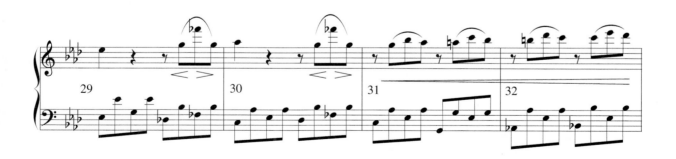

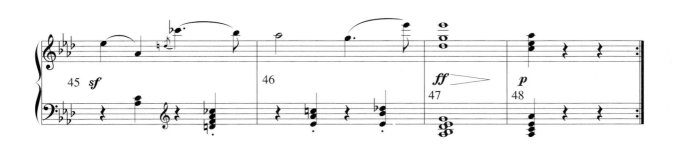

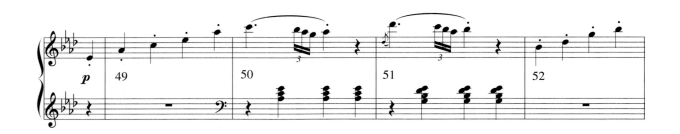

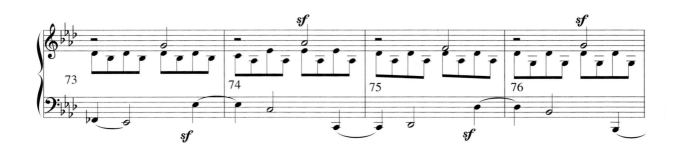

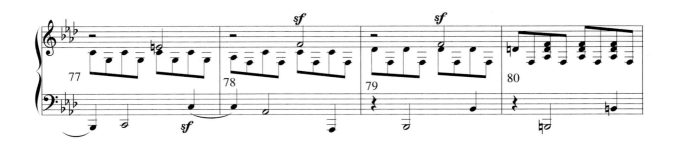

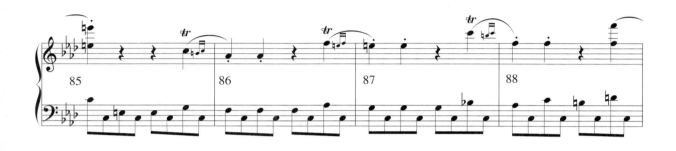

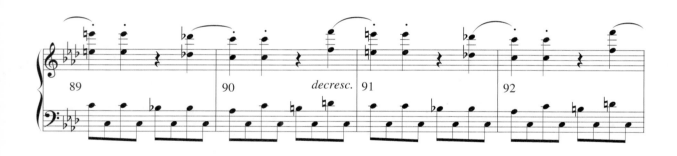

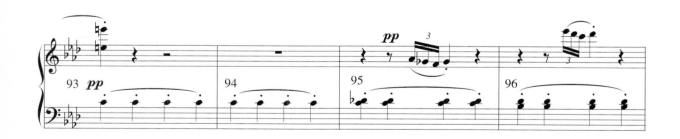

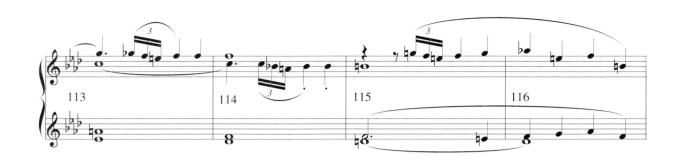

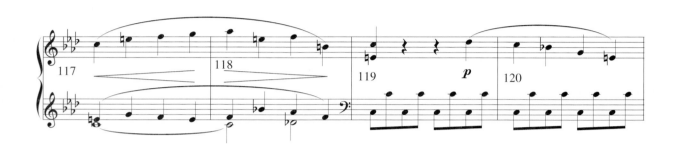

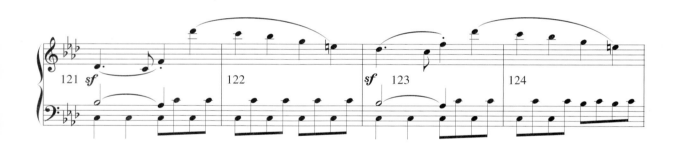

The Classical Period (1750–1825)

Assignment 8.2

1. Write the exposition of a sonata form.
2. Compose your own first and second theme. (Add a third theme if you wish.)
3. Use the first movement of the Beethoven Sonata no. 1 in F minor as a model for the form.
4. Place the first theme in G minor.
5. Place the second theme in B-flat major.
6. The transition will probably provide the greatest difficulty. It may be wise to write the transition after composing the first and second themes. Plot harmonic progressions backward from the beginning of the second theme to ensure that the transition will be smooth and logical.
7. Use the first movement of the Beethoven piano sonata as a guide for form, but write the composition for any instrument or combination of instruments that interests you.
8. Perform your composition in class.
9. Have members of the class identify the various sections of the exposition just by listening.
10. Continue the composition through the development section.
11. Complete the movement by adding the recapitulation.

CHAPTER 9

Rondo Forms

Topics	*Refrain*	*Retransition*	*Seven-part rondo*
	Episode	*Three-part rondo*	*Sonata rondo*
	Transition	*Five-part rondo*	

Important Concepts

Rondo form is one of the larger classical forms, consisting of recurring sections called *refrains* interspersed with contrasting sections called *episodes*.

Refrain

The refrain (also known as the rondo theme) is repeated from one to four times during the course of the composition, almost always in the tonic key, and often with variations.

Episode

The episode is inserted between repeats of the refrain. Episodes are typically in contrasting keys. A typical rondo form is as follows:

	A = Refrain	**B** = Episode 1	**C** = Episode 2	
Sections:	**A**	**B**	**A**	**C**	**A**
Keys:	CM	GM	CM	am	CM

Transition

A *transition* sometimes connects a refrain to an episode.

A	(transition)	**B**	**A**

Retransition

Often a *retransition* is used to make the return from an episode to the refrain as smooth as possible. A retransition may be included even in instances where a transition is not present.

A	(transition)	**B**	(retransition)	**A**

159

Rondo Types

The following four formal outlines represent the most common types of rondo.

Three-part rondo:	**A B A** (transition and retransition is optional)
	If both transition and retransition are absent, the three-part rondo is indistinguishable from the three-part form.
	Three-part form is often found in slow movements from sonatas and symphonies of the classical period.
Examples:	Beethoven: Sonata in E-flat Major, op. 7 (II)
	Haydn: Symphony no. 100 (II)
Five-part rondo:	**A B A C A** (transitions and retransitions are optional)
	The five-part rondo occurs most often in slow movements of sonatas, symphonies, and string quartets.
Examples:	Mozart: Sonata in C Minor, K. 457 (II)
	Beethoven: Sonata in C Major, op. 2, no. 3 (II)
	Beethoven; Sonata in C Minor, op. 13 (II)
Seven-part rondo:	**A B A C A B A** (transitions and retransitions are optional)
	Possibly the most common rondo type; it occurs in the final movement of classical symphonies, string quartets, and solo sonatas.
Examples:	Beethoven: Sonata in A Major, op. 2, no. 2 (IV)
	Beethoven: Sonata in C Minor, op. 13 (III)
	Beethoven: Symphony no. 6, op. 68 in F Major (V)
Sonata rondo:	**A B A Development A B A**
	A mixture of sonata and rondo forms. It is like a rondo with the A B C sections and like the sonata form with the development between the exposition and recapitulation.
Examples:	Beethoven: Sonata in E-flat Major, op. 27, no. 1 (IV)
	Haydn: Symphony no. 94 in G Major (IV)

Departures from Standard Rondo Form

In no other form is there more latitude for flexibility than in the rondo forms. The following table shows some of the variants:

Type	Standard Outline	Variant
Three-part	A B A	A B C A
Five-part	A B A C A	A B A B A
Seven-part	A B A C A B A	A B A C B A
Sonata rondo	A B A Dev. A B A	A B A Dev. B A

History

The rondo of the classical period developed from the *rondel,* a vocal form of the medieval period (500–1450). The troubadours of Provence (southern France) employed a type of composition with a recurring section, also called *rondeau.* These *rondeaux* (plural) were composed throughout the Renaissance (1450–1600). In the baroque period (1600–1750) a similar rondolike form (again *rondeau*) was used by Bach in some of his instrumental suites. Other composers of the same period also adopted the form.

The rondo forms discussed in this chapter are those of the classical period (1750–1825), the era that developed and perfected the form. The preclassical form is often called *rondeau.* Its sections were generally shorter and more numerous than those of the classical rondo.

Application

The third movement of Mozart's Sonata in C Major, K. 545, is analyzed in figure 9.1 in its entirety. Following that is a summary outline of the form.

Refrain 1

The first section (refrain) of the rondo form is measures 1 to 8. Notice that nearly all progressions are circle progressions. The refrain is only two phrases, which form a parallel period.

Figure 9.1

Mozart: Sonata in C Major, K. 545, III.

- *Episode 1*
- *Retransition*

The first episode (B) is in the key of G major, the dominant key. This section (mm. 13–16) contains material that is similar to the A section and closes with a retransition (mm. 16–20). Notice the modulation, which is an important feature of most retransition sections.

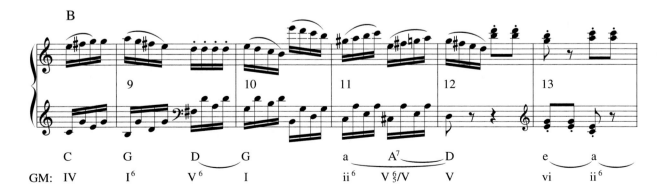

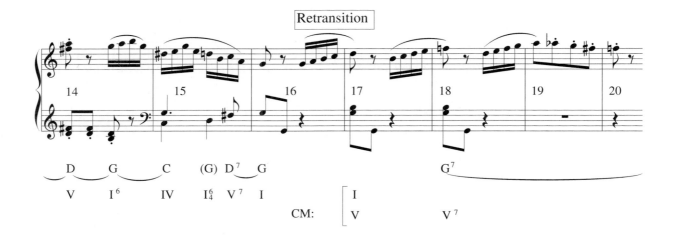

- *Refrain 2* The refrain returns unaltered from its first appearance (mm. 21–28).

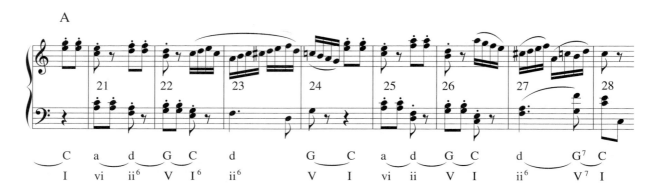

- *Episode 2* The second episode (C) is in the key of A minor, the relative minor key (mm. 29–48).
- *Retransition* Again, as in the first episode, the melodic materials are similar to those of the refrain. The section closes with a short codetta that becomes a retransition (mm. 48–52).

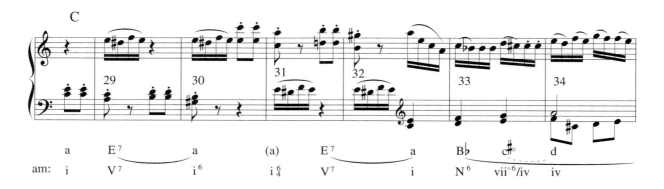

• **Refrain 3**   A second return of the refrain is again unaltered from its first appearance (mm. 53–60).

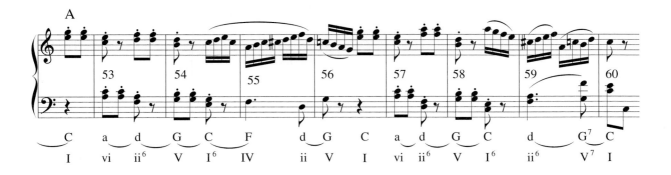

Coda

The coda section (mm. 61–73) consists entirely of cadence formulas in the tonic key. The melodic materials show some relationship with the codetta that closed the second episode (mm. 48–51).

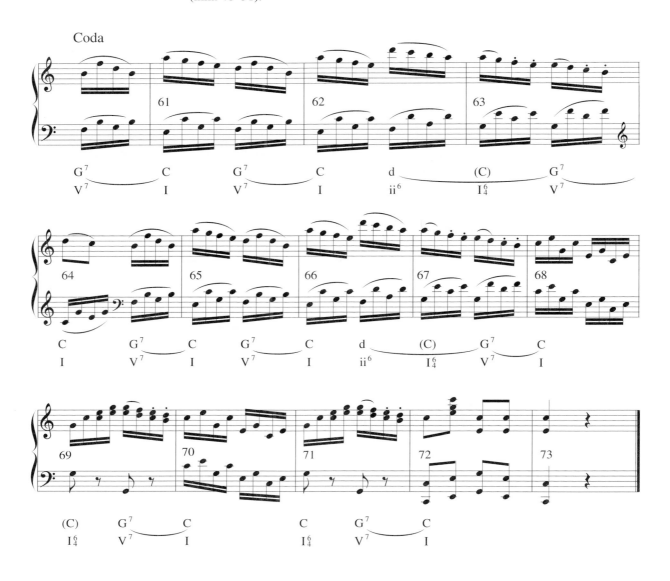

Summary

The composition in figure 9.1 is a very clear example of five-part rondo form. The three statements of the refrain are exact repetitions of one another, and the two episodes are in contrasting keys (the dominant and the relative minor). Following is a summary outline of the work.

FORMAL OUTLINE

	Measures	Keys	Remarks
Refrain 1 (A)	1–8	CM	Parallel period
Episode 1 (B)	8–16	GM	Contrasting period
Retransition	16–20	to CM	Four-measure phrase based entirely on the G chord
Refrain 2 (A)	20–28	CM	Exact restatement of refrain 1
Episode 2 (C)	28–48	am	Three-phrase period with irregular phrase lengths (8, 4, and 8 measures)
Codetta/ retransition	48–52	to CM	Cadence repetition in A minor ending with the dominant in C major
Refrain 3 (A)	52–60	CM	Exact restatement of refrain 1
Coda	60–73	CM	Repeated cadence formulas in the tonic key

The following composition is in rondo form.

1. Complete the analysis as shown in measures 1 to 8.
2. Prepare an analysis outline as shown on page 165.
3. Discuss the general characteristics of the movement and compare it with the rondo analyzed beginning on page 161.
4. Look through the macro analysis and find as many patterns as you can that might assist a performer in memorizing the composition.

Haydn: Sonata in C Major, Hob. XVI:35, III. CD Track 23

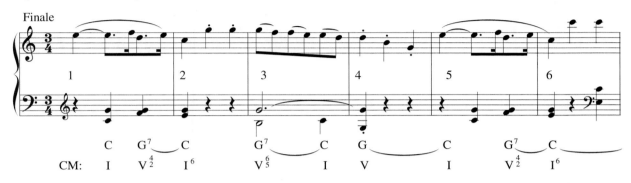

The Classical Period (1750–1825)

The Classical Period (1750–1825)

Extended and Chromatic Harmony

The chord vocabulary introduced in the following chapters represents the outer limits of tertian (third-based) harmony. These harmonic devices, which increase the dissonance level and chromaticism of the musical landscape, were much favored by composers in the nineteenth and twentieth centuries for their colorful and dramatic effects. The 9th, 11th, and 13th chords developed as logical extensions of the tertian system by piling additional thirds above the 7th chords. Altered dominants and chromatic mediants represent the triumph of chromaticism over the diatonic system. These harmonic devices will be presented in a four-part chorale setting for the most part, but they usually occur in music that goes beyond this basic texture.

CHAPTER 10

9th, 11th, and 13th Chords

Topics	*V⁹*	*V¹¹*	*V¹³*	*Nondominant 9th, 11th, and 13th chords*

Important Concepts

9th, 11th, and 13th chords are created by adding additional thirds to chords (figure 10.1). Because these chords contain more than four notes, it is necessary to omit some notes in four-voice writing.

Figure 10.1

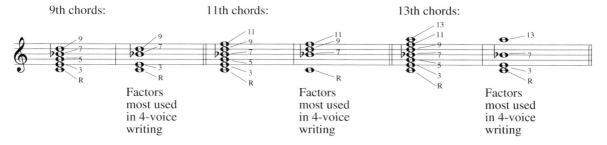

Position

9th, 11th, and 13th chords tend to lose their identity when inverted, so they are generally found in root position.

Mode

9th, 11th, and 13th chords are found in both major and minor keys. Note that in the major, V^9 and V^{13} contain a major 9th and major 13th, respectively, whereas in the minor mode both are minor intervals. The 11th in V^{11} is unaffected by changes of mode.

Function

Most 9th, 11th, and 13th chords are dominant chords (V^9, V^{11}, V^{13}), although they occur with other chords, such as I and IV. They occur most often in a series of circle progressions.

As Secondary Dominants

9th, 11th, and 13th chords also occur as secondary dominants—V^9/V, V^{11}/V, V^{13}/V, V^9/ii, V^{11}/ii, V^{13}/ii, and the like (figure 10.2).

Figure 10.2

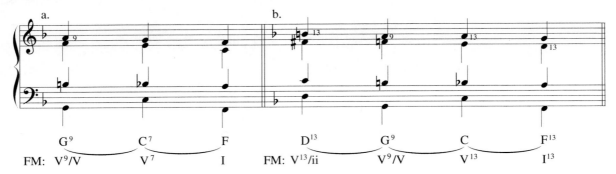

Progression

The addition of a 9th, 11th, or 13th to chords does not change their function. For example, V^{13} chords still resolve to I or i; ii^9 chords normally progress to dominant (V) function, and so on.

History

Baroque Period (1600–1750)

True 9th, 11th, or 13th chords are rare in music of the baroque period. However, there are many instances where 9th, 11th, and 13th factors appear as nonharmonic tones. These dissonances (9th, 11th, 13th) usually resolve before the chord changes and are analyzed as triads or 7th chords with nonharmonic tones.

Classical Period (1750–1825)

As in the baroque period, 9th, 11th, and 13th chords were not a significant part of the style of the classical period.

Romantic Period (1825–1900)

It was in the romantic period that the 9th, 11th, and 13th chords became common. Figure 10.3 illustrates a V^{13} that proceeds immediately to I. The 13th factor (B) moves down a 3rd to G, the root of the tonic triad.

Figure 10.3

Schumann: *Kleine Studie* (Short Study) from *Album for the Young*, op. 68, no. 14, mm. 60–64.

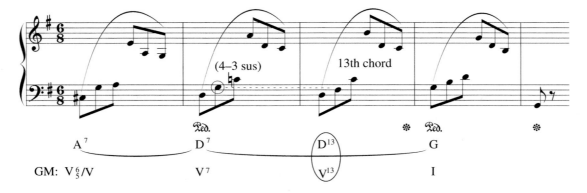

Extended and Chromatic Harmony

In figure 10.4 the 9th resolves before a change of harmony but achieves the strength of a true chord factor through its duration (two measures).

Figure 10.4

Wagner: *Tristan und Isolde,* Act II, scene 2 (voice part omitted), mm. 610–613.

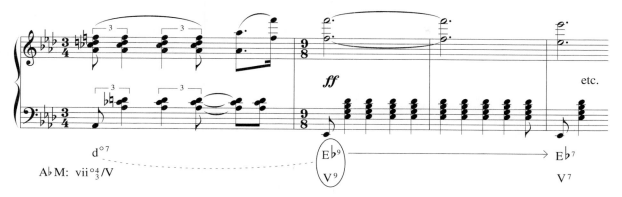

Post-Romantic and Impressionistic Period (1875–1920)

In the period from 1875 to 1920, 9th, 11th, and 13th chords reached their greatest use. The excerpt in figure 10.5 illustrates a V^{11} at a cadence point. The 11th (C) does not resolve downward, as it is a common tone with the tonic triad.

Figure 10.5

Ravel: *Valses nobles et sentimentales* (Noble and Sentimental Waltzes).

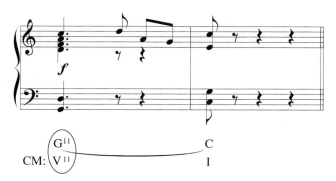

Jazz and Popular Music (1900–Present)

Figure 10.6 is from a composition written in 1901 by Scott Joplin. Although Joplin used most of the harmonic vocabulary of the late romantic period, he used 9th, 11th, and 13th chords somewhat sparingly.

9th, 11th, and 13th Chords

Figure 10.6

Joplin: "The Augustine Club Waltz," mm. 125–132.

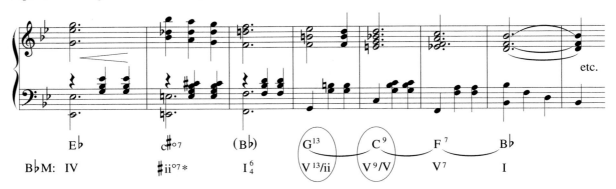

*This chord is discussed in chapter 13, p. 210.

In later jazz styles, the 9th, 11th, and 13th chords became very common. In some styles nearly all chords are 9th, 11th, 13th, or added-tone chords. Figure 10.7 is an illustration of a typical cadence found in the music of the 1950s.

Figure 10.7

Jazz of the 1950s.

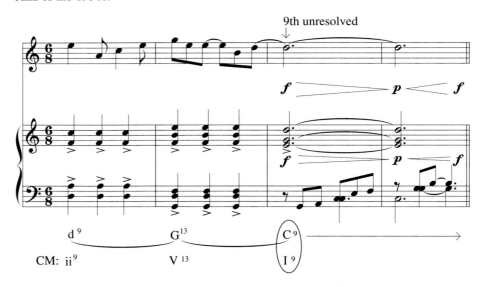

Applications

Voice Leading

Chord	Most Common Factors Present	Voice-Leading Guides
V^9	Root, 3rd, 7th, 9th	The 9th and 7th resolve downward to the 5th and 3rd of tonic triad (figure 10.8a).
V^{11}	Root, 7th, 9th, 11th	The 11th is usually retained as a common tone when V^{11} resolves to I or i (figure 10.8b).
V^{13}	Root, 3rd, 7th, 13th	The 13th is most often in the soprano and usually resolves a 3rd downward to the tonic factor of I or i (figure 10.8c). If the tonic following V^{13} is a 9th chord, the 13th of V^{13} sometimes resolves to the 9th of I^9 (figure 10.8d).

Figure 10.8

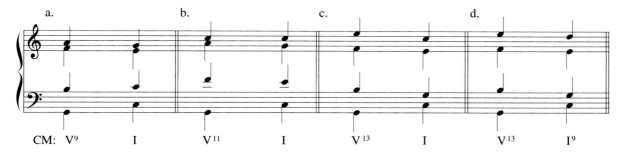

CM: V^9 I V^{11} I V^{13} I V^{13} I^9

Assignment 10.1

Write all the factors of the requested 9th chord. If you forget what the popular music chord symbols mean, consult the chart in Appendix B.

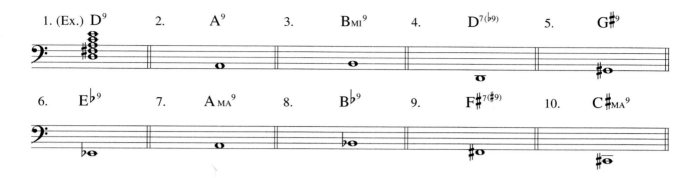

1. (Ex.) D⁹   2. A⁹   3. B$_{MI}$⁹   4. D$^{7(♭9)}$ 5. G$^{♯9}$

6. E♭⁹   7. A$_{MA}$⁹   8. B♭⁹   9. F♯$^{7(♯9)}$ 10. C♯$_{MA}$⁹

Assignment 10.2

Write the requested 11th and 13th chords. The first five are shown with Roman numerals and the second five with popular music chord symbols.

Analysis symbols					Popular music symbols				
1.	2.	3.	4.	5.	6. B♭^{11}	7. D♯^{13}	8. F♯^{11}	9. E^{13}	10. G^{13}

FM: V^{13} DM: I^{13} cm: V^{11} A♭M: V^{11} D♭M: V^{13}

Assignment 10.3   Add alto and tenor to the following phrases and analyze each chord.

1. Follow voice-leading recommendations on page 177.
2. Observe all previous suggestions regarding doubling, spacing, voice order, and voice range.
3. Avoid large skips (skips greater than a P5th).

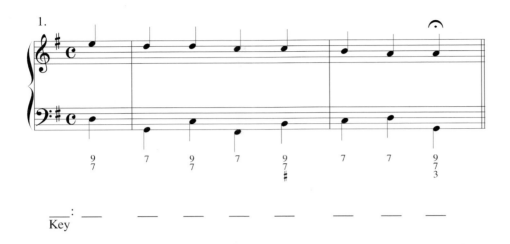

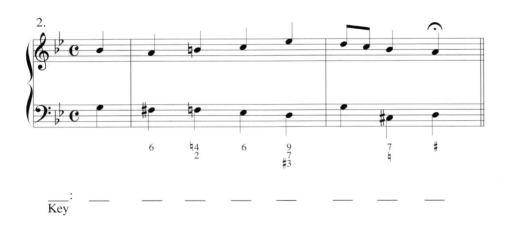

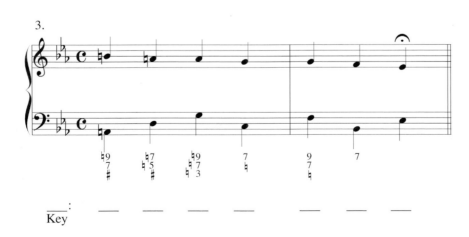

4.

♮9
7
♯

♮13
7
♯

♮9
7

♮13
7
♮

13
9
♮

13
7

13
9

Key: ___ ___ ___ ___ ___ ___ ___

5.

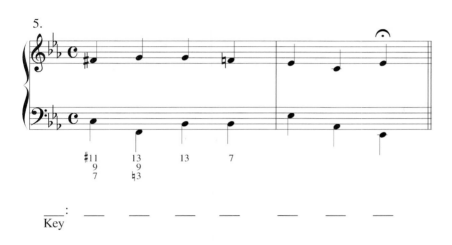

♯11
9
7

13
9
♮3

13

7

Key: ___ ___ ___ ___ ___ ___ ___

Assignment 10.4

The following is an excerpt from *Pavane pour une Infante défunte,* written in 1899 by Maurice Ravel.

1. Make a complete analysis (macro or traditional) according to the directions of your instructor.
2. When you find a 9th, 11th, or 13th chord, circle the analysis.
3. In class or on a separate sheet, discuss the harmonic rhythm (how often chord changes occur); the kinds of 9th, 11th, and 13th chords that are present; the tonality; and the general use of dissonance.

Ravel: *Pavane pour une Infante défunte* (Pavane for a Dead Princess), mm. 1–12. CD Track 24

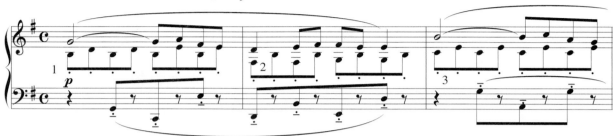

CHAPTER 11

Altered Dominants

Topics	V^+	$V^{5\flat}$	$v^{\varnothing 7}$
	V^{+7}	$V^7_{5\flat}$	

Important Concepts

Altered dominants are dominant triads or 7th chords that contain a raised or lowered 5th factor. One altered dominant type ($v^{\varnothing 7}$) contains both lowered 3rd and 5th factors. Figure 11.1 illustrates the five altered dominant types in common use.

Figure 11.1

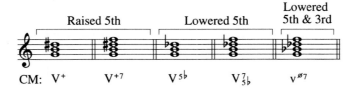

Position

Altered dominants are found most frequently in root position, but they occasionally occur in any inversion.

Mode

Most altered dominants are found in both major and minor keys. However, the altered dominant with a raised 5th does not occur in minor mode (the raised 5th is enharmonic with the 3rd scale degree).

Progression

Altered dominants, like diatonic dominants, proceed in a circle progression to the tonic.

Secondary Dominants

Altered dominants are often used as secondary dominants.

History

Baroque Period (1600–1750)

Altered dominants were virtually nonexistent during the baroque period.

Classical Period (1750–1825)

The use of altered dominants was just beginning during the classical period.

Romantic and Post-Romantic Period (1825–1920)

Altered dominants represented a colorful and exotic addition to the harmonic vocabulary of the nineteenth century. Figure 11.2 is from *Mörike Lieder,* a set of songs by Hugo Wolf. In the five measures shown, there are three altered dominants.

Figure 11.2

Wolf: *Das verlassene Mägdlein* (The Forsaken Maiden) from *Gedichte von Eduard Mörike*, no. 7, mm. 26–30.

Altered dominants were employed in popular music and jazz of the 1930s through the 1960s. Figure 11.3 illustrates typical usage.

Figure 11.3

Mercer and Arlen: "My Shining Hour."

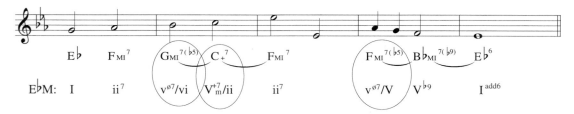

Doubling and Voice Leading

Altered dominants require careful treatment with regard to doubling and voice leading.

Doubling

Altered tones are almost never doubled. Triads in this category typically double the pitch other than the altered pitch—the root of a root position chord, for example.

Resolution

Resolve the altered 5th in the direction of the alteration—raised pitches up, lowered pitches down.

7th Resolution

In altered dominant 7th chords, resolve the 7th factor down one scale degree. This may result in either a doubled third or tripled root in the tonic triad that follows.

Never Double Altered Tones

Altered tones are almost never doubled.

Applications

Figure 11.4 illustrates that the altered 5th resolves in the direction of the alteration: raised pitches resolve upward and lowered pitches resolve downward. In altered dominant 7th chords, remember to resolve the 7th factor down one scale degree. This may result in either a doubled third or a tripled root in the tonic triad that follows (figure 11.4a, b, c).

Figure 11.4

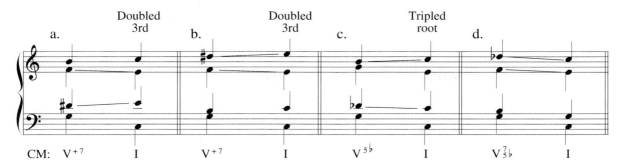

Assignment 11.1   Write the requested chord above the given tone. Indicate the major key in which this chord is found. The example illustrates the correct procedure.

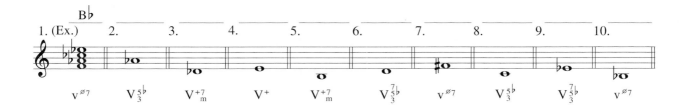

Assignment 11.2   Add alto and tenor voices to the following phrases. Observe the voice-leading strategies listed in this chapter. Make a complete harmonic analysis of each exercise. In class or on paper, discuss different analyses that might be possible for some chords.

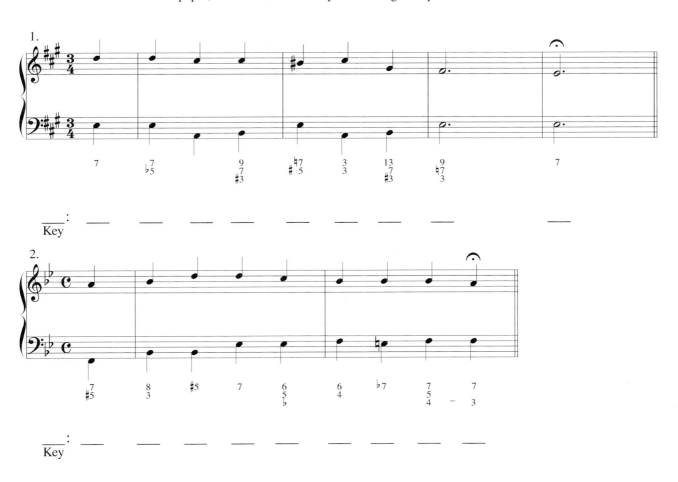

3.

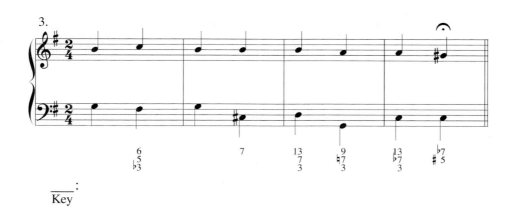

Key: _____

Assignment 11.3

The following excerpt is from a popular song by Duke Ellington. Make a complete analysis (macro or traditional). The excerpt contains several chords discussed in this chapter, but also some that will test your ingenuity. Consider the possibility of more than one analysis and enharmonic spelling of chords. In class, discuss differences in analysis.

Ellington and Strayhorn: "Day Dream." CD Track 25

CHAPTER 12

Chromatic Mediants

Topics	*Chromatic mediants in major keys:*	*Chromatic mediants in minor keys:*
	III, ♭III or ♮III, and ♭iii or ♮iii	*iii, ♯III or ♮III, and ♯iii or ♮iii*
	VI, ♭VI or ♮VI, and ♭vi or ♮vi	*vi, ♯VI or ♮VI, and ♯vi or ♮vi*

Important Concepts

Chromatic mediants are altered mediant and submediant triads and sometimes 7th chords (figure 12.1).

Figure 12.1

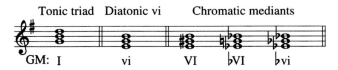

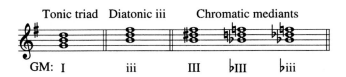

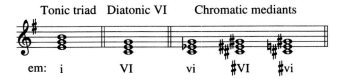

Some chromatic mediants are spelled the same as other altered chords.

Key	Chord	Other Function
Major	♭VI	Also a borrowed chord—from parallel minor, (see chapter 4)
Major	VI	Also secondary dominant of ii (see Volume 1, chapter 15)
Major	III	Also secondary dominant of vi (see Volume 1, chapter 15)

The analysis of these chords should reflect whatever function is evident from their relationship to surrounding harmony. Figure 12.2 illustrates correct analysis. In example 12.2a, an E major triad (E G♯ B) resolves to a ii triad, leaving no doubt that the chord is a secondary dominant, whereas in example 12.2b the same E major triad returns to the tonic triad, thus demonstrating the characteristics of a chromatic mediant.

Figure 12.2

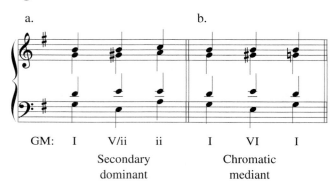

Any position is possible, but root position is most frequent.

As seen in the preceding examples, chromatic mediants and submediants may appear in either major or minor keys.

Chromatic mediants are usually mediant or submediant chords that have been altered.

Chromatic mediants usually have a 3rd relationship (of chord roots) with tonic and most often proceed from and to the tonic triad. Less often, the dominant (V) is the pivot around which chromatic mediants move. Sometimes chromatic mediants are preceded or followed by their own secondary dominant and, in other instances, create a full-fledged modulation. Figure 12.3 shows:

a. A minor chromatic mediant.
b. A major chromatic submediant.
c. A major chromatic mediant.
d. A minor chromatic mediant with its secondary dominant.

Figure 12.3

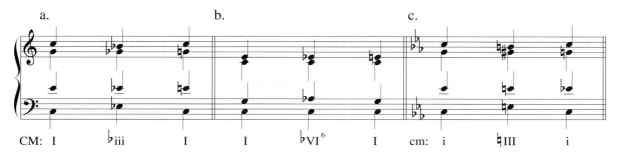

History

Baroque (1600–1750) and Classical (1750–1825) Periods

Chromatic mediants were rarely used during the baroque and classical periods.

Romantic and Post-Romantic Period (1825–1920)

Chromatic mediants became much more common in the romantic and post-romantic periods.

Figure 12.4 is from Brahms' Symphony no. 3. A chromatic mediant (♭VI) in C Major occurs in the third measure. In this instance the A♭ major triad is both a chromatic mediant (because it returns to a C major triad immediately) and a borrowed chord (because it is borrowed from the parallel minor [C minor]).

Figure 12.4

Brahms: Symphony No. 3 in F Major, op. 90, II (Andante), mm. 128–131.

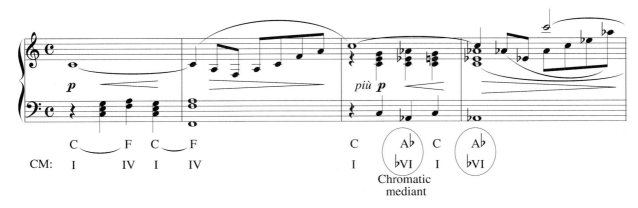

Applications

Doubling and Voice Leading

Because chromatic mediants are reached by 3rd-relationship progressions, chromatic movement, such as B to B♯, A to A♭, and F♯ to F in melodic lines, is common (figure 12.3).

Chromatic mediants are either major or minor triads, so doubling patterns are often the same as for diatonic triads. Double the root whenever possible (figure 12.3).

Assignment 12.1   Write the six chromatic mediants related to the tonic triad for each of the following keys:

1. D major (example)
2. B harmonic minor
3. G harmonic minor
4. A major

1. Tonic   Chromatic mediants   2. Tonic   Chromatic mediants

I   VI ♭VI ♭vi   III ♮III ♮iii

3. Tonic   Chromatic mediants   4. Tonic   Chromatic mediants

Assignment 12.2   Add alto and tenor voices to the following phrases. Analyze each chord.

1. Instead of figured bass, chord symbols are given above the soprano voice.
2. The bass melody is given and should not be altered. The placement of bass notes may indicate an inversion of the chord described by the chord symbol.
3. To refresh your memory regarding chord symbols, see Appendix B.
4. If your instructor requests, be prepared to categorize each altered chord—whether secondary dominant, altered dominant, borrowed chord, or chromatic mediant.

1.   A   F   A   E¹³   F♯MI C♯¹³   D   D   A

AM: __   __   __   __   __   __   __   __   __

2.

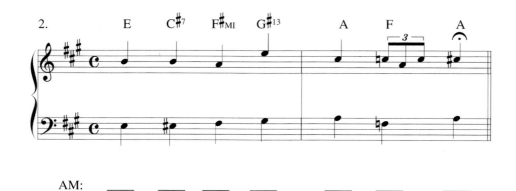

AM: ___ ___ ___ ___ ___ ___ ___ ___

3.

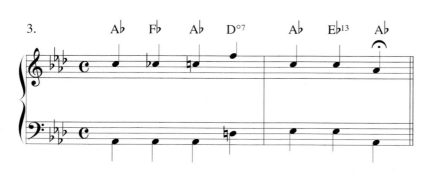

A♭M: ___ ___ ___ ___ ___ ___ ___

4.

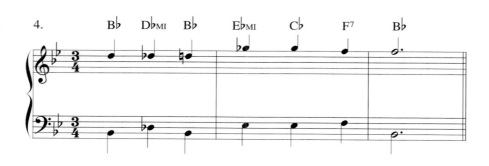

B♭M: ___ ___ ___ ___ ___ ___ ___

Assignment 12.3

1. The following excerpt contains chromatic mediants. In this short composition, Chopin includes chromatic mediants preceded by their secondary dominant. Be aware that some chromatic mediants may be enharmonically spelled. Neapolitan harmony also plays a role in the analysis.
2. Provide a complete analysis (macro or traditional) of the composition with a single chord for each bracket.
3. Measures 4 (brackets 12–15) and 7 (brackets 22–25) are particularly difficult.
4. In one area that includes three adjacent brackets, the chords appear to be a by-product of linear motion—circle progressions are absent. Besides indicating the chord analysis, label the area "linear."
5. Because there is more than one correct analysis for this composition, discuss alternative viewpoints and the merits of each in class.

Chopin: Prelude, op. 28, no. 9. CD Track 26

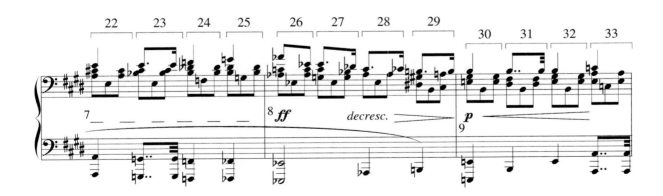

Chromatic Mediants

Extended and Chromatic Harmony

The Nineteenth and Twentieth Centuries

Romantic Period (1825–1900)

Music of the romantic period was dominated by a wider range of emotional expression, more individual styles, and greater subjectivity than the music of the classical period. Musical forms, such as the sonata and symphony, became longer and more involved, but shorter forms, especially piano compositions, were also numerous. Harmony and orchestration expanded to create a more colorful sound palette, which was used to create dramatic musical effects.

In contrast to the classic ideals of organization, symmetry, control, and perfection within acknowledged limits, romanticism sought independence, movement, and passion. It pursued the mysterious or exotic because they represented a distant and unattainable goal.

Post-Romantic and Impressionistic Period (1875–1920)

The post-romantic composers developed and extended the techniques of the romantic composers, resulting in a still more dramatic musical style. In contrast, a group of French composers, the impressionists, developed a musical style that renounced the clear phrases and goal-oriented harmonic idiom of romantic music. They replaced them with purposeful understatement and ambiguity that was evocative of, but very different in effect from, the romantic style. These impressionist composers abandoned traditional thematic development and became more concerned with the color or mood of a particular moment.

Contemporary Period (1920–Present)

The period from 1920 to the present has seen the development of great diversity in musical styles and techniques. Much of this development can be traced back to the upheavals caused by World War I (1914–1918) and World War II (1939–1945), which caused disruption of the established cultural institutions in Europe and at the same time brought people of diverse cultural backgrounds together for the first time. The development of recording technology, radio and television transmission, and rapid transportation created a sense of world community in which disparate cultures could freely intermingle. Modern technological advances have made possible the development of electronic and computer instruments for the composition, synthesis, and performance of music.

Popular song as we know it in the United States evolved during this period. Some notable composers of popular song were George Gershwin, Cole Porter, Richard Rodgers, Irving Berlin, Vernon Duke, and Burt Bacharach. Popular songs by these and other composers were the dominant popular music until rock music became firmly established in the 1960s.

African-American music is among the most notable expressions of religious, folk, and art music in the United States. The blues, which arose from the gospel music of the South, has been perpetuated as a unique style of its own. It has also infused and inspired nearly all types of African-American music, some twentieth-century classical music, and the popular songs and rock music of the present day. Jazz, a general term for particular kinds of African-American music, has undergone many changes in its brief history. It has now been accepted as a substantive art form and a unique American contribution to world culture.

In the 1960s, rock music, which developed out of the traditions of the blues, jazz, and popular music, became the dominant form of music with mass appeal. More recent popular music has been influenced extensively by electronics and the mass media, with developments such as MTV, new age music, and rap.

CHAPTER 13

The Romantic Period (1825–1900)

Topics	Romanticism	Nonfunctional harmony	Enharmonic spelling
	Modal mixture	Chromatic nonharmonic	Common-tone diminished
	Foreign modulation	tones	7th chords

Romanticism is the term applied to much of the music written between 1825 and 1900. The period could be seen as little more than an extension of the classical period, judging by the works of the more conservative composers such as Franz Schubert (1797–1828) and Johannes Brahms (1833–1897), or as a major change in style, if the works of the more progressive composers such as Franz Liszt (1811–1886) and Richard Wagner (1813–1883) are considered. In spite of various national styles evident in the music of Polish composer Frédéric Chopin (1810–1849), Russian composer Alexander Borodin (1833–1887), and others, the music of the romantic period was dominated by German-speaking composers.

Important Concepts

The harmonic materials discussed in the previous chapters—including borrowed chords; 9th, 11th, and 13th chords; the Neapolitan 6th; augmented 6th chords; chromatic mediants; and altered dominant chords—were used much more frequently during the romantic period.

Modal Mixture

The increasing use of borrowed chords resulted in a blending of the major and minor modes, sometimes to the point of modal ambiguity (figure 13.1).

Figure 13.1

Schubert: Waltz from *Original Tänze für Klavier* (Original Dances for Piano), op. 9, no. 22, D. 365, mm. 1–4.

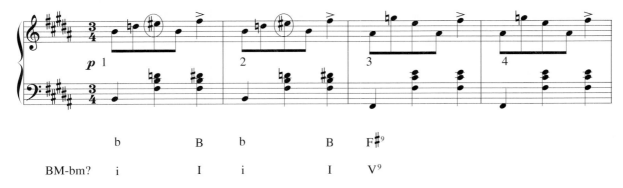

Modulation

Romantic composers often imply several keys in rapid succession. This has the effect of decreasing the influence of the central tonic. Notice the sudden modulation after only one measure and the equally sudden return in measure 3 in figure 13.2 (see also figure 13.7 on p. 206).

Figure 13.2

Chopin: Prelude, op. 28, no. 20, mm. 1–3.

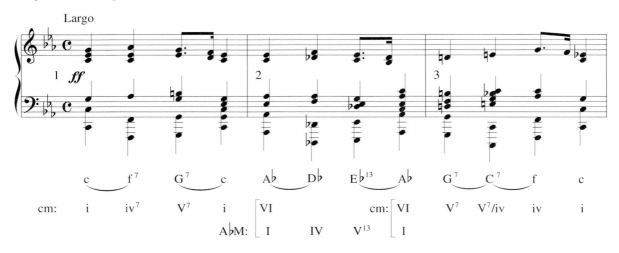

Foreign Modulation

The full spectrum of keys was exploited by nineteenth-century composers, with modulations to keys quite distant from the tonic of the composition. These often necessitate enharmonic spellings of chords. The enharmonic relationship between the German 6th chord and the dominant 7th was a favorite device for modulation to foreign keys. In figure 13.3, notice that the German 6th chord in the first measure is respelled as a dominant 7th in the third measure and resolves in a circle progression. (This passage is discussed more fully on p. 207.)

Figure 13.3

Schumann: *Am leuchtenden Sommermorgen* (On a Shining Summer Morning) from *Dichterliebe* (Poet's Love), op. 48, no. 12, mm. 6–9.

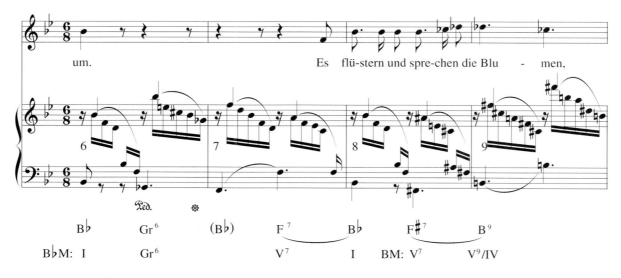

<table>
<tr><td>**Unresolved
Dissonance**</td><td>Dissonant chords, which required resolution in earlier periods, were sometimes left unresolved by nineteenth-century composers. These unresolved dissonances were often exploited for their dramatic effect, as figure l3.4 illustrates.</td></tr>
</table>

Figure 13.4

Schubert: Symphony in B Minor ("Unfinished"), D. 759, I, mm. 60–64.

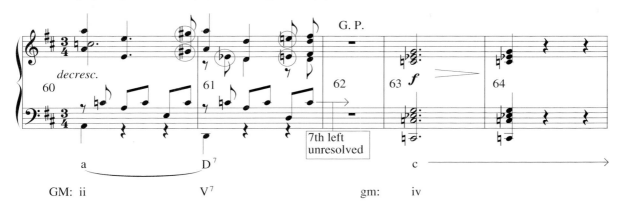

The tonic chord is clearly implied in measure 62 by the progression in the previous two measures (ii, V⁷). If this "missing chord" is filled in, a circle progression emerges (figure 13.5).

Figure 13.5

Schubert: Symphony in B Minor ("Unfinished"), D. 759, I, mm. 60–64.

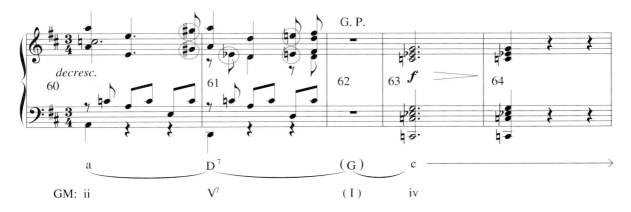

<table>
<tr><td>**Nonfunctional
Harmony**</td><td>Romantic composers occasionally abandoned functional harmony for short periods. These passages were often organized around a segment of the chromatic scale, as figure 13.6 illustrates. The chords have been given Roman numerals, but it is clear that they are not functionally related to each other. The passage is built around a descending chromatic pattern from the tonic in measure 5 to the dominant in measure 6.</td></tr>
</table>

The Romantic Period (1825–1900)   **205**

Figure 13.6

Chopin: Prelude, op. 28, no. 20, mm. 5–6.

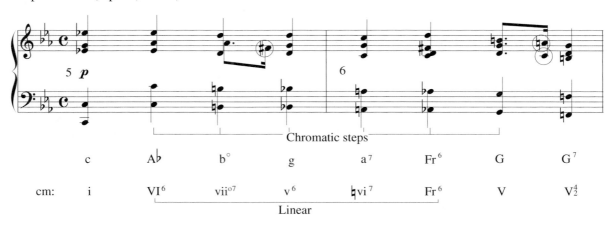

Chromaticism

The increased use of borrowed chords and augmented 6th chords along with modal mixture caused a general increase in chromaticism in the period. There also was an increase in the use of *chromatic nonharmonic tones,* particularly chromatic appoggiaturas and passing tones. Notice the chromatic appoggiaturas in measure 10 of figure 13.7.

Figure 13.7

Schumann: *Im wunderschöen Monat Mai* (In the Wonderful Month of May) from *Dichterliebe* (Poet's Love), op. 48, no. 1, mm. 8–12.

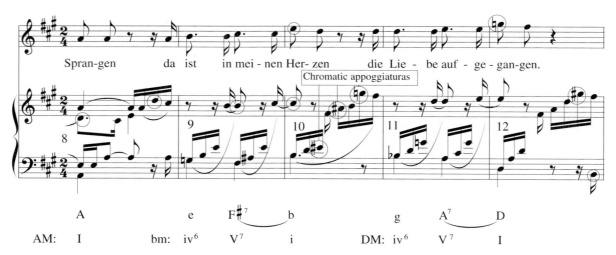

Chromatic passing tones are the central decorative devices in Chopin's Prelude (figure 13.8), occurring in nearly every measure of the work.

Figure 13.8

Chopin: Prelude, op. 28, no. 21, mm.1–4.

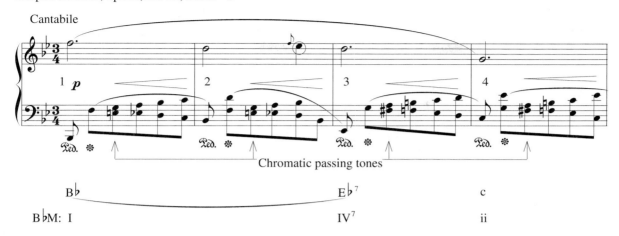

Increased Dissonance

More frequent use of 7th, 9th, 11th, and 13th chords and augmented 6th chords increased the general level of dissonance in nineteenth-century music. Composers came to favor the accented dissonances more and more, and these dissonances were often sustained much longer than their resolutions. In figure 13.9, notice the accented appoggiatura on the downbeat of measure 17 and the appoggiatura to the 9th of a dominant 9th chord in measure 16. These nonharmonic tones greatly increase the dissonance level of the passage.

Figure 13.9

Wagner: *Tristan und Isolde,* Prelude to Act I, mm. 15–17.

Enharmonic Spelling

The increased chromaticism of the nineteenth century complicated the notation of music, with the result that enharmonic spellings of chords and melodic lines became more frequent. (See measure 8 of Schumann's *Am leuchtenden Sommermorgen,* figure 13.3, on page 204, where the vocal part remains in flats while the accompaniment is written in sharps.) It is important that you develop skill in thinking enharmonically when analyzing the music of the nineteenth and twentieth centuries. The examples of enharmonic spelling of chords in figure 13.10 by no means exhaust the possibilities, but they furnish models of what you will need to be aware of in future analyses.

Diminished 7th Chords

Because all diminished 7th chords result from enharmonic spellings of three basic chords, composers often write them enharmonically.

Figure 13.10

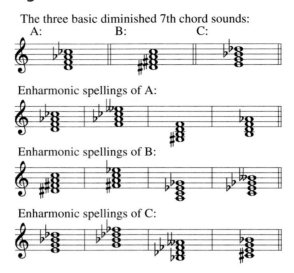

The three basic diminished 7th chord sounds:

Enharmonic spellings of A:

Enharmonic spellings of B:

Enharmonic spellings of C:

Any tone of a diminished 7th chord is a potential leading tone, and the chord may resolve to any of four roots. The chord may or may not be spelled to agree with its resolution, and enharmonic spelling must be considered in arriving at a correct analysis (figure 13.11).

Figure 13.11

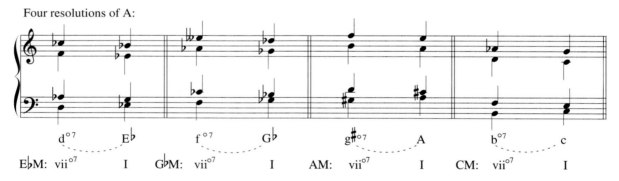

Four resolutions of A:

Figure 13.12 illustrates the enharmonic spelling of a diminished 7th chord to make a modulation from A minor to E-flat major.

Figure 13.12

Schubert: String Quartet, op. 29, D. 804 in A Minor, I.

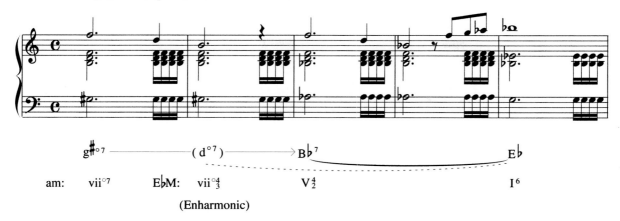

$g\sharp^{\circ 7}$ ——————— ($d^{\circ 7}$) ——————→ $B\flat^7$ $E\flat$

am: vii°⁷   E♭M: vii°$^4_3$ V$^4_2$ I⁶

                   (Enharmonic)

Common-Tone Diminished 7th Chords

An alternate resolution of a diminished 7th chord is to a major triad or major–minor 7th chord whose root is one of the tones of the diminished 7th sonority. In figure 13.13a, a single diminished 7th chord is resolved to four different major triads. In figure 13.13b it is resolved to four different major–minor 7th chords. (The diminished 7th chord is respelled enharmonically to facilitate the voice leading.)

Figure 13.13

a. Common-tone resolutions to major triads:

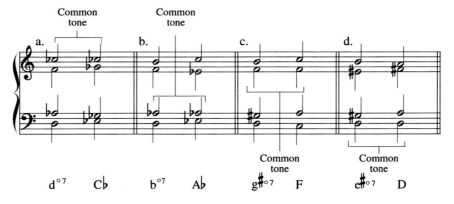

        $d^{\circ 7}$ $C\flat$ $b^{\circ 7}$ $A\flat$ $g\sharp^{\circ 7}$ F $e\sharp^{\circ 7}$ D

b. Common-tone resolutions to major–minor 7th chords

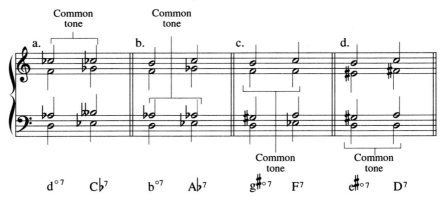

        $d^{\circ 7}$ $C\flat^7$ $b^{\circ 7}$ $A\flat^7$ $g\sharp^{\circ 7}$ F^7 $e\sharp^{\circ 7}$ D^7

Although these chords can function in a number of ways, the most common are (1) the raised supertonic 7th, which resolves to the tonic chord in major keys (figure 13.14a), and (2) the raised submediant, which resolves to the dominant triad or 7th chord in major keys (figure 13.14b).

Figure 13.14

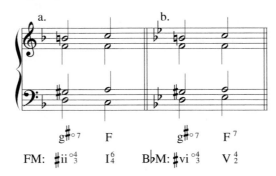

Notice in figure 13.14 that the tones that are raised resolve a half step upward. This follows the general principles outlined in previous chapters for resolving altered tones. Although these chords were known to composers in the baroque and classical periods, they became much more common during the nineteenth century (see figure 13.15a and b).

Figure 13.15

a. Josephine Lang: *Fee 'n-Reigen* (The Dance of the Fairies), mm. 18–22.

b. Tchaikovsky: Nutcracker Suite, op. 71a, III (*Valse des Fleurs*), mm. 1–4.

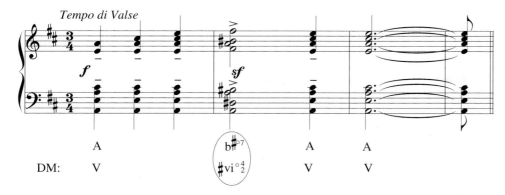

The raised supertonic and raised submediant diminished 7th chords are very common in twentieth-century "barbershop" quartet music, as shown in figure 13.16.

Figure 13.16

"In the Good Old Summertime," from Strictly Barbershop, S. P. E. B. S. Q. S. A., Folio 6049.

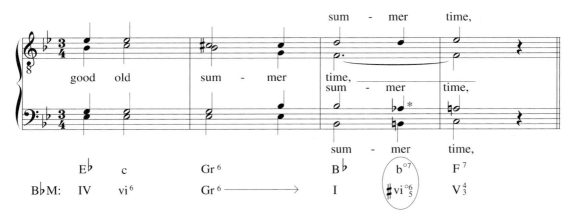

*A♭ should be read enharmonically as G♯ for purposes of analysis.

German 6th Chords

The enharmonic relationship between the Italian 6th and the German 6th chords and the dominant 7th led composers to spell these chords enharmonically (figure 13.17). Be alert for dominant 7th chords where the root resolves downward by a half step. Most of these chords are functioning as German 6th chords. When the enharmonic relationship between dominant 7ths and the augmented 6th chords is used as a modulatory device (see figure 13.3 on p. 204), the chord may be spelled correctly in one key but not in the other.

Figure 13.17

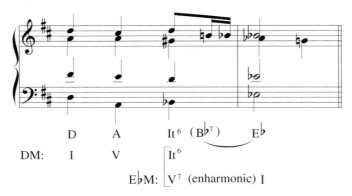

Assignment 13.1

Because enharmonic spelling of diminished 7th chords is quite common, it is important that you become accustomed to thinking of the enharmonic equivalents of these chords. The chord below represents one spelling of a diminished 7th chord. Analyze this chord (or its enharmonic equivalent) in as many ways as possible in each of the given keys. The first problem is completed as an example.

1. FM: $\underline{\text{vii}^{\circ 7}/\text{V}}$ $\underline{\sharp\text{ii}^{\circ 7}}$ $\underline{\text{vii}^{\circ 7}/\text{N}^6}$ $\underline{\text{vii}^{\circ 7}/\text{iii}}$

2. CM: _____ _____

3. DM: _____ _____ _____ _____

4. GM: _____ _____ _____

5. A♭M: _____ _____ _____ _____

6. B♭M: _____ _____ _____

7. E♭M: _____ _____

Assignment 13.2

Resolve each of the following "common-tone" diminished 7th chords to its normal chord of resolution using figure 13.14 as a model. Provide a Roman numeral analysis of the second chord.

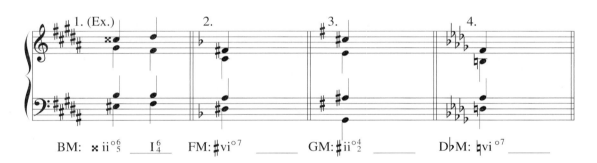

BM: $\times\text{ii}^{\circ \frac{6}{5}}$ $\underline{\text{I}^{\frac{6}{4}}}$ FM: $\sharp\text{vi}^{\circ 7}$ _____   GM: $\sharp\text{ii}^{\circ \frac{4}{2}}$ _____   D♭M: $\natural\text{vi}^{\circ 7}$ _____

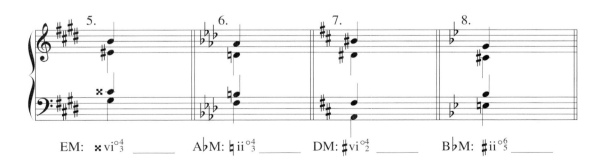

EM: $\times\text{vi}^{\circ \frac{4}{3}}$ _____   A♭M: $\natural\text{ii}^{\circ \frac{4}{3}}$ _____   DM: $\sharp\text{vi}^{\circ \frac{4}{2}}$ _____   B♭M: $\sharp\text{ii}^{\circ \frac{6}{5}}$ _____

Assignment 13.3   Because the German augmented 6th and the dominant 7th chords sound the same (B♭ D F G♯ = B♭ D F A♭—see figure 13.17, p. 212—German 6th chords), composers of this period occasionally spelled these chords enharmonically. Analyze each of the following chords as either dominant 7th or German 6th chords in the keys indicated and resolve each chord to the logical diatonic chord in the key. Some augmented 6ths may be spelled as dominant 7ths and vice versa, so it is important that you consider various spellings in completing the exercise.

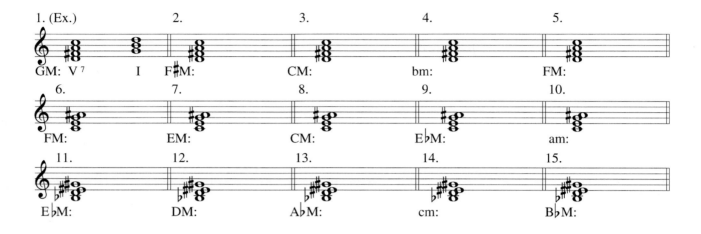

Assignment 13.4   Complete each of the following figured basses and do a Roman numeral analysis. Each progression involves a foreign modulation and may involve enharmonic spelling of chords. Analyze each modulation with a pivot chord. These progressions may be transposed to a variety of keys as a keyboard assignment.

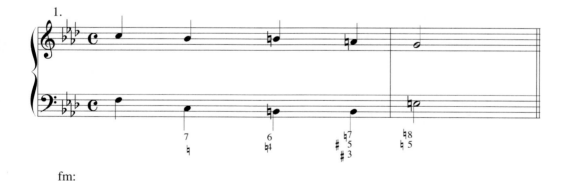

fm:

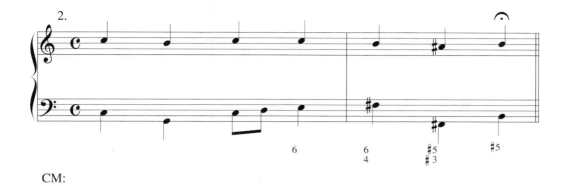

CM:

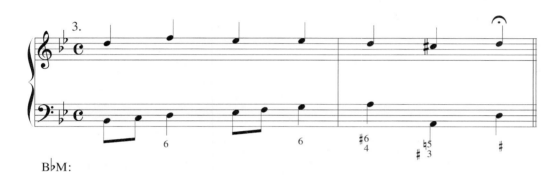

B♭M:

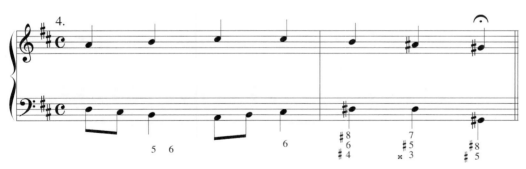

DM:

Assignment 13.5

Make an analysis (traditional or macro) of Chopin's Prelude, op. 28, no. 4, which follows. This work contains nonfunctional harmony and enharmonic spelling of chords. Compare your analysis with that of other class members and discuss the relative merits of the various analyses. There is no single "correct" analysis of this work.

Chopin: Prelude, op. 28, no. 4. CD Track 27

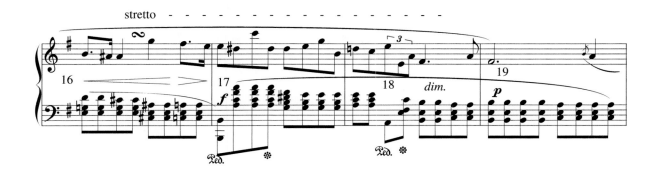

Assignment 13.6

Make an analysis (traditional or macro) of Franck's *Choral no. 1 pour Grand Orgue,* which follows, using the same strategy you used in completing assignment 13.5.

Franck: *Choral no. 1 pour Grand Orgue* (excerpt), mm. 1–23. CD Track 28

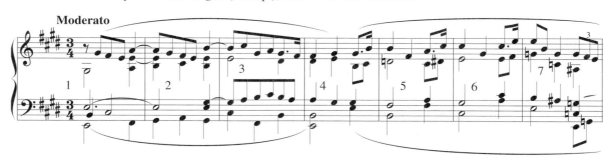

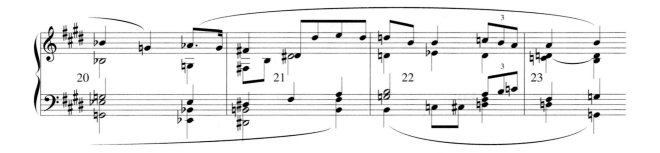

Assignment 13.7

The following excerpt is from the opera *Tristan und Isolde,* completed by Wagner in 1859.

1. Provide a complete analysis (traditional or macro) for the passage.
2. The first six measures are analyzed for you. These measures form the basis of a pattern that continues throughout the excerpt. Trace this pattern.
3. Discuss the general style of the music. Indicate salient features that make the style distinctive.
4. Perform the excerpt in class, with piano accompaniment. Have the men sing the part of *Tristan* and the women the part of *Isolde.*
5. Listen to this excerpt on recordings.

Wagner: *Tristan und Isolde,* Act II, scene 2, mm. 615–631. CD Track 29

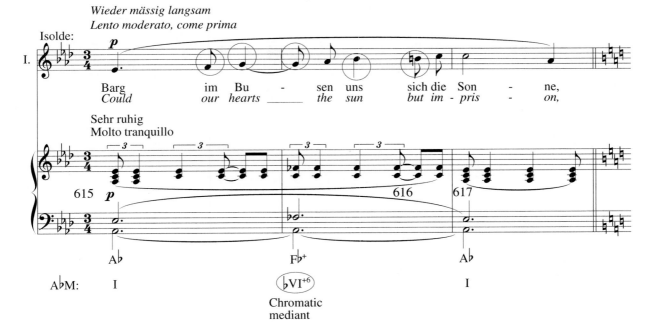

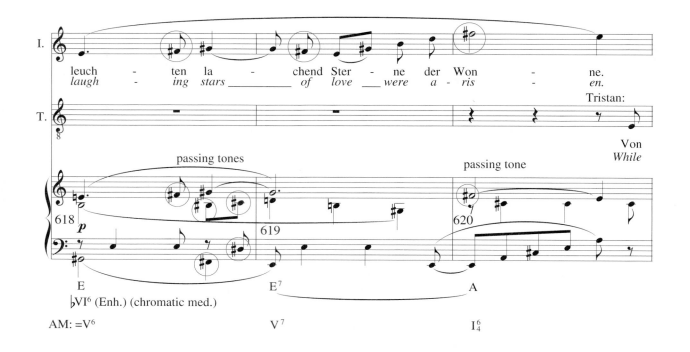

CHAPTER 14

The Post-Romantic, Impressionistic, and Related Styles

Topics	Post-Romanticism	Pentatonic scale	Traditional cadences
	Impressionism	Whole-tone scale	Linear cadence
	Tonal instability	7th, 9th, 11th, and	3rd-relationship cadence
	Nonfunctional harmony	13th chords	Cadences with added or
	Omnibus progression	Chords of addition	omitted tones
	Blurred cadence	and omission	Melodic doubling at
	Augmented triads	Split 3rds	various intervals
	Church modes	Quartal/quintal chords	Parallel chords (planing)

Important Concepts

Post-Romanticism

The term *post-romantic* is applied to the music of composers such as Hugo Wolf (1860–1903), Gustave Mahler (1860–1911), and Richard Strauss (1864–1949), who carried the musical style developed by the romantic composers (Richard Wagner in particular) to the outer limits of a tonal system based on the major and minor scales and functional harmony.

Impressionism

The term *impressionism* was first applied to a group of French painters, including Édouard Manet, Claude Monet, and Auguste Renoir. Their interest in light and color led to a style characterized by blurred images that convey the "impression" of a scene instead of an actual representation. The term was first used in music to describe the work of Claude-Achille Debussy (1862–1918) and his followers, principally Maurice Ravel (1875–1937).

Characteristics of Post-Romanticism

Tonal Instability

The post-romantic composers were greatly influenced by the music of Richard Wagner, who was able to sustain high levels of tension for long periods of time by avoiding resolution of the dominant function. Notice that each dominant 7th in figure 14.1 is followed by silence and not resolved in the expected way.

Figure 14.1

Wagner: *Tristan und Isolde,* Prelude to Act I, mm. 1–11.

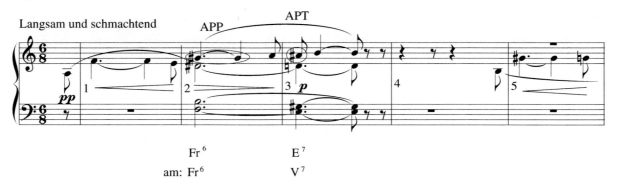

The use of chromatic harmony and nonharmonic tones, plus the absence of the tonic chord, creates tonal instability in this passage. This passage is one of the most discussed and analyzed passages in all Western music, and the analysis just presented is only one possible interpretation.

The following excerpt from a Wolf song (figure 14.2) creates tonal instability at the outset of the song through thin textures, chromaticism, incomplete chords, and lack of strong moves toward the tonic. The music arrives at a clear tonal center only in measure 9 through a circle progression in the previous measure (V/V, V^7, i), and even here the tonic is somewhat obscured by nonharmonic tones.

Figure 14.2

Wolf: *Der Knabe und das Immlein* (The Boy and the Bee) from *Gedichte von Eduard Mörike,* mm. 1–9.

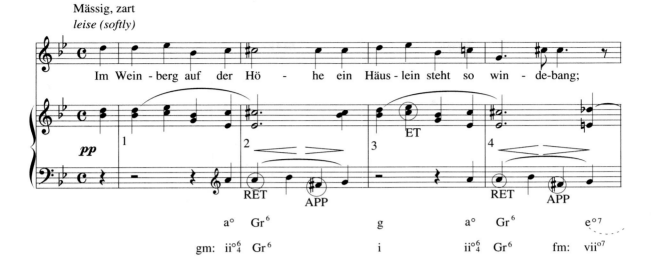

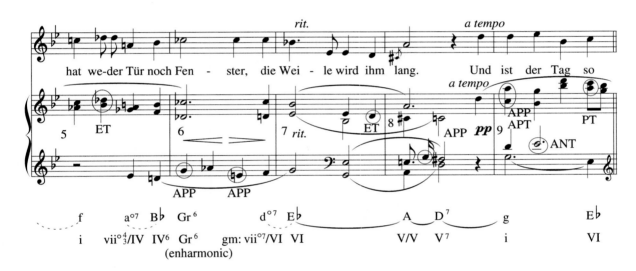

Nonfunctional Harmony

The post-romantic composers often used foreign modulation to create tonal instability. Figure 14.3 is the beginning of a passage that does not return to the tonic for 16 measures. Notice the moves toward G major and D-flat major and the chromatic passage in measures 13 to 15.

Figure 14.3

Strauss: *Allerseelen* (All Souls Day), op. 10, no. 8, mm. 11–17.

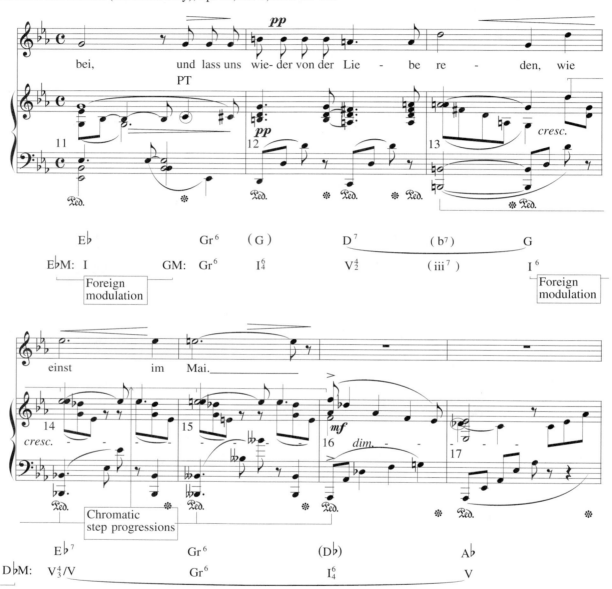

Omnibus Progression

The so-called omnibus progression is a specific harmonic progression based on the chromatic scale (figure 14.4).

Figure 14.4

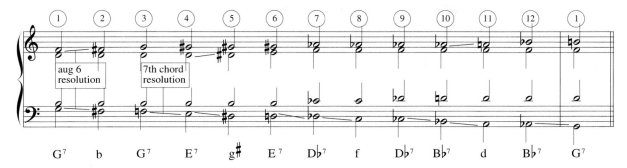

This progression, which occurred occasionally in romantic period music and more frequently in post-romantic music, takes advantage of the dual resolution tendencies of the major–minor 7th/German 6th. In chord I, the minor 7th (G–F) is resolved as an augmented 6th (G–E♯). In chord 3, the F is resolved as the 7th of a chord. At the point of resolution in chord 4, another German 6th/dominant 7th sonority is created, and the process continues until the first chord returns, creating an endless cycle. Figure 14.5 shows a passage from Mussorgsky's *Boris Godunov* that uses seven chords of the omnibus cycle.

Figure 14.5

Mussorgsky: *Boris Godunov,* Act III, scene I, mm. 205–212.

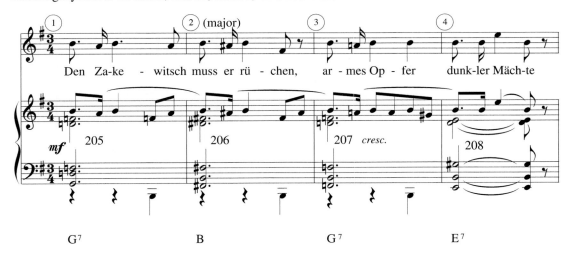

Blurred Cadence

The tonic is sometimes in doubt during most of a composition in this period, but it normally returns at the end to create closure. At the end of a composition, strong cadences are often blurred by inserting other chords (particularly the V/IV) between the dominant and the tonic chord, as shown in figure 14.6. The authentic cadence was too simple, following the highly chromatic music earlier in this song.

Figure 14.6

Strauss: *Zeitlose* (Meadow Saffron), op. 10, no. 7, mm. 22–27.

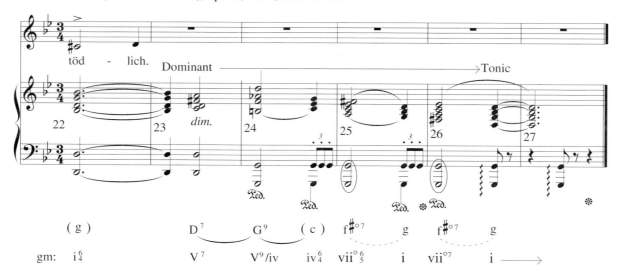

Augmented Triads

The post-romantic composers added the augmented triad to their vocabulary of ambiguous chords. It appeared both as an altered dominant and as a nonfunctional chord. In figure 14.7 nonfunctional augmented chords are treated with the same sliding chromaticism as the diminished 7th chord in earlier times.

Figure 14.7

Wolf: *Das verlassene Mägdelein* (The Forsaken Maiden) from *Gedichte von Eduard Mörike*, mm. 19–26.

Debussy also felt the influence of Wagner, but his response was a conscious attempt to remove "Wagnerisms" from his music. In a letter to a friend during the composition of his opera *Pelléas et Mélisande,* he complained, "I was too hasty to crow over *Pelléas et Mélisande.* . . . The ghost of old Klingsor, alias *R. Wagner,* appeared at the turn of a measure, so I tore it all up." Debussy created a unique musical style that has come to be called *impressionism.* It is a blend of elements borrowed from Eastern and Western music as well as those of his own invention. Many composers in the early twentieth century were influenced by impressionism.

Scale Resources
Church Modes

Composers of this time often utilize modal resources to create new and unusual melodic effects. Figure 14.8 illustrates the use of the Dorian mode.

Figure 14.8

Dorian mode beginning on A:

Bloch: "Chanty" from *Poems of the Sea.*

Copyright © 1923 G. Schirmer, Inc. Used by permission.

Figure 14.9 illustrates the use of the Phrygian mode beginning on A.

Figure 14.9

Respighi: *Trittico Botticelliano* (Botticelli Triptych).

Pentatonic Scale

The pentatonic (five-tone) scale was frequently used in compositions of this period. Because it is a gapped scale (containing intervals larger than a whole step between adjacent tones), there are several possible forms available. Two of the more frequently used pentatonic scales are shown in figure 14.10.

Figure 14.10

Figure 14.11, from Debussy's Preludes, demonstrates the use of the pentatonic scale.

Figure 14.11

Pentatonic scale:

Debussy: *Voiles* (Sails*) no. 2 from Preludes, Book I, mm. 43–45 (Modified).

Voiles can also be translated as "Veils."

The Nineteenth and Twentieth Centuries

Whole-Tone Scale

The whole-tone scale is a scale in which each degree is a whole step from the next. The whole-tone scale has only six tones—it is a hexatonic scale. Only two different whole-tone scales are possible. An aggregate of the chromatic scale is formed by the two scales illustrated.

Figure 14.12 is a whole-tone scale utilizing the tones C, D, E, F♯/G♭, G♯/A♭, and A♯/B♭ (any pitch may be spelled enharmonically).

Figure 14.12

Figure 14.13 shows the remaining tones of the chromatic scale (any pitch may be spelled enharmonically).

Figure 14.13

There are no P5ths or P4ths between any two degrees of the whole-tone scale. The whole-tone scale is not diatonic—it contains no key or tonal center and may begin on any of the six tones. Figure 14.14 illustrates Debussy's use of the whole-tone scale.

Figure 14.14

Debussy: *Voiles* (Sails) no. 2 from Preludes, Book I, mm. 1–4.

Chords

7th, 9th, 11th, and 13th Chords

The 7th, 9th, 11th, and 13th chords are employed with considerably greater frequency during the impressionistic period and with much less tendency to resolve the dissonant factors. Figure 14.15, from Ravel's *Sonatine* (1903), illustrates the use of 7th and 9th chords in succession. Note the circle progression, a vestige of the baroque, classical, and romantic periods.

The Post-Romantic, Impressionistic, and Related Styles   **231**

Figure 14.15

Ravel: *Sonatine,* II, mm. 6–12.

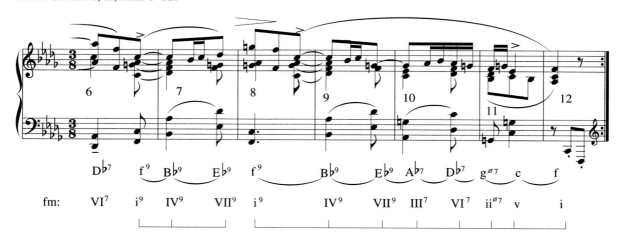

Successive circle progressions

Chords of addition and omission are chords with added or deleted tones. To enrich the sound of some sonorities, composers of the period often added a 6th, a 4th, or a 2nd to the traditional triad. Similarly, tones were, on occasion, deleted from chords, thus thinning the sound. Some common examples are found in figure 14.16.

Figure 14.16

Added 6th   Added 4th   Added 2nd   Omitted 3rd   Omitted 3rd

Chords with added tones often appear very similar to 9th, 11th, and 13th chords, but when the highest factor (9th, 11th, or 13th) is in a lower voice, the tendency is to hear it as an added tone (figure 14.17).

Figure 14.17

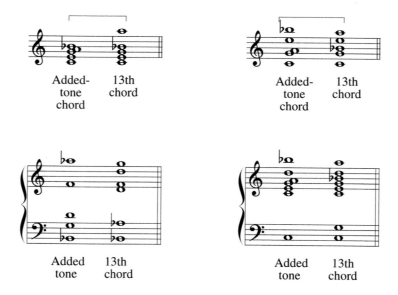

In this book we will use the word ᴼᴹᴵᵀ plus the chord factor missing to indicate tones omitted from chords and the word ᴬᴰᴰ plus the interval added for tones added to chords. For example, a chord with a missing third will be labeled ⁽ᴼᴹᴵᵀ ³⁾, and a chord with an added sixth will be labeled ⁽ᴬᴰᴰ ⁶⁾.

The added 6th chord is especially prominent in figure 14.18.

Figure 14.18

Ravel: *Sonatine*, I, mm. 22–26.

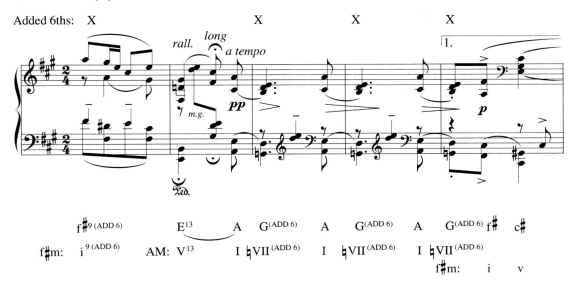

Split 3rds

The preceding examples of added tones were diatonic, but chromatic added tones are also found. Such chromatic tones often produce double inflections of chord tones. Double inflection of the 3rd of the chord produces a combination of major and minor, which is called a *split 3rd*. Figure 14.19 contains five chromatic added tones.

Figure 14.19

Ravel: *Valses nobles et sentimentales* (Noble and Sentimental Waltzes), I, mm. 57–58.

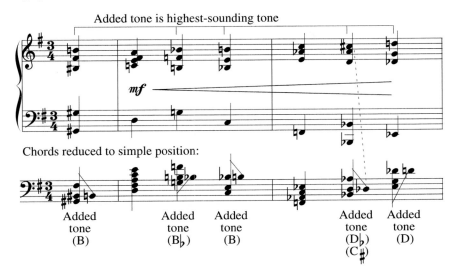

The excerpts in figure 14.20 contain both chords of omission and added tones.

Figure 14.20

Debussy: *La Soirée dans Grenade* (Evening in Granada) from *Estampes* (Prints), mm. 1–4.

Debussy: *La Soirée dans Grenade* (Evening in Granada) from *Estampes* (Prints), mm. 38–39.

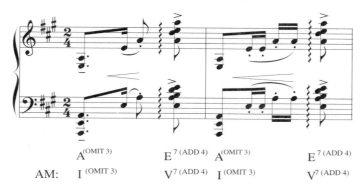

Quartal/Quintal Chords

Quartal chords are chords built in 4ths, whereas quintal chords are based on 5ths. Although by no means a common occurrence, quartal/quintal chords can be found in this style period. Two distinct types can be identified: "consonant" and "dissonant" quartal/quintal sonorities. Consonant quartal/quintal chords usually contain three to five factors built in P4ths (or P5ths), whereas dissonant quartal/quintal chords contain one or more A4ths (or d5ths) or five or more P4ths (or P5ths). Examples are shown in figure 14.21.

Figure 14.21

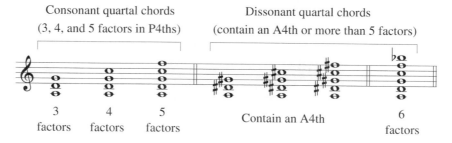

The Nineteenth and Twentieth Centuries

Quartal/quintal chords are not particularly common in impressionistic music, although they sometimes appear as parallel chords in nonfunctional harmony. Figure 14.22 illustrates such use.

Figure 14.22

Debussy: *La Cathédrale engloutie* (The Engulfed Cathedral), no. 10 from Preludes, Book I, mm. 85–86.

Copyright © 1910, Durand et Cie. Used by permission of the publisher. Elkan-Vogel, Inc., sole representative, United States.

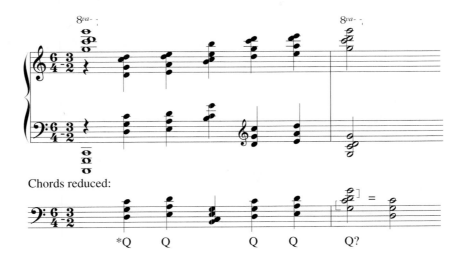

*Quartal chords

Cadences
Traditional Cadences

A wide variety of cadences are found in this style period, ranging from the traditional authentic cadence to the 3rd-relationship cadence. The traditional authentic cadence is frequently adorned with 7th, 9th, 11th, or 13th chords (figure 14.23).

Figure 14.23

Debussy: *Pelléas et Mélisande,* Act I, scene 1, mm. 131–132.

The Post-Romantic, Impressionistic, and Related Styles

235

Linear Cadences

A linear cadence consists of melodic lines that converge or diverge to form cadence points. These cadences are reminiscent of cadences in early music, before the development of the major–minor tonal system. (See *clausula vera,* chapter 1.) Figure 14.24 contains examples of linear cadences.

Figure 14.24

In figure 14.25, the final cadence results from oblique motion.

Figure 14.25

Debussy: *Le vent dans la plaine* (Wind on the Plain) no. 3, from Preludes, Book I, mm. 57–59.

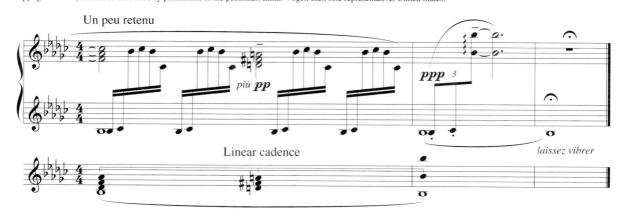

3rd-Relationship Cadences

A cadence that results from a harmonic progression in which the roots lie a 3rd apart is very common. Figures 14.26 to 14.28 illustrate 3rd-relationship cadences.

Figure 14.26

Ravel: *Sonatine,* II, mm. 77–82.

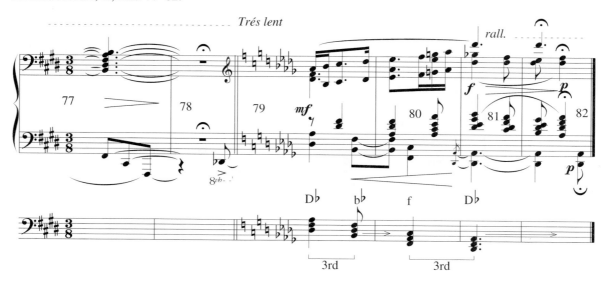

Figure 14.27

Debussy: *Clair de lune* (Moonlight) from *Suite Bergamasque*, mm. 70–72.

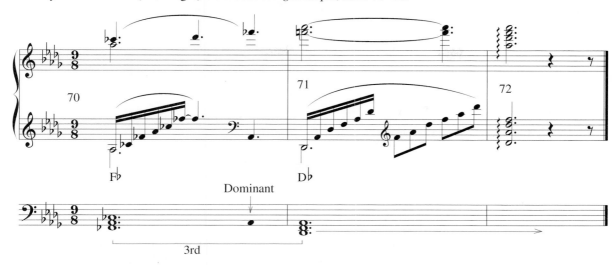

Figure 14.28

Ravel: *Sonatine,* I, mm. 79–84.

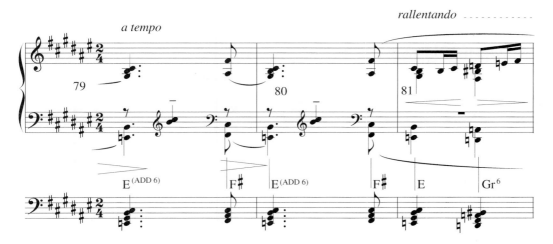

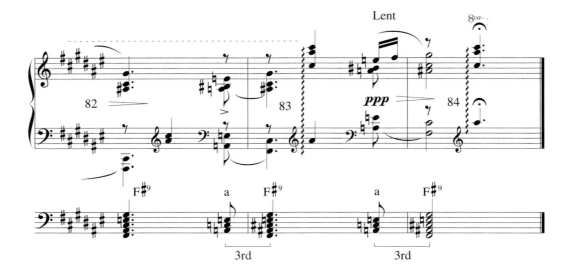

Cadences with Added or Omitted Tones

Although the authentic cadence of the late eighteenth and nineteenth centuries is sometimes found in its unaltered state in this style period, the dominant–tonic function is often camouflaged by chords to which additional factors have been added or from which they have been deleted. The final cadence in figure 14.29 contains a dominant 7th chord with an added 4th. This chord thus contains elements of both dominant and tonic harmony.

Figure 14.29

Debussy: *Six Morceaux Choisis,* no. 3, Menuet, mm. 86–88.

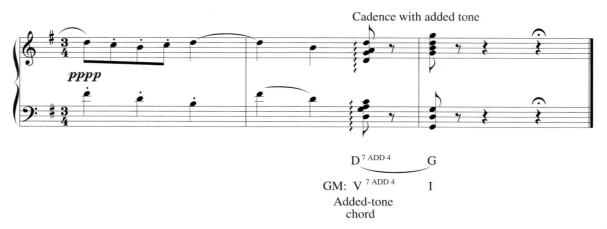

Other Cadences

A variety of other cadences are also a part of the late nineteenth- and early twentieth-century style. Most are simply variations of traditional cadences. Figure 14.30 ends with a dominant–tonic cadence in the Mixolydian mode.

Figure 14.30

Satie: *Gymnopedie,* no. 2, mm. 61–65.

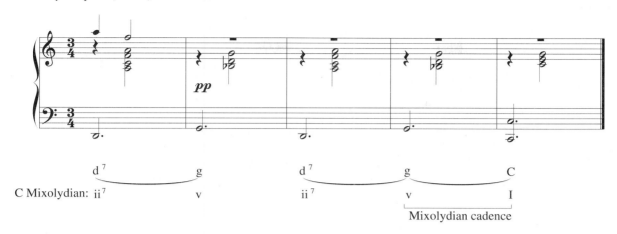

C Mixolydian:

ii⁷ ... v ... ii⁷ ... v ... I

Mixolydian cadence

Textural Considerations
Melodic Doubling at Various Intervals

Melodic doubling in parallel refers to the doubling of melodic lines to create parallel movement. The doubling may be simply the addition of a single tone at a fixed harmonic interval (figure 14.31).

Figure 14.31

Melody:

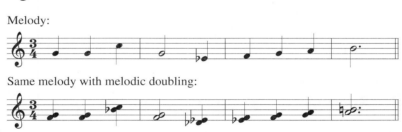

Same melody with melodic doubling:

   Although treated in a unique way in this period, melodic doubling is by no means the invention of twentieth-century composers. Such doubling has been in existence for many centuries and can be found in fauxbourdon and English descant of the fifteenth century (figure 14.32).

Figure 14.32

Dufay: *Missa Sancti Jacobi,* IX (*Communio*), mm. 21–23.

Figure 14.33 illustrates the use of melodic doubling at the interval of the 2nd.

Figure 14.33

Debussy: *Ce qu'a vu le vent de l'Ouest* (What the West Wind Saw), no. 7 from Preludes, Book I, mm. 10–13.

Copyright © 1910, Durand et Cie. Used by permission of the publisher. Elkan-Vogel, Inc., sole representative, United States.

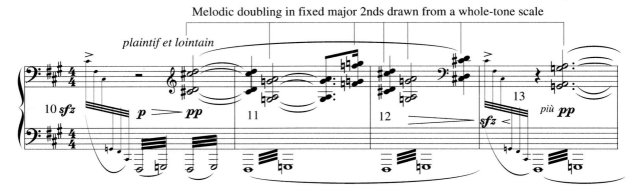

Parallel Chords (Planing)   Similar to melodic doubling, parallel chords are chords in which all factors or voices move in parallel motion. This motion is called *planing*. Generally, planing reduces or negates the effect of harmonic progression, but occasionally chords such as the tonic and dominant may create the sense of harmonic progression (figure 14.34).

Figure 14.34

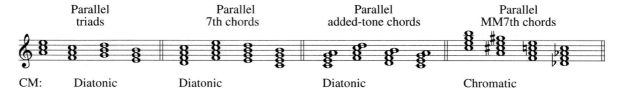

The example of planing in figure 14.35 contains only Mm 7th chords.

Figure 14.35

Debussy: *Sarabande* from *Pour le Piano* (For the Piano), mm. 9–12.

Parallel major–minor 7th chords

Figure 14.36 contains mixed major and minor triads in first inversion.

Figure 14.36

Debussy: *La Soirée dans Grenade* (Evening in Granada) from *Estampes* (Prints), mm. 80–81.

Chords reduced:

Planed 1st inversion M and m triads

History

The romantic period's emphasis on individual expression rested heavily on composers at the turn of the twentieth century. The farthest reaches of the major–minor tonal system had been explored by Wagner, and the music of all cultures was becoming known. (It is well known, for example, that Debussy was influenced by the pentatonic music of the Javanese *gamelan,* which he heard at the Paris *Exposition Universelle* in 1889.) The study of history had brought much of the music of earlier times to the attention of musicians. The composer was faced with the daunting task of creating a "new" music. The statements of Ferruccio Busoni are typical of the period: "The function of the creative artist consists in making laws, not in following laws ready made. He who follows such laws, ceases to be a creator. Creative power may be the more readily recognized, the more it shakes itself loose from tradition. But an intentional avoidance of the rules cannot masquerade as creative power, and still less engender it" (from *Sketch of a New Esthetic of Music*). The paradox of "not following laws ready made," although not "intentionally" avoiding tradition, was a nearly insurmountable obstacle and may be responsible, in part, for the note of regret and nostalgia that comes through in much late nineteenth-century music. The music of this period presents unique challenges to analysis. It is much more diverse and not as systematized as the music of the baroque, classical, and early romantic periods. It should not be surprising that new analytical strategies must be created to deal with music from the late nineteenth century to the present.

Applications

Scale Vocabulary

In previous analyses the major or minor scales could be assumed to be the tonal basis, but no such assumption can be made with music of the late nineteenth and early twentieth centuries. Instead, the identification of the scale basis (major, minor, modal, chromatic, pentatonic, or whole tone) will be an important step in analysis. If the music is not based in some way on the major–minor tonal system, then traditional Roman numeral analysis is not likely to prove fruitful. (In some cases, modal materials can be successfully analyzed with Roman numerals.)

Chord Vocabulary

The introduction of quartal chords raises questions concerning the interval basis of harmony. Roman numeral analysis assumes a tertian system (a harmonic system based on thirds) and is not appropriate for quartal harmonic materials. Chords of addition and omission present new problems in chord labeling.

The following suggestions are intended to help you recognize and label the tonal materials you will encounter in studying the music of this period.

Suggested Approach to Analysis

1. Establish the scale basis by examination of the music. If the music is chromatic, try to determine if the chromaticism is the result of functional chromatic harmony or is nonfunctional. If the music seems diatonic, check first to see if it may be pentatonic. Because the pentatonic scale is a subset of the diatonic scale, it is easily overlooked. If the music proves to be diatonic, check for a modal versus a major–minor basis.
2. Examine the harmonic vocabulary by looking at prominent chords. Check particularly for quartal/quintal sonorities.
3. If the music is major–minor or functional chromatic, then Roman numeral analysis is appropriate. Complete an analysis (traditional or macro) below the staff.
4. If the music contains passages of nonfunctional harmony, do a harmonic reduction and identify each chord by quality, with either Roman numerals or direct labeling (A^7, $d°$, etc.). Check carefully for functional relationships that may be masked by enharmonic spellings.
5. If the music falls outside steps 3 and 4, do a harmonic reduction and resort to direct labeling of scales and chords.
6. Melodic and rhythmic analysis is little affected by the introduction of new tonal materials and can be done in the usual way.

Specimen Analysis: *La Cathédrale engloutie,* by Debussy

Figure 14.37

This excerpt (figure 14.37) from a well-known work of Debussy should be examined as an example of the analysis of late nineteenth- and early twentieth-century music.

Debussy: *La Cathédrale engloutie* (The Engulfed Cathedral), no. 10 from Preludes, Book I.

Copyright © 1910, Durand et Cie. Used by permission of the publisher. Elkan-Vogel, Inc., sole representative, United States.

Peu à peu sortant de la brume

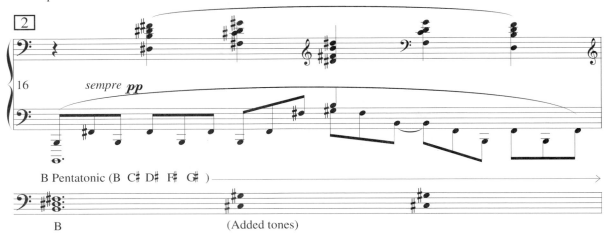

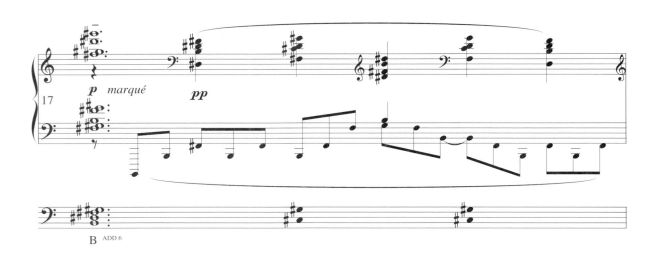

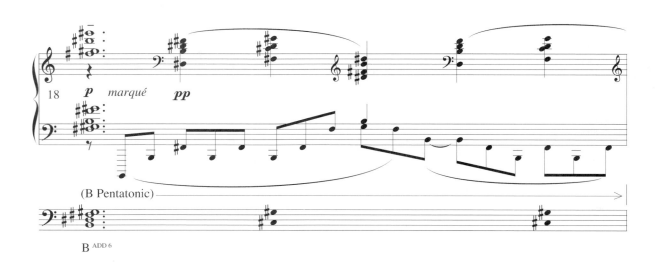

The Nineteenth and Twentieth Centuries

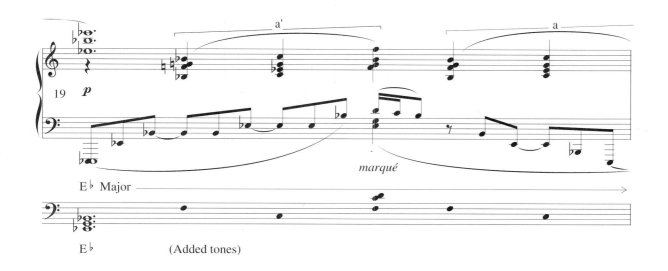

E♭ Major

E♭   (Added tones)

Augmentez progressivement (Sans presser)

(E♭ Major)

E♭

(E♭ Major)

E♭

The Post-Romantic, Impressionistic, and Related Styles

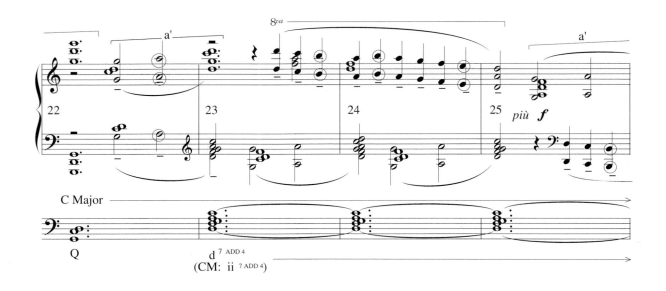

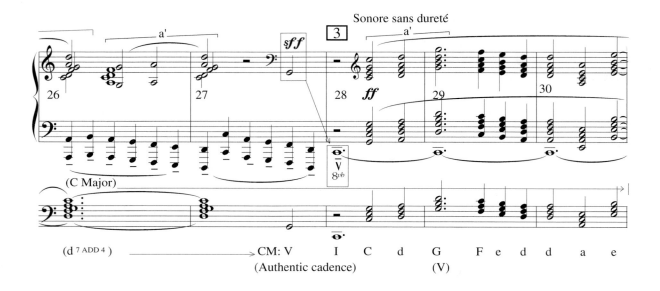

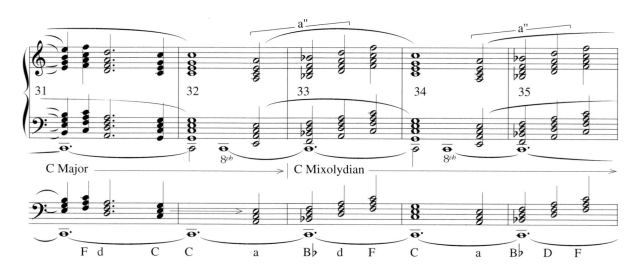

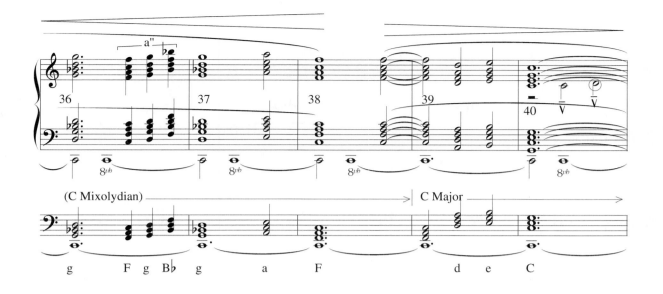

(C Mixolydian) ——————————————————→ | C Major ——————————————→

g   F   g   B♭   g   a   F   d   e   C

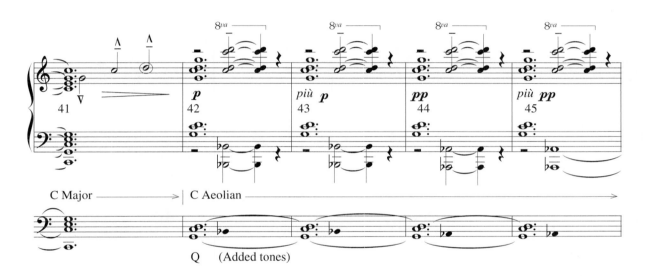

C Major ——————→ | C Aeolian ——————————————————————→

Q   (Added tones)

☐4 Un peu moins lent (Dans une expression allant grandissant)

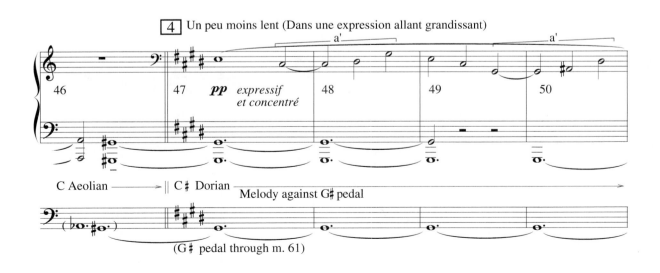

C Aeolian ——————→ ‖ C♯ Dorian ——————————————————→

Melody against G♯ pedal

(G♯ pedal through m. 61)

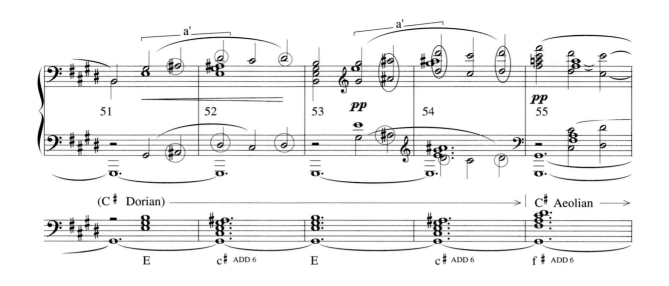

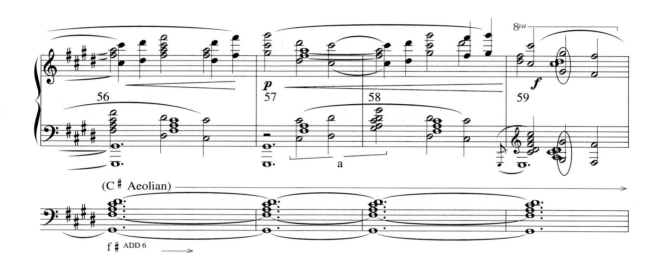

The Nineteenth and Twentieth Centuries

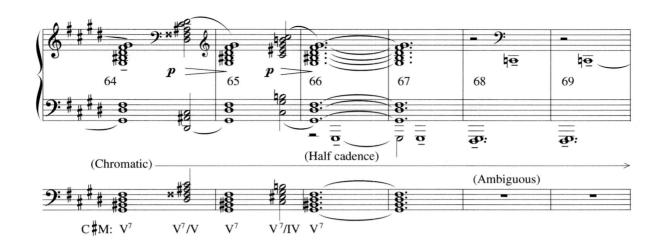

(Chromatic) ——————————————————————————————————————→

(Half cadence)

(Ambiguous)

C♯M: V⁷   V⁷/V   V⁷   V⁷/IV   V⁷

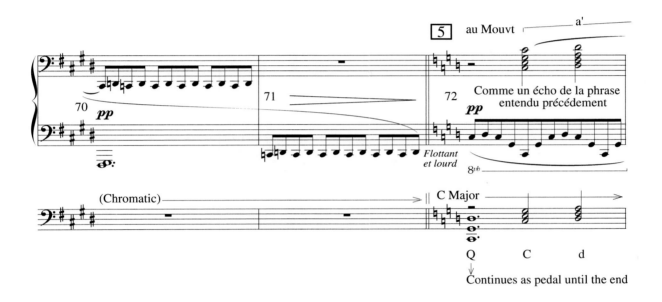

5 au Mouvt   a'

Comme un écho de la phrase
entendu précédement

*Flottant
et lourd*

(Chromatic) ———————————————————————————→ ‖ C Major ——————————————→

Q   C   d

↓
Continues as pedal until the end

(C Major) ——→

G   F   e   d   d   a   e   F   d   C

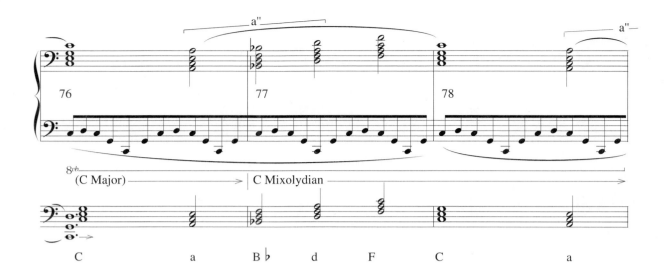

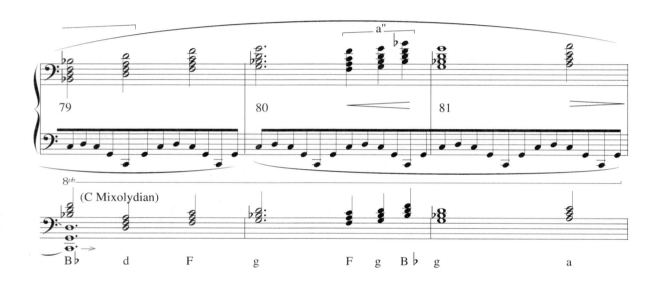

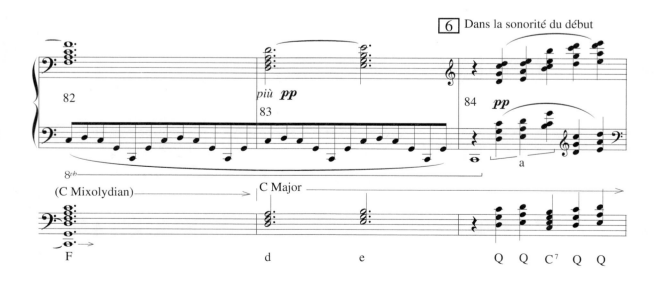

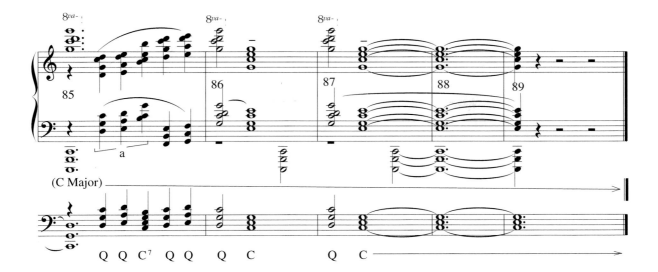

Tonality

Although not based, for the most part, on functional harmony, an overall tonal center of C emerges. This is primarily due to a bass line in the opening section that descends in stepwise motion from G to C (figure 14.38a), a strong authentic cadence in measures 27 to 28 (figure 14.38b), and sustained C pedals in measures 28 to 41 and 72 to 89.

Figure 14.38

The C tonal center is relieved by passages centered around B (mm. 16–18), E♭ (mm. 19–21), and G♯ (mm. 47–67). Notice the extensive 3rd relationships among these centers (C–E♭, B–E♭, G♯–C), even though they may be spelled enharmonically.

Chord Progressions

The effect of regularly recurring harmonic progressions is minimized in this composition. The reasons are as follows:

1. The actual progressions occur at widely spaced intervals of at least 2 measures, and in one instance at a distance of 13 measures. The harmonic rhythm is extremely slow.
2. Some of the harmonic progressions (such as from measures 18 to 19 and 21 to 22) contain chords whose roots lie in 3rd relationship to each other. When the 3rds are ascending, the harmonic strength is weakened considerably.

Cadences

Traditional harmonic cadences are suggested but are seldom stated clearly as in earlier styles. (The authentic cadence at measures 27 to 28 is veiled with added-tone chords and a running figure in the lower voice.) The cadence points are as follows:

Measures	Cadence Type	Tonality	Chords
27–28	Authentic	C	V (implied) to I
39–40	Linear (parallel motion)	C	I (pedal)
64–66	Half	C♯	V^7/V to V^7
86–89	Authentic (modified dominant)	C	V (or quartal) to I

The Post-Romantic, Impressionistic, and Related Styles   **251**

Melodic Material

The melodic material is quite similar throughout the work. There is a prominent three-note motive that appears in various guises in most sections of the piece (figure 14.39). The similarity of melodic material creates an organic unity that ties the work together.

Figure 14.39

Meter and Rhythm

The meter $\frac{6}{4}$ $\frac{3}{2}$, indicated at the beginning of this composition, is normally interpreted to mean that the quarter-note values remain fixed and that in some measures they will be grouped in duples and in others as triplets. However, in his own performance of this work, Debussy played in a fashion that would indicate the following:

$$\text{♩ in } \tfrac{6}{4} \text{ meter} = \text{♩ in } \tfrac{3}{2} \text{ meter}$$

Because the meter vacillates somewhat between groupings of two and groupings of three, the rhythm, although interesting and diverse, is not stressed. In its subtler aspects, however, rhythm plays a role as part of the total "color" in this work.

Texture

The texture of this composition is the antithesis of polyphony. With the numerous pedal tones and the parallel movement of chords (planing), conflict of opposing melodies is almost totally absent. The motion is predominantly parallel or oblique, as shown in figure 14.40, in a typical measure (14).

Figure 14.40

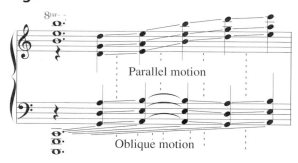

Form

In 1907 Debussy wrote to his publisher, "I am more and more convinced that music is not, in essence, a thing that can be cast into a traditional and fixed form. It is made up of colors and rhythms." Any attempt to cast this music into a traditional form would seem doomed to failure. Nevertheless, several points within the work seem to be the beginnings of important statements or seem to contrast in one way or another with previous sections. These points are identified in the score as points of formal articulation. The following table lists these points and musical elements that support the perception of the beginning of a statement.

Articulation Point	Measure	Elements Creating the Formal Articulation
1	1	Beginning of the work
2	16	New accompaniment texture; tonal center B
3	28	Strong cadence; new planed triad texture
4	47	Tonal center G♯; previous passage is "transitional"
5	72	Return to C tonal center; previous passage is "transitional"
6	84	Eighth-note accompaniment texture replaced by quarter-note motion; planed quartal texture

It is clear that articulation point 6 is like number 1 (the beginning of the work), creating a sense of return. Articulation point 3 is also similar to number 5 (compare right-hand parts). This has led at least one theorist to see an arch form in which the second part of the work represents a mirror image of the first part of the work.

Articulation point	1	2	3	4	5	6
Formal	A	A′	B	C	B′	A″

Although it may not be possible to state with certainty which formal outline best fits this prelude, it is clear that the work is carefully constructed and presents a unified impression. Judging by Debussy's statements on the subject of form, this should be sufficient.

Assignment 14.1

Using the suggestions in the applications section of this chapter (p. 241), do an analysis of *Der Mond hat eine schwere Klag erhoben,* by Hugo Wolf. Before preparing the analysis, have two students perform the song in class or listen to a recording until the work is familiar. (It is fruitless to attempt the analysis of a composition unless you know it thoroughly.)

Wolf: *Der Mond hat eine schwere Klag erhoben* (The moon hath been most grievously complaining) from *Italienisches Liederbuch.* CD Track 30

die mich ver - blen - det.

my heart's un - do - ing. (Lily Henkel)

Assignment 14.2

Using the suggestions in the applications section of this chapter, do an analysis of the following excerpt from *Pour le Piano,* by Debussy. Before preparing the analysis, have a student perform the composition several times in class or listen to a recording until the work is thoroughly familiar to you.

Debussy: *Sarabande* from *Pour le Piano* (For the Piano), mm. 1–22. CD Track 31

Avec une élégance grave et lente

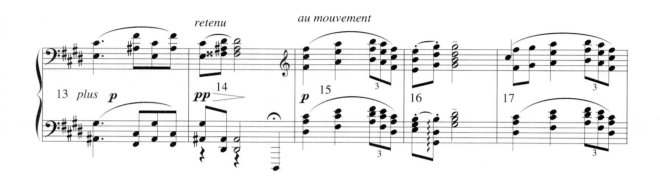

Assignment 14.3

Using the suggestions in the applications section of this chapter, do an analysis of *Je garde une médaille d'elle,* by Lili Boulanger (1893–1918). Before preparing the analysis, have a student perform the composition several times in class or listen to a recording until the work is thoroughly familiar.

Boulanger: *Je garde une médaille d'elle* (I Keep a Medal of Hers). CD Track 32

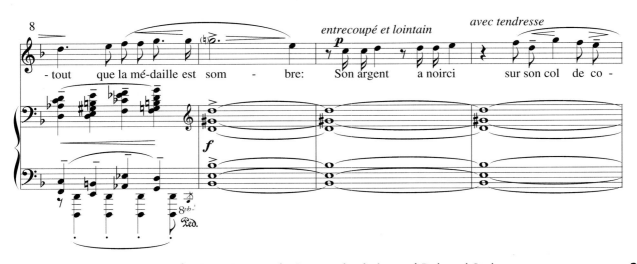

The Post-Romantic, Impressionistic, and Related Styles

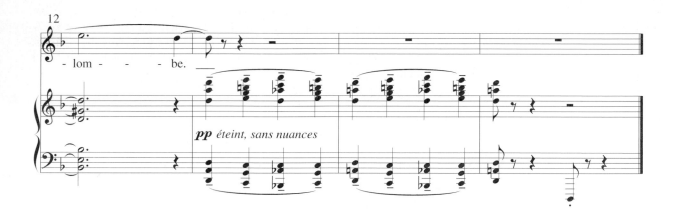

*I keep a medal of hers on which are engraved a date, and the words: "pray, believe, hope." But, as for me, I see above all that the medal is dark; its silver has tarnished on her dovelike neck.

Assignment 14.4

Using some of the devices listed below, write a short composition of 16 to 30 measures in the style of Debussy.

3rd-relationship cadence	Melodic doubling
Parallelism (planing)	Altered dominants or tonics
Modal melody	Changing meters
Pedal tones	7th, 9th, 11th, and 13th chords
Chords of addition and omission	Pentatonic scale

1. Write for any combination of instruments played by class members.
2. Perform the compositions in class.
3. After each student composition is performed, members of the class should enumerate (from listening only) the various devices employed in the work.

CHAPTER 15

The Contemporary Period (1910–1945)

Topics	*Primitivism*	*Polychords*	*Set theory*
	Neoclassicism	*Quartal chords*	*Pitch classes*
	Pandiatonicism	*Clusters*	*Set*
	Polytonality	*Changing meter*	*Set types*
	Dual modality	*Additive rhythm*	*Inversion*
	Shifted tonality	*Asymmetric meters*	*Normal order*
	Free tonality	*Nonaccentual rhythms*	*Best normal order*

Important Concepts
Contemporary Period

Concurrent with the surge of post-romantic and impressionistic music, several other, quite different styles began to surface. These are generally grouped together as *contemporary music.* At the same time that the works of Debussy, Delius, Wolf, Fauré, and Richard Strauss were receiving their premieres, other composers such as Arnold Schoenberg (1874–1951), Charles Ives (1874–1954), Béla Bartók (1881–1945), and Igor Stravinsky (1882–1971) were writing music in distinctly different idioms. Some composers maintained tertian chord structures but abandoned functional harmony, whereas others experimented with chords constructed in 4ths, 5ths, or combinations of several intervals. Some preserved tonality, others discarded it in favor of atonality. Experimentation ranged even to the tuning system itself, leading to the development of microtonal systems based on more than 12 different pitches per octave. This chapter will deal with the music of Stravinsky, Bartók, and composers with similar styles and the following chapter with the work of Schoenberg and the other composers who evolved a music based on *twelve-tone technique,* a compositional technique in which all pitches are related to a fixed ordering of the 12 tones of the chromatic scale.

Major Styles
Primitivism

Primitivism provided a contrast to the extremely refined and fragile music of such composers as Debussy and Ravel. Rhythm was the primary structural element of this music, and driving rhythms were combined with simple and clearly defined melodies, often of a folk nature, that operated within a narrow pitch range. Sharp percussive effects with thick chords and much parallel movement typified the style. Bartók's *Allegro Barbaro* (1911) and Stravinsky's *The Rite of Spring* (1913) represent examples of this movement, which flourished in the early years of the twentieth century.

Neoclassicism

The term *neoclassicism* refers to the music of composers such as Stravinsky and Hindemith who sought to return to the classical values of symmetry and balance while maintaining more contemporary tonal materials. This movement, which began just after World War I, was quite important through the first third of the twentieth century.

Tonal Basis

Pandiatonicism

Pandiatonicism is the use of the tones of a diatonic scale in such a way that each tone is stripped of its traditional function. The style is characterized by the absence of functional harmony, little or no chromaticism, and thick harmonies. Figure 15.1 is a typical example of pandiatonicism.

Figure 15.1

Stravinsky: Sonata for Two Pianos, II (Theme with Variations), Variation 1, mm. 4–7.

Polytonality

Polytonality is the use of two or more tonalities at the same time. (The simultaneous use of two tonalities is often called *bitonality* [figure 15.2].)

Figure 15.2

Dual Modality

The simultaneous use of a pair of major and minor modes or combinations of Gregorian modes is called *dual modality*. Usually the two modes have the same tonic (figure 15.3).

The Nineteenth and Twentieth Centuries

Figure 15.3

Bartók: *Major and Minor*, no. 59 from *Mikrokosmos,* vol. 2, mm. 1–3.

Treble clef notes: Dorian

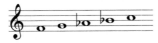

Bass clef notes: Lydian

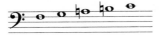

Shifted Tonality

Shifted tonality refers to a sudden change of tonality without preparation, as occurs in the excerpt in figure 15.4.

Figure 15.4

Prokofiev: Piano Sonata no. 8 in B-flat Major, op. 84, II (Andante sognando), mm. 7–10.

Free Tonality

Free tonality has the following characteristics:

1. No conventional mode or key is used.
2. A clear tonal center is present.
3. Any combination of the 12 tones of the octave may be used.
4. The traditional functioning of the diatonic tones of a key based on that same tonal center is minimized or avoided entirely.
5. The dominant-tonic relationship of key-centered tonality is absent.

In figure 15.5, eleven of the 12 tones are present, the tonality of F is achieved without a single dominant-tonic progression, and the Phrygian mode is suggested but not confirmed.

Figure 15.5

Hindemith: Piano Sonata no. 2, I, mm. 41–48.

Copyright © 1936. Used by permission of Belwin Mills Publishing Corp., Melville, NY. United States distributor for B. Schott's Soehne, Mainz, Germany.

Harmony

Polychords

A *polychord* consists of two or more triads, 7th chords, or other chords sounded simultaneously and spaced far enough apart to make each recognizable as a separate structure. Two triads containing common tones and spaced a distance apart may not be perceived as separate structures if the combination of the two forms a chord very familiar to us. But if the triads contain no common tones and are of sufficiently contrasting nature, fusion will not result, and each triad will maintain its identity, as shown in figure 15.6.

Figure 15.6

Polychord   Polychord

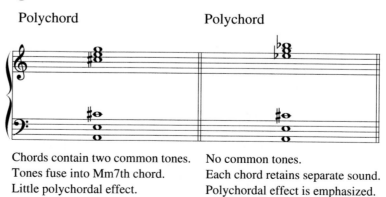

Chords contain two common tones.   No common tones.
Tones fuse into Mm7th chord.   Each chord retains separate sound.
Little polychordal effect.   Polychordal effect is emphasized.

Figure 15.7 illustrates the wide spacing and contrasting nature of the simultaneous chords making up polychords.

Figure 15.7

Schuman: No. 2 from *Three Score Set*, mm. 1–4.

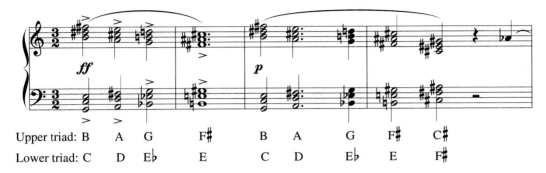

| Upper triad: | B | A | G | F♯ | B | A | G | F♯ | C♯ |
| Lower triad: | C | D | E♭ | E | C | D | E♭ | E | F♯ |

Quartal Chords

Quartal chords are common in contemporary music. Figure 15.8 contains pure quartal chords almost exclusively throughout the composition, which makes it a rare example of quartal chord treatment.

Figure 15.8

Ives: "The Cage" (no. 64 of 114 Songs).

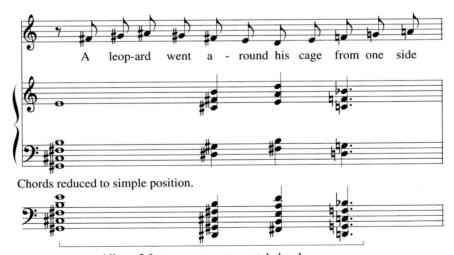

A leop-ard went a - round his cage from one side

Chords reduced to simple position.

All are 5 factor consonant quartal chords.

Frequently, quartal chords are not pure—that is, other intervals are included in the chord, thus creating a mixture of quartal and tertian harmony. The following excerpt (figure 15.9) from Alban Berg's opera *Wozzeck* (1921), illustrates the intermixing of 3rds and 4ths. The parallel 4ths in contrary motion (treble against bass) create a counterpoint that adds to the interest of the composition.

The Contemporary Period (1910–1945)

265

Figure 15.9

Berg: *Wozzeck,* op. 7, Act I, scene 3, "Marie's Lullaby," mm. 372–374.

*Predominantly quartal.

Figure 15.10 also illustrates the mixing of quartal with tertian (triadic) harmony. Note that the melody contains a motif made up of two intervals, the m2nd and the tritone. In its last two appearances in this excerpt, the m2nd is maintained, but the tritone gives way first to a P5th and then to an M3rd.

Figure 15.10

Pisk: "Nocturnal Interlude" from New Music for the Piano.

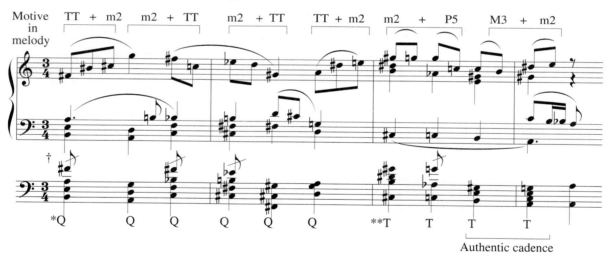

*Quartal/quintal chords.
**Tertian (triadic).
†Grace notes are not part of the chords.

Both quartal and tertian harmony often contain the same tones, each distinguished only by the arrangement of the chord factors (figure 15.11).

Figure 15.11

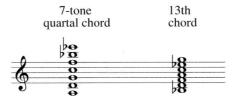

7-tone
quartal chord

13th
chord

Both contain the same pitches

Clusters

Chords containing three or more factors of which each is no more than a whole step from its adjacent factor are called *clusters* (figure 15.12).

Figure 15.12

Rhythm

Changing Meter

Meter changes from measure to measure within a composition show shifting rhythmic patterns more clearly than would a single governing meter. The signature is changed as often as necessary to clarify rhythms. *Changing meter* often occurs in music with *additive rhythm* (where the pulse is irregular in length, varying between groups of two and three regular divisions) (figure 15.13).

Figure 15.13

Stravinsky: Triumphal March of the Devil from *l'Histoire du Soldat* (The Soldier's Tale), (violin part), mm. 1–7.

Asymmetric Meters

Asymmetric meters, also known as irregular meters or combination meters, are meters in which the beats are not grouped into units divisible by two or three. These meters are a common way of notating additive rhythm, particularly when there is a recurring pattern of beats (figure 15.14).

Figure 15.14

Nonaccentual Rhythms

Nonaccentual rhythms are characterized by the absence of dynamic accents, which focuses the listener's attention on agogic accents (accents by virtue of duration) (figure 15.15).

Figure 15.15

History

The music of the contemporary period was marked by increasing stylistic divergence. In the twentieth century, rapid transportation, radio communication, and the development of audio recording technology and the sound film brought the rich diversity of the world's cultures to the attention of the general public. At the same time, World War I in Europe devastated established cultural institutions, leaving a culture that was undergoing rapid change while losing some of its own traditional base. The composers of this period were affected in many ways by these upheavals, as the brief biographies in this and the following chapters will illustrate.

Igor Stravinsky (1882–1971)

Igor Stravinsky's professional activity lasted nearly 60 years and evolved through many styles. Born in St. Petersburg, Russia, in 1882, he began studying with Rimsky-Korsakov in 1907. By 1911 Stravinsky had achieved success in Paris with two ballets, *The Firebird* and *Petrushka*. A third ballet, the initially controversial *The Rite of Spring,* received its first performance in 1913 and has since become one of the landmarks of twentieth-century music. Just before World War I, Stravinsky left Russia and took up residence in Switzerland, where he remained until 1920. After a long residence in France (1920–1939), he moved to the United States and became an American citizen in 1945. Perhaps the capstone of his career are the 21 works for the theater and 19 orchestral compositions, but he published chamber music, concertos, sacred choral–orchestral works, solo songs, and piano music. Stravinsky is considered by many to be the most important figure in twentieth-century music.

The following chart provides an overview of the various phases of Stravinsky's professional life.

Approximate Years	Period	Representative Compositions	Brief Description of Techniques
1904–1913	Post-Romantic Nationalistic	*The Firebird, Petrushka, The Rite of Spring*	Extreme modulations; rich harmonic schemes; full orchestral sounds; changing and asymmetrical meters.
1913–1923	Transition to Neoclassic	*l'Histoire du Soldat, Les Noces*	Chromaticism, polytonality; more dissonant harmony; use of polyrhythms; thinner textures.
1923–1951	Neoclassic	*Symphony of Psalms, Symphony in Three Movements*	Somewhat less chromaticism; use of pandiatonicism; thin textures; use of song and sonata-like forms.
1952–1971	Serial technique	*In Memoriam Dylan Thomas, Orchestral Variations*	Tone rows of five to seven tones; also fully developed serial technique; suggested by a study of Webern's music.

Béla Bartók (1881–1945)	A composer of considerable stature in the twentieth century, Béla Bartók was born in a farming region of Hungary and emigrated to the United States in 1940. He was beset most of his life with financial difficulties and eventually died almost penniless in a New York hospital in 1945. Almost all his music is in some way influenced by folk music material. He collected in excess of six thousand Magyar, Slovak, Transylvanian, and Rumanian folk tunes, and they often appear in his works. Bartók developed his own unique compositional techniques, working and experimenting as he went along. He avoided the twelve-tone technique, did not imitate major composers of his own era, and showed only passing interest in the native styles of America. Important works include *Music for Strings, Percussion and Celesta* (1936), *Concerto for Orchestra* (1943), and six string quartets, which are regarded among the greatest twentieth-century works for that medium.

Applications

Analysis of Contemporary Music

The diversity of style in the music of the twentieth century requires more than one system of analysis. Several systems have been proposed, but none appears to be useful for all styles of music. In the face of such diversity it becomes important to choose analytical methods that reveal the underlying structure of a given work. Thus the choice of analytical method becomes the first and most important decision you must make when approaching a contemporary composition. Two specimen analyses, one of the *Marche du Soldat* from Stravinsky's *l'Histoire du Soldat* (1919) and the other of "Chromatic Invention" no. 91 from *Mikrokosmos,* volume 3, by Béla Bartók, will illustrate two approaches to the analysis of twentieth-century music.

Marche du Soldat

l'Histoire du Soldat (The Soldier's Tale), a work intended "to be read, played, and danced," was written in 1918 for a small touring theater company composed of a few actors, dancers, and a chamber ensemble consisting of clarinet in A, bassoon, cornet in A, trombone, percussion, violin, and double bass. The percussion instruments include two snare drums, two tenor drums, bass drum, cymbals, tambourine, and triangle, all to be played by one player. This limited ensemble was clearly chosen to emphasize diversity of color, but the woodwinds, brass, and string sections are each represented by one high- and low-pitched instrument, and the entire orchestral range is covered by the ensemble. Swiss author C. F. Ramuz prepared the libretto and, as he was not a dramatist, a mimed narration (narrator and mime) supported by dancers and orchestra was prepared. Currently the work is sometimes performed without the staging.

Because the work is heterogeneous (consisting of many diverse elements), a descriptive analysis is the best choice (figure 15.16).

Figure 15.16

Stravinsky: *Marche du Soldat* (Soldier's March) from *l'Histoire du Soldat* (The Soldier's Tale).

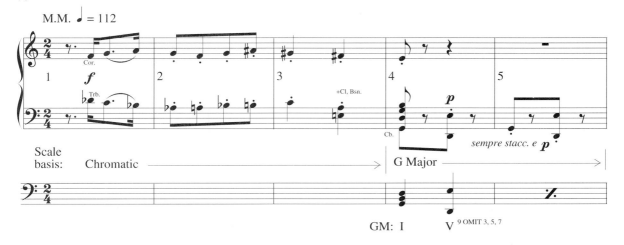

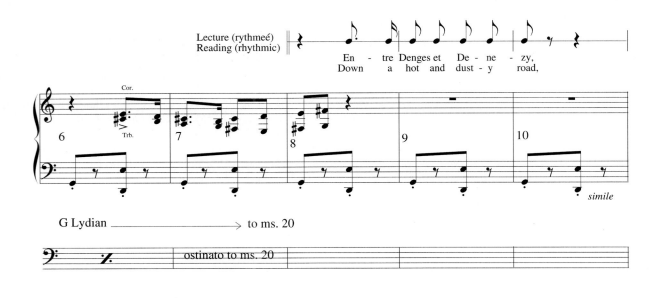

G Lydian ——————————→ to ms. 20

ostinato to ms. 20

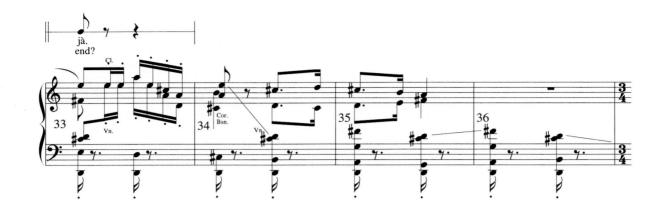

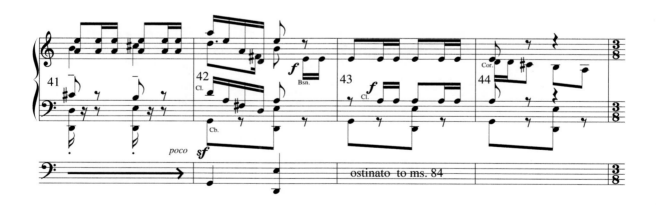

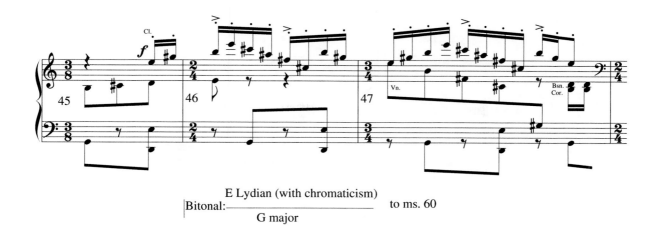

E Lydian (with chromaticism)
Bitonal:—————————————— to ms. 60
          G major

G major to ms. 64

Bitonal: Chromatic (D related) to ms. 84

G major

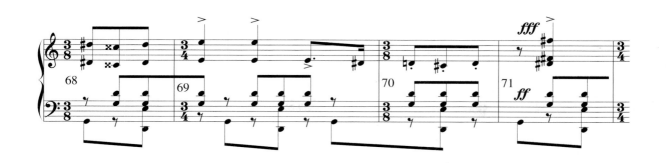

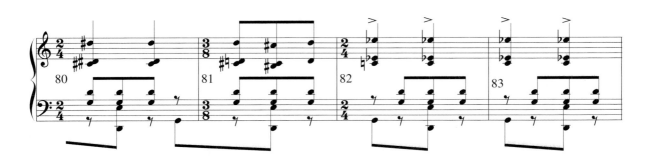

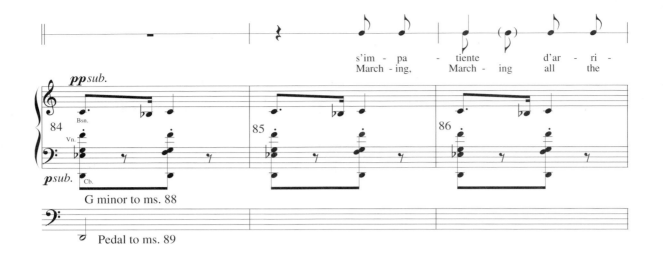

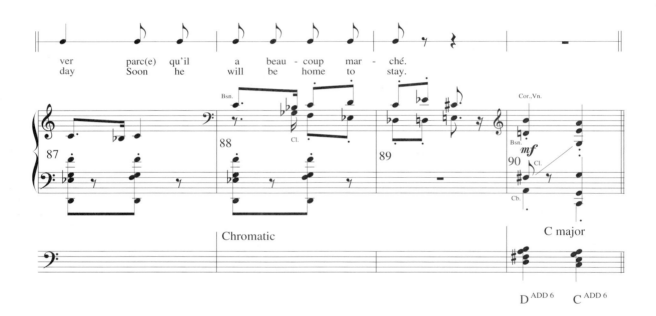

Melody

The characteristics of the melody are as follows:

1. The melody is in the top part, often with contrapuntal accompaniment.
2. A mixture of homophonic and contrapuntal texture applies throughout most of the composition.
3. The melody is based essentially on diatonic scales.

The Motives

The melody utilizes three motives. Motive A is simply a diatonic, conjunct passage that first descends and then ascends. Figure 15.17 shows examples of variations of this motive.

Figure 15.17

Motive A:

Motive B, by contrast, consists of outlined chords (figure 15.18).

Figure 15.18

Motive B:

Motive C is very similar to motive A but differs in that it is made up entirely of repeated notes and half steps (figure 15.19).

Figure 15.19

Motive C:

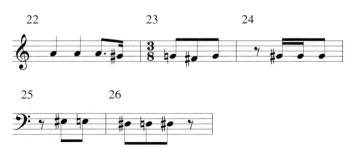

A close look at measures 64 to 79 reveals the technique of phrase extension using motive C. Figure 15.20 compares measures 64 to 70 with measures 71 to 79. Whole notes are used to represent all tones so that rhythmic factors will not obscure the pitch relationships.

Figure 15.20

Phrase extension (melodic extension):

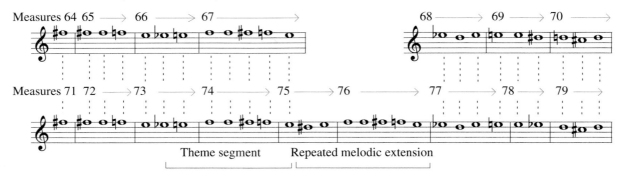

Theme segment   Repeated melodic extension

Form

The composition does not divide itself easily into clearly defined sections because it is strongly influenced by the spoken narrative (The Soldier's Tale). It is designed to accompany and strengthen the plot. An ostinato figure and a pedal tone on D are two of the most easily identified musical components of the work. If these two factors were considered alone, the form might suggest the following:

Measures	Lower Voice	Section
1–30	Ostinato figure	A
31–41	Pedal tone	B
42–83	Ostinato figure	A
84–90	Pedal tone	B

Another approach would use motive order as a way of organizing the composition:

Measures	Motive	Measures	Motive
1–18	A	39–43	B
20–21	B	44–46	A
22–26	C	45–47 (overlap)	B
26–30	B	47–57	A
31–32	A′	57–59	B
33–34	B	64–83	C
34–38	A′ (inv.)	84–90	Related to A

Harmony	The harmonic material is mostly the result of the bitonal mix, except for clear chords in measures 4, 20 to 21, and 90.
Phrase Structure	Melodic cadences, such as in figure 15.21, often mark the end of phrases in the upper voices but are not often supported by the lower voices because of the continuing ostinato figure.

Figure 15.21

Melodic cadence:

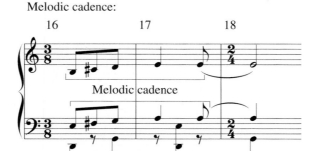

Overlapping phrases are fairly common. A melodic cadence is completed in one voice while a new phrase begins in another voice (figure 15.22).

Figure 15.22

Overlapping phrase:

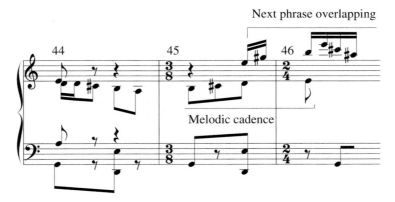

Meter	There are frequent meter changes, but in most instances the steady ostinato figure disregards these and plods on as if the $\frac{2}{4}$ meter had not been altered. Figure 15.23 is an example showing Stravinsky's actual notation along with another version illustrating how it might have been written keeping the steady $\frac{2}{4}$ meter intact.

Figure 15.23

The passage as written:

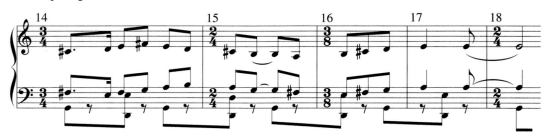

The same passage in strict **2/4** meter:

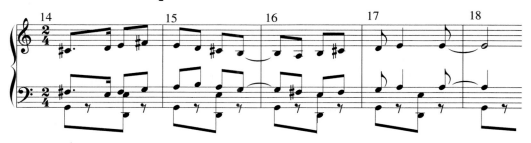

Texture

A thin, homophonic texture persists throughout. The upper voices occasionally engage in counterpoint (as in mm. 11–18).

Chromatic Invention no. 91 from Mikrokosmos, vol. 3, by Béla Bartók

The series of compositions known as the *Mikrokosmos* is a group of 153 piano compositions in six volumes, graded from easy to difficult. They are often assigned as "teaching pieces" and illustrate in miniature form the compositional techniques Bartók used in his larger works. The *Mikrokosmos* was written in an 11-year period (1926–1937).

Because this work is much more homogeneous in its materials than the "The Soldier's March," it will be given an analysis based on set theory. These methods were developed by such theorists as René Leibowitz, Milton Babbitt, and Allen Forte to analyze compositions that are not based on the diatonic scales but that exhibit a great deal of internal consistency of musical materials.

Set Theory

Set theory analysis is based on a collection of pitch classes. A *pitch class* is any particular pitch (such as C or F) in any octave. Thus, pitch class G refers to the pitch G regardless of the octave in which it may appear.

Set

The term *set* means an unordered group of pitch classes such as C, D, and E. A set may contain any number of pitch classes from two through twelve (figure 15.24).

Figure 15.24

Set   Set   Set   Set

The advantage of the system as applied to this composition lies in its capacity to include groupings of pitch classes (sets) outside the traditional diatonic scales. (The diatonic scales may also be thought of as sets. See p. 281.) As an example, the first five notes of the *Chromatic Invention* are A, G♯, E♭, D, and G—notes that, taken together, do not conform to any of the diatonic scale systems.

Set Types

Sets are classified according to the interval between the first pitch class of the set and each successive pitch class expressed as the number of half steps in the interval (figure 15.25).

Figure 15.25

Some typical sets:

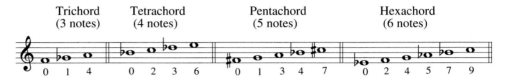

The "0" indicates the lowest pitch in the set, and the remaining pitches are named by the interval they form with the lowest pitch. For example, the 0 1 4 trichord contains the following:

Interval	From	To
0	F	F
1	F	G-flat
4	F	A

The major scale can be considered to be a heptachord (a seven-tone set) (figure 15.26).

Figure 15.26

Major scale:

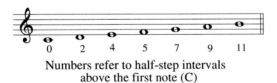

Numbers refer to half-step intervals
above the first note (C)

Sets are usually written with the pitches in ascending order, but in compositions they are often transposed or written in different orders. Figure 15.27 shows the tetrachord **0 1 2 5** followed by the same set reordered and transposed.

Figure 15.27

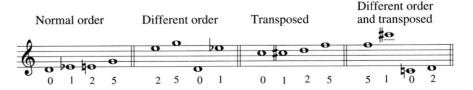

Sets, like chords, can be inverted. In *inversion,* the original direction of the intervals is turned upside down. Consider the three-note set in figure 15.28.

Figure 15.28

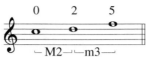

Set 025

The inversion of this set is shown in figure 15.29.

Figure 15.29

Because sets are usually written starting with the lowest note, the inversion set would be written in reverse order, as shown in figure 15.30.

Figure 15.30

The pentachord and its inversion shown in figure 15.31 are found in the "Chromatic Invention" by Bartók.

Figure 15.31

0 1 5 6 7 Pentachord: Its inversion: 0 1 2 6 7:

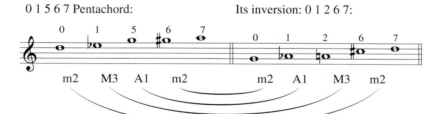

To find out whether one set is the inversion of another (e.g., the 0 1 5 6 7 pentachord in figure 15.31), do the following:

1. Subtract all the numbers of the set from 12. This procedure will invert all the intervals, just as the inversion of a major 2nd (two half steps) is a minor 7th (10 half steps):

Inversion of 0 1 5 6 7				
12	12	12	12	12
−0	−1	−5	−6	−7
12	11	7	6	5

2. These numbers represent the inversion, but they are confusing because the set does not begin with "0." To convert the set to the lowest possible numbers, just subtract from all the numbers the lowest one. Here the lowest number is 5:

$$
\begin{array}{ccccc}
12 & 11 & 7 & 6 & 5 \\
\underline{-5} & \underline{-5} & \underline{-5} & \underline{-5} & \underline{-5} \\
7 & 6 & 2 & 1 & 0
\end{array}
$$

3. Now, put the numbers in order from the lowest to highest, and the inversion of 0 1 5 6 7 = 0 1 2 6 7.

Normal Order

As mentioned before, composers employ sets in a variety of configurations. To understand the compositional techniques employed, it is necessary to trace the derivation and development of such structures. The fundamental ordered form of a set is the *normal order*. To reduce a set to its normal order, do the following:

1. Begin with any note in the set and rearrange the remaining notes in ascending order within an octave. Change the order of the notes as needed (figure 15.32).
2. At the end of the set, add the first note an octave higher.

Figure 15.32

Set as it appears in a composition:

Set rearranged within an octave:

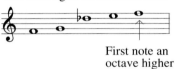

First note an octave higher

3. Bracket the largest interval, as in figure 15.33.

Figure 15.33

Largest interval

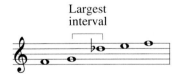

4. Begin the set with the second note of the bracketed interval, and the set will be in its normal order, as shown in figure 15.34.

Figure 15.34

Normal order:

0   3   4   6

The Contemporary Period (1910–1945) **283**

5. Occasionally a set will contain two larger intervals of the same size. Add the numbers (interval classes) of both possibilities. The *best normal order* is the arrangement with the lowest total (i.e., the most small intervals at the beginning of the set). Another way of thinking of best normal order is the arrangement that is most densely packed to the left of the set (figure 15.35).

Figure 15.35

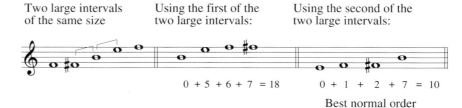

Two large intervals of the same size	Using the first of the two large intervals:	Using the second of the two large intervals:
	$0 + 5 + 6 + 7 = 18$	$0 + 1 + 2 + 7 = 10$
		Best normal order

For a more complete treatment of set theory, refer to Allen Forte, *The Structure of Atonal Music* (New Haven, Conn.: Yale University Press, 1973); John Rahn, *Basic Atonal Theory* (New York: Longman, 1980); or Joseph Straus, *Introduction to Post-Tonal Theory* (Englewood Cliffs, N.J.: Prentice Hall, 1990).

Figure 15.36 shows the distribution of the sets found in Bartók's *Chromatic Invention*: the 0 1 5 6 7; its inversion, the 0 1 2 6 7 set; and the 0 1 2 set.

Figure 15.36

Bartók: *Chromatic Invention,* no. 91 from *Mikrokosmos,* vol. 3.

Analysis of Bartók's *Chromatic Invention*

The Theme

The sets in this composition could be analyzed in a variety of ways. We have chosen the following analysis because it accounts for every single note in the composition.

The composition is based entirely on one theme, shown in figure 15.37.

Figure 15.37

Complete theme:

The theme is divided into two sections, with each containing five notes, as shown in figure 15.38.

Figure 15.38

Theme—first section: Theme—second section:

First Section

The first section of the theme is made up of the 0 1 5 6 7 pentachord (five notes). Its inversion, 0 1 2 6 7, also occurs in the composition (figure 15.39).

Figure 13.39

Theme—first section: Inversion (mm. 4–5):

Prime form: Inversion:

In figure 15.40, the notes of the 0 1 5 6 7 and 0 1 2 6 7 (inversion of 0 1 5 6 7) sets as they appear in the composition are extracted on the upper staff, and the normal order of each is listed on the staff beneath it.

Figure 15.40

Theme—second section:

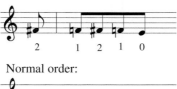

Normal order:

Note that the 0 1 2 trichord fills in pitches not found in the 0 1 5 6 7 pentachord to form a chromatic set. Thus the aggregate (combination) of both sets is a chromatic scale from D to A (figure 15.41).

Figure 15.41

Theme, first section—whole notes
Theme, second section—black notes

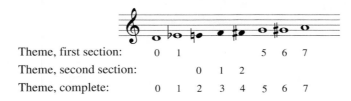

Theme, first section:	0	1				5	6	7
Theme, second section:			0	1	2			
Theme, complete:	0	1	2	3	4	5	6	7

Figure 15.42 shows each instance of the second section of the theme in the composition. The notes of the 0 1 2 set (with occasional added half steps) as it appears in the first six measures of the composition are extracted on the upper staff, and the normal order of each is listed on the staff beneath it.

Figure 15.42

Measures: 1–2   2   3–4   5–6

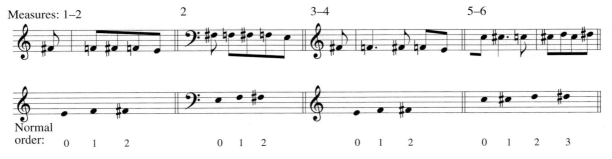

Figure 15.43 shows a further analysis of Bartók's *Chromatic Invention*.

Figure 15.43

Bartók: *Chromatic Invention*, no. 91 from *Mikrokosmos,* vol. 3.

Imitation is used in the composition (figure 15.43) as follows:

1. With the exception of measure 11 and parts of measures 10 and 12, the entire composition utilizes canonic imitation.
2. Imitation in the first 10 measures is by similar motion.
3. Imitation in the last seven measures is by contrary motion (melodic inversion).
4. Most of the composition employs imitation at the octave, but imitation at the M6th, M9th, and P4th also occurs.

*Influence
of the Tritone*

The tritone relationship is prominent in the composition.

1. The tritone is one of the intervals contained in the first section (0 1 5 6 7) of the theme.
2. Indicated in the score along with the imitation are four conspicuous step progressions that emphasize the tritone. Each outlines portions of the whole-tone scale, which is rich in tritone relationships.

Form

The composition divides neatly into three sections as follows:

Measures	Description
1–6	The complete theme occurs six times, four times derived from the normal order and twice from the inversion.
6–11	Canon at the octave with overlapping entrances of the first section of the theme. The second section of the theme is found only at the end, in measures 10 and 11.
11–17	The complete theme occurs three times in the upper voice, whereas the lower voice, containing an inversion of the theme, occurs in canon (by contrary motion) with the upper voice.

The sections are not set apart from each other. Each contrasts with the others through the compositional techniques employed.

Tonality

Naming the tonal center of the *Chromatic Invention* is a hazardous venture indeed. Certainly there are few clues—no highly organized key system present, no long pedal tones to influence a decision—and the highly chromatic nature of the theme renders little assistance. Thus a definitive answer, acceptable to all, is unlikely.

One might argue that because the theme outlines a perfect 4th (see figure 15.44), a suggestion of tonality might be gained from that relationship. Although the *Chromatic Invention* begins with the theme clearly stated, the ending (mm. 15–17) seems bent on destroying any tonal hints that might have accrued up to that point.

Figure 15.44

Theme outlines P4th

Summary

A unique and highly organic invention, the *Chromatic Invention* is held together through a single theme constructed from the 0 1 5 6 7 pentachord, along with its inversion, the 0 1 2 6 7 pentachord, and its chromatic complement, the 0 1 2 trichord. These sets, with some extensions of the 0 1 2 trichord, are used exclusively throughout. Imitation, both in similar and contrary motion, further helps to weld the work into a tightly knit and eminently unified whole.

Assignment 15.1

Make a complete analysis using the same approach as the analysis of *Marche du Soldat* of an excerpt from one of the following works by Stravinsky. Select a small section that can be treated thoroughly.

Le Sacre du Printemps (The Rite of Spring) (either full score or a piano arrangement).
Petruchka (either full score or excerpts arranged for two pianos by Victor Babin).
Circus Polka (either full score or arranged for piano solo, violin and piano, or two pianos).
L'Oiseau de Feu (The Firebird) suite.

Assignment 15.2

1. Using the following three compositional devices (found in *Marche du Soldat*), write a short composition of 16 to 30 measures:

   Changing meters
   Ostinato
   Bitonality (polytonality)

2. Write for any combination of instruments played by class members.
3. Perform the composition in class.
4. The class should discuss each composition, its strengths and weaknesses, its resemblance to the style of the *Marche du Soldat,* and its general musical qualities.

Assignment 15.3

Beneath each of the following intervals, write the number representing the interval.

Assignment 15.4

Furnish the interval numbers for each of the following sets.

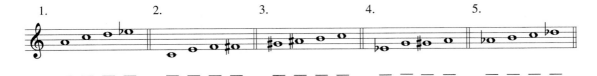

Assignment 15.5   Below are six tetrachords. Three are inversions of the remaining three. Indicate the pairs.

Set _____ is the inversion of _____ Set

_____

_____

_____

_____

Assignment 15.6   Below are five sets in scrambled order. Find the best normal order of each set.

The sets:

   1. Rearrange the notes of the above sets within an octave and bracket the largest interval:

   2. Write the best normal order on the blanks below.

1.   2.   3.   4.   5.

— — — — —   — — — —   — — — —   — — — —   — — — —

Assignment 15.7

1. On a separate sheet of paper, make a complete analysis of the following composition, using the same approach as is used for the *Chromatic Invention* of Bartók.
2. The violin duo is based on a tetrachord. Trace its development throughout the composition.
3. As an alternative analysis, consider the two sets that occur simultaneously as a single eight-pitch set (an octachord!). Do you recognize the scales formed by these eight-pitch sets?
4. Before preparing the analysis, have two students perform the composition two or three times in class or listen to a recording until the work is thoroughly familiar.

Bartók: *Song of the Harvest*, no. 33 from *Forty-Four Violin Duets.* CD Track 33

Assignment 15.8

1. Using the following compositional techniques (found in the *Chromatic Invention*), write a short two-voice composition (16 to 30 measures):
   a. Asymmetric divisions of the meter.
   b. A tetrachord or pentachord as a basis.
   c. Transpositions of the theme or motive.
2. Write for any combination of instruments played by class members.
3. Perform the composition in class.
4. After each student composition is performed, members of the class should enumerate (from listening only) some of the various devices employed in the work.

Assignment 15.9

Analyze a section of Debussy's *La Cathédrale engloutie* (p. 244, CD Track 34) using set theory analysis. As a beginning point, convert the melodic motives shown in figure 14.39 (p. 252) into set form and trace these sets through a section of the composition. How well does set theory account for the pitch material of this work?

CHAPTER 16

Twelve-Tone Technique

Topics	Prime	Retrograde inversion	Pitch class
	Retrograde	Row	The matrix
	Inversion	Series	Segments

Important Concepts

Twelve-Tone Technique

Twelve-tone technique, a method of composition based on a fixed order of the 12 chromatic tones, was widely adopted by composers during the mid–twentieth century. It was developed by Arnold Schoenberg around 1920 as a means of providing a coherent basis for highly chromatic music. According to Schoenberg, "The method of composing with twelve tones grew out of necessity. In the last hundred years the concept of harmony has changed tremendously through the development of chromaticism. The idea that one basic tone (the root) dominated the construction of chords and regulated their succession—the concept of *tonality*—had to develop first into the concept of *extended tonality*. Very soon it became doubtful whether such a root still remained the center to which every harmony and harmonic succession must be referred. Furthermore, it became doubtful whether a tonic appearing at the beginning, at the end, or at any other point really had a constructive meaning." Schoenberg saw clearly that innovations of the postromantic period had had the effect of weakening the constructive force of functional harmony. He sought a means to return order to music, to replace the lost power of tonal harmony that had been used to regulate the relationships among tones. He said, "After many unsuccessful attempts during a period of approximately twelve years I laid the foundations for a new procedure in musical construction which seemed fitted to replace those structural differentiations provided formerly by tonal harmonies. I called this procedure the *Method of Composing with Twelve Tones Which Are Related Only with One Another*." Schoenberg provided the following guides for his twelve-tone technique (dodecaphonic composition):

Order

The set of all 12 tones contained within the octave in a particular order (tone row) forms the basis for the method. Except for immediate repetitions, there is no return to a particular tone until all the succeeding tones in the row have been sounded.

Register

The tones of the series (tone row) may appear in any octave.

Forms

The tone series may appear in any of the following four forms:

Symbol		Form	Description
P	=	Prime	The series as it is originally constructed.
R	=	Retrograde	The prime series sounded in reverse order.
I	=	Inversion	Starting with the first tone of the prime series, the direction (up or down) of each successive interval is inverted.
RI	=	Retrograde-Inversion	The inversion of the series is sounded in reverse order.

Transposition

Any of the four forms of the series can be transposed. The prime form untransposed is P^0, one half step up is P^1, another half step up P^2, and so on. As a further illustration, note the following:

P^8 = Prime form of the series transposed up eight half steps (m6th).
R^8 = Retrograde form of the series transposed up eight half steps (m6th).
RI^2 = Retrograde inversion transposed up two half steps (M2nd).
I^{11} = Inverted series transposed up 11 half steps (M7th).

Row or Series

The term *row* is a literal translation of the German word *Reihe*. Another term, *series,* is used by later authors who believe that *row* denotes certain properties not in keeping with the true nature of the original German term. Despite controversies over subtleties in translation, *row* and *series* are used synonymously in this book.

Numbering

Earlier writers also numbered the series from 1 to 12, but later theorists adopted a numbering system from 0 to 11 to facilitate mathematical calculation.

Pitch Class

Pitch class is another term frequently found in contemporary writing. This term is used in preference to *tone* or *pitch* because it is broader in meaning and includes a single pitch together with its octave duplications.

The Matrix

A *matrix* is a convenient analytical device for showing all forms and transpositions of a row. The matrix (described in detail later) was not invented by Schoenberg himself, but its use by later writers has made it a standard device for analysis of twelve-tone music.

History

Schoenberg invented twelve-tone technique around 1920. This development was preceded by the independent invention of a similar method in 1919 by Josef Matthias Hauer that was based on unordered sets of six pitches that he called *tropes*. Anton Webern (1883–1945) was a student of Schoenberg from 1904 until 1910. He adopted twelve-tone technique around 1924, and his work fully exploits the potential of the system. Webern wrote in such a concentrated style that most of his works are quite brief, and his complete works can be played in less than six hours (any two of Wagner's operas would consume more). Alban Berg (1885–1935), another student of Schoenberg, also adopted twelve-tone technique but with much less rigor. Schoenberg, Webern, and Berg were at the center of artistic and intellectual circles in Vienna, and their work was a major force in the development of musical style in the mid–twentieth century.

Application

As an example of twelve-tone technique, figure 16.1 will be given a detailed analysis.

Figure 16.1

Webern: *Wie bin ich froh!* (How Happy I Am!), no. 1 from *Drei Lieder* (Three Songs), op. 25.

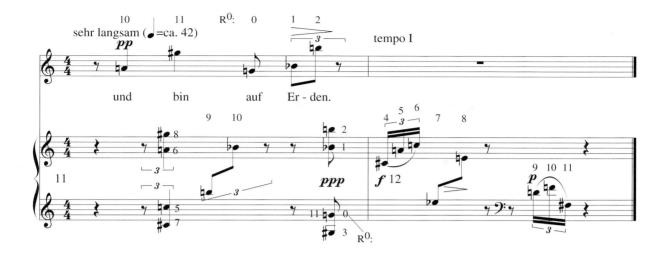

The Matrix

The following matrix shows the possible series forms and their transpositions (48 possibilities in all). This particular matrix represents the series that is the basis of Webern's *Wie bin ich froh!* (figure 16.1).

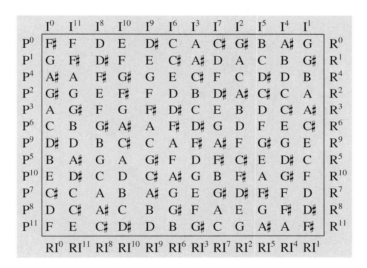

The matrix is created by first listing the P^0 form along the top:

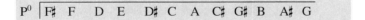

List the inversion beginning with the first pitch of the original row down the left side of the chart:

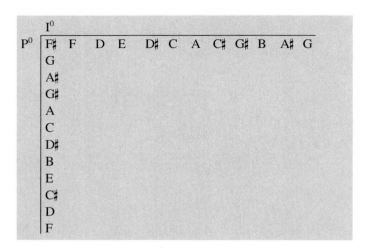

	I⁰											
P⁰	F♯	F	D	E	D♯	C	A	C♯	G♯	B	A♯	G
	G											
	A♯											
	G♯											
	A											
	C											
	D♯											
	B											
	E											
	C♯											
	D											
	F											

Label the left side of the chart beginning with P⁰ according to the number of half steps each tone of the I⁰ series is above the first tone:

	I⁰											
P⁰	F♯	F	D	E	D♯	C	A	C♯	G♯	B	A♯	G
P¹	G											
P⁴	A♯											
P²	G♯											
P³	A											
P⁶	C											
P⁹	D♯											
P⁵	B											
P¹⁰	E											
P⁷	C♯											
P⁸	D											
P¹¹	F											

Write the P¹ series, which will be one half step above the P⁰ series:

	I⁰											
P⁰	F♯	F	D	E	D♯	C	A	C♯	G♯	B	A♯	G
P¹	G	F♯	D♯	F	E	C♯	A♯	D	A	C	B	G♯
P⁴	A♯											
P²	G♯											
P³	A											
P⁶	C											
P⁹	D♯											
P⁵	B											
P¹⁰	E											
P⁷	C♯											
P⁸	D											
P¹¹	F											

Fill in the remaining transpositions in order (P^2, P^3, etc.). Each row will be one half step above the previous row:

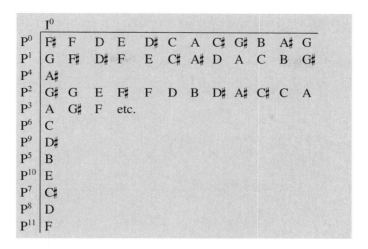

	I^0											
P^0	F♯	F	D	E	D♯	C	A	C♯	G♯	B	A♯	G
P^1	G	F♯	D♯	F	E	C♯	A♯	D	A	C	B	G♯
P^4	A♯											
P^2	G♯	G	E	F♯	F	D	B	D♯	A♯	C♯	C	A
P^3	A	G♯	F	etc.								
P^6	C											
P^9	D♯											
P^5	B											
P^{10}	E											
P^7	C♯											
P^8	D											
P^{11}	F											

Finally, add the remaining labels (I, R, and RI) to complete the matrix:

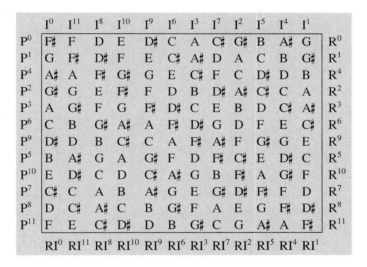

	I^0	I^{11}	I^8	I^{10}	I^9	I^6	I^3	I^7	I^2	I^5	I^4	I^1	
P^0	F♯	F	D	E	D♯	C	A	C♯	G♯	B	A♯	G	R^0
P^1	G	F♯	D♯	F	E	C♯	A♯	D	A	C	B	G♯	R^1
P^4	A♯	A	F♯	G♯	G	E	C♯	F	C	D♯	D	B	R^4
P^2	G♯	G	E	F♯	F	D	B	D♯	A♯	C♯	C	A	R^2
P^3	A	G♯	F	G	F♯	D♯	C	E	B	D	C♯	A♯	R^3
P^6	C	B	G♯	A♯	A	F♯	D♯	G	D	F	E	C♯	R^6
P^9	D♯	D	B	C♯	C	A	F♯	A♯	F	G♯	G	E	R^9
P^5	B	A♯	G	A	G♯	F	D	F♯	C♯	E	D♯	C	R^5
P^{10}	E	D♯	C	D	C♯	A♯	G	B	F♯	A	G♯	F	R^{10}
P^7	C♯	C	A	B	A♯	G	E	G♯	D♯	F♯	F	D	R^7
P^8	D	C♯	A♯	C	B	G♯	F	A	E	G	F♯	D♯	R^8
P^{11}	F	E	C♯	D♯	D	B	G♯	C	G	A♯	A	F♯	R^{11}
	RI^0	RI^{11}	RI^8	RI^{10}	RI^9	RI^6	RI^3	RI^7	RI^2	RI^5	RI^4	RI^1	

For prime series (P), read from left to right.
For inverted series (I), read down.
For retrograde series (R), read from right to left.
For retrograde-inversion Series (RI), read up.

Webern selected the series forms and transpositions (from the preceding matrix) seen in figure 16.2 for *Wie bin ich froh!*

Figure 16.2

Prime series untransposed (P^0):

Retrograde series untransposed (R^0):

Inverted series transposed up one whole step (I^2):

Pitch class: 0 1 4 2 3 6 9 5 10 7 8 11

Order: 0 1 2 3 4 5 6 7 8 9 10 11

Inverted series in retrograde transposed up one whole step (RI^2):

Pitch class: 0 9 8 11 6 10 7 4 3 5 2 1

Order: 0 1 2 3 4 5 6 7 8 9 10 11

Segments

The series itself is very carefully planned to include a three-tone figure (trichord) with two transpositions (figure 16.3).

Figure 16.3

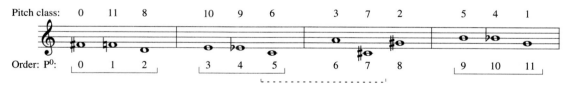

The Text

The composition is based on a poem of two strophes by Hildegard Jone:

Wie bin ich froh!   How happy I am!
noch einmal wird mir alles grün   Once more all around me grows
und leuchtet so!   green and shimmers so!
noch über bluhn die Blumen mir die   Blossoms still cover the world for me!
Welt!
noch einmal bin ich ganz ins   Once again I am at the center
Werden hingestellt   of Becoming
und bin auf Erden.   and am on earth.

The voice line is divided as follows:

First strophe: The retrograde inversion (RI) of the series followed by the first four notes of the same

Second strophe: The retrograde of the original series followed by the complete retrograde inversion

Form

While an internal balance and symmetry in the voice line is obtained through the use of RI^2, then R^0, and finally a return to the RI^2, a two-part form emerges from the two strophes of the poem:

Strophe	Section	Measures
1	A	1–5
2	B	6–12

Accompaniment

The selection of series forms and transpositions in the accompaniment is as follows:

Strophe 1	Strophe 2
P^0 RI^2 P^0 RI^2	R^0 I^2 I^2 P^0 R^0

(Notice that the accompaniment is created from complementary forms of the row in the two strophes—P^0 vs. R^0, RI^2 vs. I^2, etc.)

Rhythmic and Harmonic Figures

The accompaniment consists for the most part of three figures, two of which are rhythmic and the other harmonic (figure 16.4).

Figure 16.4

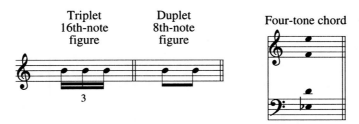

Triplet 16th-note figure   Duplet 8th-note figure   Four-tone chord

The 16th-Note Triplet Figure

There is a direct relationship between the figures and the pitches contained in them (figure 16.5). All 16th triplet figures are based on a minor 2nd plus a minor 3rd (the 0 1 4 set).

Figure 16.5

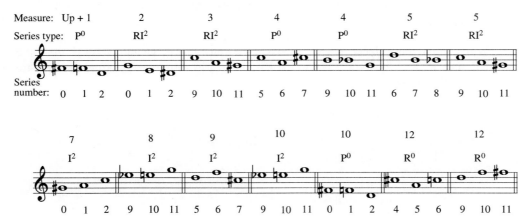

The 8th-Note Figure

Most two-tone eighth-note figures are made up of half-step intervals, with the exception of two examples indicated by an asterisk (*) in figure 16.6.

Figure 16.6

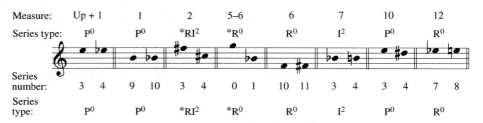

The Four-Tone Chord Figure

In most four-tone chord figures, the lower two tones form a major 7th (with the exception of m. 2) and the upper two tones form a major 7th (with three exceptions) (figure 16.7).

Figure 16.7

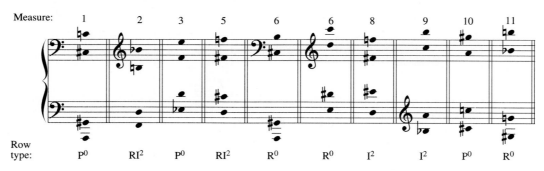

Dynamics and Tempo Indications

The dynamics and tempo indications follow this pattern:

1. The third line of each strophe is marked with a soft dynamic.
2. The first line of each strophe begins loud and ends soft.
3. For each strophe, accompaniment begins loud and ends soft.
4. The tempo is usually slowed at the end of each line or strophe.

Assignment 16.1

On a separate sheet of paper, make a complete analysis of the following composition using the same approach as for *Wie bin ich froh!*

Before preparing the analysis, have a singer and an accompanist from the class perform the composition two or three times or listen to a recording until the work is thoroughly familiar.

This work is based on the same twelve-tone row as the song analyzed in the chapter. The matrix on p. 301 can be used. (This song begins with a statement of RI⁷.) As an alternative, you may consider the row presented in measures 1 to 3 in the piano to be a new row and create a matrix for it.

Webern: *Des Herzens Purpurvogel fliegt durch Nacht* (The Heart's Purple Eagle Flies by Night), no. 2 from *Drei Lieder* (Three Songs), op. 25, mm. 1–20. CD Track 35

Assignment 16.2

1. On a separate sheet of paper, make a complete analysis of the "Theme" from Schoenberg's Variations for Orchestra, op, 31, using the same approach as for *Wie bin ich froh!*
2. The row for this work is as follows:

3. Make a matrix for this row, following the instructions on p. 301.
4. Before preparing the analysis, listen to a recording until the work is thoroughly familiar.

Schoenberg: Variations for Orchestra, op. 31, mm. 34–57. CD Track 36

Theme*

* Concert score.

The Nineteenth and Twentieth Centuries

Assignment 16.3

1. Write a short song with text for solo voice and piano employing the following twelve-tone series:

P⁰:

2. Examine the series for motivic cells that might lend themselves to the kind of technique found in the Webern song.
3. Prepare a matrix for this series (see p. 301).
4. Select four compatible series forms.
5. Prepare (without score paper) a plan for the form of the composition. Use techniques discovered in the Webern song analyzed in this chapter.
6. Select two rhythmic figures for the accompaniment.
7. Sketch in the voice part and add the accompaniment.
8. Add dynamics and other marks of interpretation as well as phrasing.
9. Perform the composition in class.
10. After each performance, the composer will lead a discussion concerning the techniques employed in the composition.

The Nineteenth and Twentieth Centuries

Music since 1945

Serialism
Rhythmic series
Dynamic series
Indeterminacy
Aleatory
Chance music
Improvisation
Electronic music
Musique concrète

Live performance with
   tape
Live electronic music
Voltage-controlled
   synthesizers
Computer-assisted
   composition
Computer synthesis
Sound mass
Mikropolyphonie

Extended techniques
Rock 'n' roll
Rock music
Eclecticism
New accessibility
Minimalism
Performance art
MIDI technology
CD-ROM
CD-I

Sampling systems
Fusion
Punk
New wave
Rap music
New age music
Space music
Ambient music
World music

The years since 1945 have witnessed the greatest stylistic changes and most extensive exploration of new techniques in the history of Western music. In the popular music field, the most important development has been rock music. In art music, composers have explored new media and new methods to a greater extent than at any other time. Although it is still too early to make a definitive judgment, it appears that two distinct periods may be observed. These periods are distinguished not so much by style as by attitude.

Musical Developments from 1945–1970

The first of these two periods lasted from about 1945 to 1970. This era, dominated by the philosophy of the avant-garde, emphasized the exploration of new techniques and highly regarded innovation and experimentation. The primary paths of exploration were serialism, indeterminacy, electronic and computer music, sound mass, and extended vocal and instrumental techniques. Several of these new directions might be observed in a single work.

Serialism

Serialism (sometimes called *total serialism*) began in the years 1920–1945 as an extension of the twelve-tone technique of the Viennese atonalists, especially Anton Webern. As you saw in chapter 16, Webern's music is characterized not only by use of a pitch series but also by carefully controlling the number of rhythmic motives in the piano accompaniment. Webern was the primary inspiration for composers who chose to order or serialize other elements of music, such as rhythm, dynamics, articulations, and tone colors.

Perhaps the most important serialist is Milton Babbitt (b. 1916), who composed *Three Compositions for Piano* in 1947. An excerpt from the *First Composition* is found in figure 17.1.

Figure 17.1

Babbitt: *First Composition* from *Three Compositions for Piano,* mm. 1–6.

The *rhythmic series* Babbitt employs in this piece consists of the numbers 5 1 4 2. This series is used to articulate a rhythmic division in the statement of each hexachord. In the first measure, the lower voice consists of group of five notes ending on C, which is the first long note and fifth pitch of the hexachord, hence the "5" (note brackets in illustration) of the rhythmic series 5 1 4 2. The single remaining note (D-flat) in this measure represents "1" in the rhythmic series. The same 5 1 rhythmic grouping may be observed in the upper voice in measure 1, although the long note ending the first rhythmic subdivision of this hexachord is only an eighth note in duration.

Diagram of Rhythmic Series		
P	(prime)	5 1 4 2
R	(retrograde)	2 4 1 5
I	(inversion)	1 5 2 4
RI	(retrograde-inversion)	4 2 5 1

In the next measure, the sixteenth-note continuity of the hexachords of each voice is broken by a long note—the fourth in the hexachord. This produces a 4 2 grouping that completes the 5 1 4 2 statement—the P (prime) form of the rhythmic series.

The R (retrograde) form of the series (2 4 1 5) is found in the upper voice of measures 3 and 4. The I (inversion) form (1 5 2 4), derived by subtracting each number of the P form from 6 (the number of pitches in a hexachord), appears in measures 5 and 6, lower voice. The RI (retrograde-inversion) form (4 2 5 1) occurs in measures 3 and 4, lower voice.

The dynamic series is much simpler, associating each form of the pitch set with a different dynamic:*

Set Form	=	Dynamic
P		Mezzo-Piano
R		Mezzo-Forte
I		Forte
RI		Piano

Babbitt's approaches to rhythmic and dynamic serialism are only some of the nonpitch elements that have been serialized. Composers have experimented with articulations, timbres, and numerous other aspects of music.

Indeterminacy

Another important concept explored by composers of this period was *indeterminacy,* sometimes also called *aleatory* or *chance music.* The following characteristics are essential to indeterminacy:

1. Some aspect or aspects of the composition, the performance, or both are beyond the composer's control.
2. Some musical decisions are unpredictable or left to chance.

The stage at which chance enters the music-making process varies from work to work.

Always an innovator, the American composer John Cage (1912–1992) thoroughly explored methods by which chance could be incorporated into composition and performance. Cage's *Music of Changes* (1951), for piano, is traditionally notated but was composed in an untraditional fashion. All musical decisions (pitches, rhythm, and dynamics) were made by consulting the *I Ching* (pronounced 'e Jing'), an ancient Chinese method of soothsaying.

A very different type of indeterminacy is represented by Cage's *Aria* (1958) (figure 17.2). This work for solo voice is composed in graphic notation. Vertical contoured lines represent relative pitch; horizontal contours give the relative durations. Each page was intended to last about 30 seconds. Eight different singing styles can be determined by the soloist. The black squares indicate other sounds of the performer's choice. Because each performer has the major responsibiliy for interpreting the precise meaning of the symbols, performances vary greatly. The singer also has the option of performing the work simultaneously with either of two other Cage compositions: *Fontana Mix* (1958), for magnetic tape or instruments, or *Concert for Piano and Orchestra* (1957–1958).

---

*This analysis owes a great deal to George Perle, *Serial Composition and Atonality,* 4th ed. (Berkeley: University of California Press, 1977), pp. 132–341 and David Cope, *New Directions in Music,* 6th ed. (Madison, Wisconsin: Brown & Benchmark Publishers, 1993), pp. 41–44.

Figure 17.2

Cage: *Aria.*

© 1960 by Henmar Press Inc. Used by permission of C. F. Peters Corporation, sole selling agents.

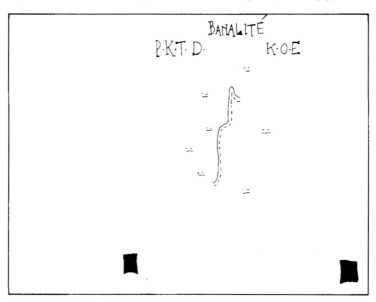

Improvisation

Improvisation is the spontaneous realization of any or all aspects of a composition and has been employed throughout most of Western music history. Beethoven's concerts, for instance, often featured his improvisations. Today, the most familiar forms of improvisation are those used in jazz performance.

Improvisation differs from other types of indeterminacy in that the composer predetermines a desired musical effect rather than detailing the notation. The performer is free to spontaneously interpret any or all of the composition.

For Pauline Oliveros (b. 1932), spontaneity is a philosophy whose benefits transcend the performed sounds. She breaks with many long-held notions of what a composition can or cannot do. As a result of her democratic philosophy, she creates music accessible to all. Sonic Meditations I, "Teach Yourself to Fly," is an example of a therapeutic, relaxing work in which anyone—not just trained musicians can participate.

> *Pauline Oliveros, Sonic Meditations I, "Teach Yourself to Fly" 1974 Smith Publications, Baltimore, Maryland.*
> *Any number of persons sit in a circle facing the center. Illuminate the space with dim blue light. Begin by simply observing your own breathing. Always be an observer. Gradually allow your breathing to become audible, then gradually introduce your voice. Allow your vocal chords to vibrate in any mode that occurs naturally. Allow the intensity to increase very slowly. Continue as long as possible naturally, and until all others are quiet, always observing your own breath cycle. Variation: Translate voice to an instrument.*

Electronic and Computer Music

Although efforts to create *electronic music* date back to the turn of the twentieth century, serious development came after World War II with the invention of plastic magnetic recording tape. Early composers worked primarily on tape, as opposed to live performance, and used either live or electronically generated sources.

Musique Concrète

Preferred by French composers, *musique concrète* (which was intended to denote a music that used natural or "concrete" sounds) used sounds recorded from the environment. Sounds were processed or modified in the following ways:

1. Splicing—cutting and rearranging the tape.
2. Playing the tape backward.
3. Varying the speed and pitch of the tape.
4. Tape loops—cutting and splicing the tape in an endless loop.
5. Tape delay—a means of creating artificial echo by rerecording a sound multiple times.

These taping techniques ranged from simple reordering of familiar sounds to complete transformations, making the original sound sources unidentifiable to the listener.

Electronic Music

The first German composers of *electronic music* generated sounds with equipment previously found in physics laboratories: oscillators, pulse generators, filters, and ring modulators. This music required even more splicing than the works of *musique concrète*.

Two of the greatest early masterpieces of electronic music combined both electronic and *concrète* techniques. It is interesting that one of these works, *Gesang der Jünglinge* (Song of the Youths in the Fiery Furnace) (1955–1956), is by the German Karlheinz Stockhausen (b. 1928) and that the other, *Poème Electronique* (1956–1958), was composed by the French-born American Edgard Varèse (1885–1965), thus demonstrating that the distinction between the two styles was not the nationality of the composer. Because a performance of either work consists of playing a tape recording, neither has a score in the conventional sense.

Live Performance with Tape

Any arbitrary limitations on the use of electronic media were short-lived. From the early years of electronic music, composers began to combine taped sounds with live instrumental or vocal performance. One of the greatest contributions to this genre is the series of six *Synchronisms* of the Argentinian-American Mario Davidovsky (b. 1934) (figure 17.3).

Figure 17.3

Davidovsky: No. 3 for Cello and Electronic Sound from *Synchronisms*.

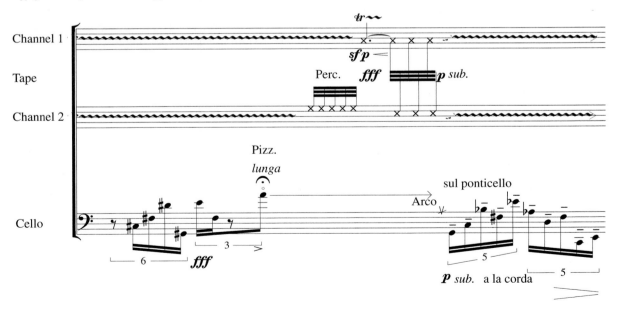

The taped sounds used in the *Synchronisms* were entirely electronically generated. The scores transcribe only as much of the tape as is needed for the synchronization of the instrumentalists.

Live Electronic Music

Although it seems that most electronic music composers preferred to work with tape, many used electronics in live performance. Alvin Lucier's (b. 1931) *I Am Sitting in a Room* (1970) required only a microphone, two tape recorders, an amplifier, and a loudspeaker. The text Lucier provided for this work is a technical description of what the audience hears.

> *Lucier: I Am Sitting in a Room**
> *"I am sitting in a room different from the one you are in now.*
> *"I am recording the sound of my speaking voice and I am going to play it back into the room again and again until the resonant frequencies of the room reinforce themselves so that any semblance of my speech, with perhaps the exception of rhythm, is destroyed.*
> *"What you will hear, then, are the natural resonant frequencies of the room articulated by speech.*
> *"I regard this activity not so much as a demonstration of a physical fact, but more as a way to smooth out any irregularities my speech might have."*
>
> *Alvin Lucier, I Am Sitting in a Room (1969) p. 30. Reprinted from Chambers © 1980 by Alvin Lucier, Wesleyan University Press by permission of University Press of New England.

Voltage-Controlled Synthesizers

The *voltage-controlled synthesizer,* introduced in the 1960s, generated and processed sound by a series of control voltages. This allowed the composer to move instantaneously rather than gradually from one setting to another. If, for example, a composer desired a melody from a nonsynthesizer oscillator, each pitch would have to be recorded separately and then spliced together. On a voltage-controlled synthesizer a melody could be played on an oscillator by a series of voltages from a keyboard or some other controlling device.

Computer-Assisted Composition

Composers have been using computers in a variety of ways since the late 1950s. The earliest use of computers in composition was as an aid in writing works for traditional instruments. Greek composer Iannis Xenakis (b. 1922) employed his Stochastic Music Program (stochasticism is a mathematical system based on the calculus of probabilities) to supply the precise details of pitch, rhythm, and timbre in a series of complex, densely textured works.

Computer Synthesis

A more popular application of computer technology was sound synthesis. Electronic or traditional instrumental sounds could be generated by a computer in either of two ways: through the sampling of natural sounds or through spectrum analysis and resynthesis. The American composer Charles Dodge (b. 1942) created a series of works featuring the electronic simulation of singing and speaking voices (figure 17.4).

Figure 17.4

Dodge: *In Celebration* (based on a poem by Mark Strand).

Sound Mass

Sound mass denotes a texture of such density and complexity that the musical effect resides in the whole rather than in the delineation of individual parts. A listener need not, and often cannot, easily distinguish between shifts in pitch, timbre, and dynamics.

Chord clusters, which have been used since the beginning of this century, form a large part of the tonal language of sound-mass compositions. Some works also employ the many-voiced, rhythmically intricate, highly chromatic counterpoint known as *mikropolyphonie*.

One of the best-known sound-mass compositions, the *Threnody to the Victims of Hiroshima* for fifty-two strings (1960) by the Polish composer Krzysztof Penderecki (b. 1933), uses both clusters and *mikropolyphonie* (figure 17.5).

Figure 17.5

Penderecki: *Threnos Den Opfern von Hiroschima (Threnody to the Victims of Hiroshima).*

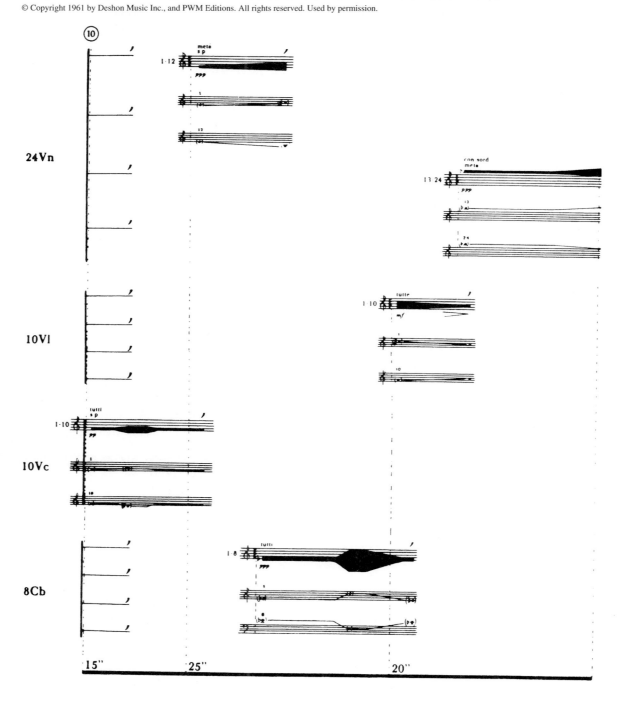

The Nineteenth and Twentieth Centuries

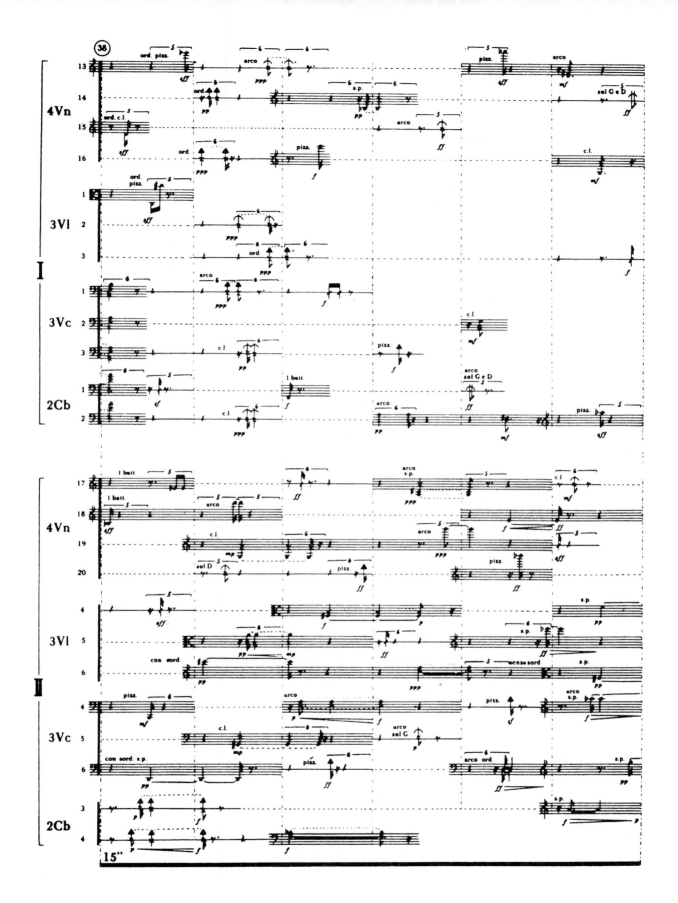

Extended Techniques

Throughout the twentieth century, composers have explored new instrumental and vocal timbral possibilities. This search for innovative techniques is an extension of a type of instrumental exploration begun much earlier in the century, most notably by Webern, who used unusual combinations of instruments rather than standard chamber ensembles. The choice of instruments has become as much a part of the creative process as the choice of pitches and rhythms. The labeling of any technique as extended is always provisional because every technique, including pizzicato and vibrato, was unusual when it first appeared. Some *extended techniques* follow:

1. Western instruments played in unusual ways, such as muting piano strings or playing piano strings with a metal instrument.
2. Unfamiliar or newly invented instruments.
3. Noninstruments such as sirens or auto horns.
4. Additional apparatus such as amplifiers.
5. Extended vocal techniques: tongue clicking, hunting, whispering, etc.

Rock 'n' Roll and Rock Music

The dominant form of white-American popular music in the period from 1955 to 1960 was *rock 'n' roll,* which fused the African-American popular music called rhythm and blues with white popular music (Tin Pan Alley and country-and-western) and a hard-driving rhythm dominated by the bass drum and electric bass. The best-known performer of the late 1950s was Elvis Presley (1935–1977), whose records sold far more than other rock 'n' roll musicians. The term *rock 'n' roll* became an umbrella term for all popular music of the late fifties and was gradually shortened to *rock* in the early 1960s. The rock music of the 1960s was an electronic medium, relying extensively on amplification, distortion, and ultimately on electronic synthesis of sound. Recording technology began to dominate rock music in the later sixties, and many bands curtailed live performance in favor of issuing albums. In the mid-sixties, the first wave of the "British Invasion" bands brought white versions of late-1950s African-American rhythm-and-blues hits back to the United States. The best known of these bands was the Beatles. Their album *Sgt. Pepper's Lonely Hearts Club Band* (1967), which incorporated sophisticated studio techniques and many extra musicians (including the London Symphony Orchestra), set the tone for the age.

Music since 1970

Although none of the new musical trends of the years 1945–1970 has disappeared, it is apparent that at about 1970 a shift in attitude took place. This new musical philosophy, called *post-modernism,* emphasizes the musical experience of the listener over innovation and experimentation.

Eclecticism

Like the avant-garde, eclectic composers experiment, but only as a tool to produce meaningful musical results. Using the cultural creations of all eras and all places, eclectic composers create unusual and fascinating combinations, borrowing passages from earlier music and freely mixing styles.

No discussion of *eclecticism* can be complete without reference to Luciano Berio (Italian, b. 1925). His early post-modern five movement masterpiece, *Sinfonia* (1968), uses a barrage of quotations from Bach, Ravel, Mahler, Stockhausen, and his own work. The vocalists sing in jazz syllables, or sing and speak a collage of texts as eclectic as the music itself.

New Accessibility

Several new styles and genres have emerged in the post-modern era. One feature that unites many of these approaches is their accessibility. The works of David del Tredici (b. 1937), George Rochberg (b. 1918), Henryk M. Gorecki (b. 1933), and others have been called neoromantic, partly because of their return to tonality. The audiences who often felt shut out by the avant-garde can comprehend and enjoy these new styles.

Minimalism

Minimalism is the gradual process of unfolding a very limited body of motivic material, often with an unprecedentedly high degree of literal repetition. Although the motivic material may be anything, it is most often simple, tonal or modal, and largely diatonic. Many minimal works owe a great deal to the influences of African and Asian music.

Steve Reich (American, b. 1936) is one of the most important of the minimalists. His *Four Organs* for four electric organs and maracas (1970) consists entirely of a single chord whose individual tones are gradually augmented while maracas keep a steady eighth-note pulse (figure 17.6).

Figure 17.6

Reich: *Four Organs,* mm. 1–4.

The maraca part consists of steady unbroken eighth notes played throughout the piece thus:

Because the maracas must be clearly heard over the four organs, it is suggested that two pairs be used, one pair in each hand.

Performance Art

Performance art is art that is performed (as opposed to object art, such as painting and sculpture). It is, like opera, a multimedia genre that may involve costumes, staging, movement or dance, video, words, and, of course, music. Laurie Anderson (American, b. 1947) is trained, as are many performance artists, in the visual arts; however, she is now known mostly as a composer/performer and has wide followings among both concert and rock music listeners. Anderson's compositions are intended specifically for her own performances, no two of which are alike. Her music tends to be modal, minimal, and rhythmically driving in the manner of rock music, and she frequently uses ostinato. Her creations involve electronics, live performance, and movement. She describes herself as a storyteller and says that "the gadgets don't matter if the emotional center, and the words, aren't there . . ."

MIDI Technology

In the early 1980s, digital technology was increasingly applied to portable keyboard synthesizers, culminating in 1983 in the establishment of an industry standard for connecting digital musical instruments called *MIDI* (Music Instrument Digital Interface). This development has facilitated the interfacing of personal computers with digital keyboards, and much software now exists for creating, editing, storing, and manipulating musical information in computer-readable form. The implications of MIDI networks involving synthesis equipment, computers, and analog or digital recording technology on the future direction of music are now being explored, but the impact has already been felt on commercial music applications, in instructional applications, and in music publishing. In recent years a thriving international community of MIDI-based musicians has formed on the World Wide Web (WWW), sharing MIDI files of their compositions and arrangements with one another and the world at large.

Computer-Assisted Composition

Computer-assisted composition has largely shifted from large mainframe computer systems to MIDI networks using personal computers, putting this technology in the hands of individual composers. In the 1980s, computer programs such as *M, Jam Factory, Music Mouse,* and *Cybernetic Composer* were developed and marketed, moving computer-assisted composition out of the realm of experimentation and into the mainstream (figure 17.7). Many amateur musicians now engage in computer-assisted composition as a form of recreation.

Figure 17.7

An example of a screen from *Jam Factory.*

© 1990 Dr. T's Music Software.

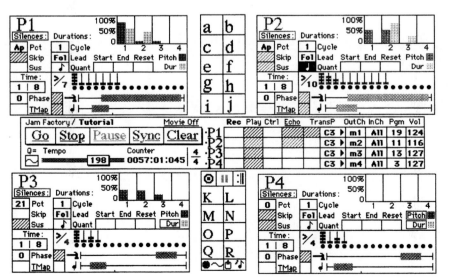

The development of *CD-ROM* (Compact Disc Read-Only Memory) has allowed composers such as Morton Subotnick (b. 1933) to create multimedia compositions involving video and audio materials that the listener can interact with in real time using personal computers. His *All My Hummingbirds Have Alibis* and *5 Scenes from an Imaginary Ballet,* both produced on CD-ROM, are examples of this interactive medium. The advent of *CD-I* (Interactive Compact Discs) in the mid 1990s allows listeners to interact with prerecorded music played on home audio equipment to change such elements as tempo, relative intensity of various elements, and other large-scale aspects of the music they are listening to. It would seem that audience interaction and participation, long a goal of the avant-garde, is well on its way to fruition through the strides made in digital technology.

Sampling Systems

An outgrowth of digital recording technology, *sampling systems* produce their sounds by recording and playing back acoustic sounds. This makes possible the electronic simulation of all acoustic instruments. The full potential of this technology was first explored in commercial music, but these systems have made their way to the concert hall in recent years. Libby Larsen (b. 1950) has employed sampling synthesizers in orchestral works such as *Ghost of an Old Ceremony* and *Schöenberg, Schenker, and Schillinger.* With the development of computer software to sample and record sounds, virtually any sound can be recorded and manipulated to create music. Composers wishing to create *musique concrète* (see p. 317) compositions now have powerful digital tools at their disposal.

Post-1970 Rock

By the early 1970s, the term *rock* was used for all popular music, regardless of style. During the 1970s and 1980s, rock music employed a basic instrumentation consisting of electric guitars, bass, keyboards, and drums. (These instruments have been gradually augmented or replaced by digital instruments with the advent of MIDI instrumentation.) Much of this music was sophisticated, being derived in part from the style of the late Beatles albums. A blending of jazz and rock began in the 1970s, resulting in a style called *fusion.* In the later 1970s, new types of rock (*punk* and *new wave*) represented a return to the simplicity and directness of rock 'n' roll. At the same time, a more commercial type of rock-based music, called *pop,* arose. The advent of music videos, MTV, and other video programs in the 1980s marked a radical departure for all commercial popular music, and popular music has become conceived in visual as well as aural terms. In the late 1980s, a type of African-American street poetry was fused by inner-city disk jockeys (DJs) with background music derived from a late-seventies African-American style known as *funk* to form a style known as *rap.* These background sounds were originally done by mixing sounds from recordings in a live setting, either in the studio or in concert. More recently, there has been an extensive use of sampling synthesizers to produce rap music.

New Age Music

In the 1980s, elements of minimalism, jazz, and electronic music were fused into a genre that has come to be called *new age,* or "space," music. This largely instrumental music is characterized by a static or very slow harmonic rhythm and an interest in complex textures with sensuous appeal; it has relaxation or reflection as its goal. Composers who have contributed to this eclectic popular music include: minimalists such as Phillip Glass (b. 1937), Terry Riley (b. 1935), and Harold Budd (b. 1936); jazz composers such as Keith Jarrett (b. 1945), Paul Winter (b. 1939), and Pat Metheny (b. 1954); experimentalists such as David Hykes (b. 1953); commercial musicians such as Chip Davis (b. 1947) (Mannheim Steamroller, Fresh Aire); and electronic composers such as Wendy Carlos (b. 1939) and Kitaro (b. 1953).

Ambient Music

Spearheaded by the work of Don G. Campbell (b. 1946) and based on the work of French physician and psychologist Alfred A. Tomatis (b. 1920), some composers are producing compositions whose purpose is to create feelings of well-being and even to effect changes in the physical and mental health of listeners.

World Music

In the 1980s, as a direct result of the availability of recordings and the tremendous increases in worldwide communication and travel, the concept of *world music* began to develop. Popular music of the West (primarily England and the United States) had been disseminated to and imitated in many countries in Asia and Africa, often superseding the traditional music of these cultures. Now the traditional music of Asia and Africa has begun to seriously influence the popular music of the West. Musicians such as Paul Winter (b. 1939), David Amram (b. 1930), Brian Eno (b. 1948), and Paul Simon (b. 1941) have incorporated much non-Western music into their compositions. Even in the concert hall, the last bastian of western European art music, composers such as John Corigliano (b. 1938), Kay Gardner (b. 1941), Toru Takemitsu (1930–1996), and R. Murray Schafer (b. 1933) have contributed works that are strongly influenced by non-Western music. Many people see the gradual emergence of a new international style, understood and appreciated by people all over the world as a result of the musical cross-fertilization that is now taking place.

Conclusions

Today's music is rich in diversity. It appears that the rigorous experimentation of the avant-garde has yielded the center stage to post-modernism, a philosophy that tolerates not only the uncompromisingly original but also innovative combinations of tradition and invention, tonality and atonality, Eastern and Western music, popular music and art music, and trained and untrained musicians.

Audiences enjoy the new music, and composers enjoy the attention. Although no one can predict which recent developments will retain their importance in the future, we can all be grateful for the enormous variety of music that is available to us now.

APPENDIX A

Macro Analysis

Symbols

Macro analysis is a sophisticated strategy that may be employed along with, or instead of, more conventional methods of analysis. An introduction to the system is presented in Volume 1. The following is a summary and continuation of the analysis system.

Macro analysis symbols are written as follows:

1. Major triads are represented by uppercase letter names.
2. Minor triads are represented by lowercase letter names.
3. Diminished triads are represented by a lowercase letter name followed by a ° symbol.
4. Augmented triads are represented by an uppercase letter name followed by a + sign.

Figure A.1

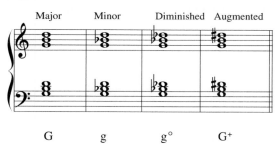

| Major   Minor   Diminished   Augmented |
| G   g   g°   G+ |

5. The numbers ^{7}, ^{9}, ^{11}, and ^{13} may be added to the above letter symbols to represent 7th, 9th, 11th, and 13th chords.

Slurs

One of the strongest driving forces in music is harmonic progression. In macro analysis, this motion is illustrated with slur markings:

1. Use a solid slur line when chord roots move by either an ascending fourth or a descending fifth.
2. Use a dotted slur line for chord progressions involving leading-tone chords. Even though the vii° chord functions in the same manner as the V, it is not a true V chord and thus is represented with a different type of slur.
3. Attach these slur markings to the letter names representing each chord.

Circle Progressions

Slurs are applied to the letter names of circle progressions in macro analysis (figure A.2). One segment of this progression does not include an ascending perfect fourth, yet is considered part of the circle progression. A tritone occurs between the second and third chord of the series in major keys and between the fifth and sixth chord in minor keys.

Figure A.2

Handel: Suite (Partita) in G Major (G 211–217).

Chromatic Harmony

Macro analysis provides the same advantage in locating chromatic harmonies as it does diatonic harmony. Analyzing the letter names of the chords simplifies the process of identifying harmonies that are not diatonic. If a letter name is not a part of the original key, it will be a chord from one of the chromatic categories.

Macro analysis is a very flexible system. You may wish to add your own symbols for other types of harmonic progressions, such as 3rd relationships, or any of the other chromatic harmonies presented on the following pages.

Borrowed Chords

Letter-name analysis: The letter name represents quality of chord.
Slurs: If the borrowed chord is substituted for a harmony that is in a position to receive a slur, the borrowed chord letter name is slurred also.

Figure A.3

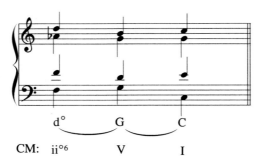

9th, 11th, and 13th Chords

Letter-name analysis: The letter name represents quality of chord and is followed by a ^{9}, ^{11}, or ^{13} as needed.
Slurs: 9th, 11th, and 13th chords are slurred like any other harmony that is in a position to receive a slur.

Figure A.4

Joplin: "The Augustine Club Waltz," mm. 128–132.

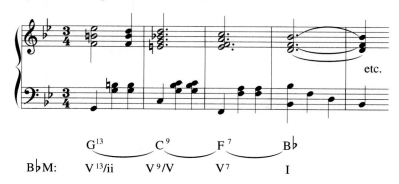

	G¹³	C⁹	F⁷	B♭
B♭M:	V¹³/ii	V⁹/V	V⁷	I

Neapolitan 6th Chord

Letter-name analysis: The letter name represents quality of chord.
Slurs: The Neapolitan 6th chord is slurred like any other harmony if it is in a position to receive a slur.

Figure A.5

Schubert: *Der Müller und der Bach* (The Miller and the Brook) from *Die schöne Müllerin* (The Beautiful Miller's Daughter), op. 25, no. 19, D. 795, mm. 22–27.

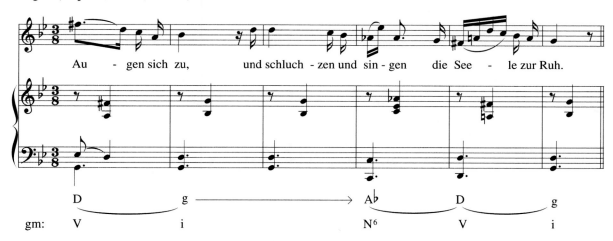

Au - gen sich zu, und schluch - zen und sin - gen die See - le zur Ruh.

	D	g	A♭	D	g
gm:	V	i	N⁶	V	i

Augmented 6th Chords

Letter-name analysis: These chords are *not* represented by a letter name but rather by the augmented 6th chord symbols: It⁶, Gr⁶, and Fr⁶.
Slurs: These chords are not slurred.

Figure A.6

Mozart: *Das Veilchen* (The Violet), K. 476, mm. 39–42.

Altered Dominants

Letter-name analysis: The letter name represents the quality of the chord. Other symbols that represent the type of alteration should be included with the letter name.

Slurs: An altered dominant is slurred like any other harmony if it is in a position to receive a slur.

Figure A.7

Wolf: *Das verlassene Mägdlein* (The Forsaken Maiden) from *Gedichte von Eduard Mörike*, no. 7, mm. 26–30.

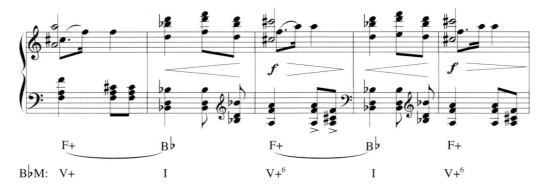

Chromatic Mediants

Letter-name analysis: The letter name represents the quality of the chord.

Slurs: Because of the way a chromatic mediant moves, it will usually not be slurred; however, if the chromatic mediant *does* occur in a position that would require a slur, it can be slurred.

Figure A.8

Brahms: Symphony No. 3, op. 90, in F Major, II (Andante), mm. 128–131.

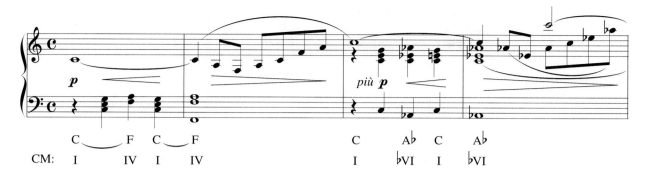

Some Questions

The following questions are issues to consider when thinking about macro analysis.

1. What is occurring in the music when there are no circle progressions? How can this be illustrated in the analysis?
2. Can melody be incorporated in the analysis?
3. How many different ways do circle progressions function? Some function as a way to move quickly from one place to another (e.g., in a sequence). Some are a part of the thematic material itself. What other functions can you identify?

Popular Music Chord Symbols

Comprehensive List of Chords Found in Popular Music

Following is a comprehensive list of chords found in popular song accompaniments. All are based on C but may be transposed to any other tone. This chart follows the recommendations of Brandt and Roemer's *Standardized Chord Symbol Notation* (Roevik Music Co., Sherman Oaks, CA, 1976).

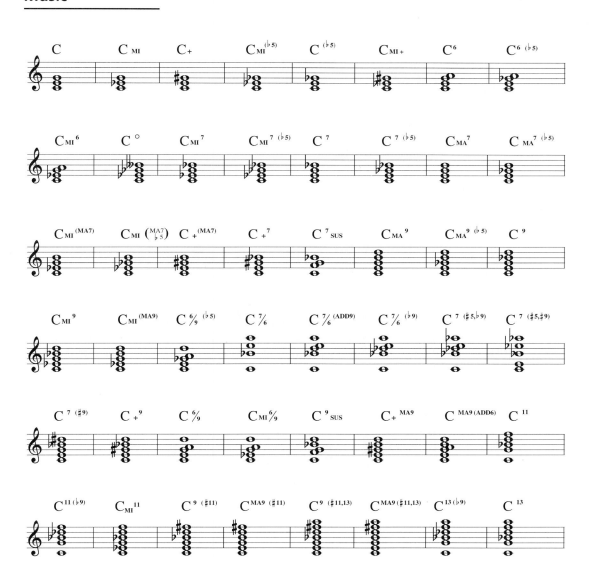

Alternate chord symbols for some common chords:

C~MI~ = Cm   c

C~MI~^(♭5)^ = Cdim   C °

C~+~ = Caug   C ^+5^

C~MI~ ^6^ = Cm6   Cmi^(6)^

C ^7^ = C7   C^7th^   C^♭7^

C~MA~^7^ = C^Δ^   C^Δ7^   CM7

C~MI~ ^7^ = Cm7   Cmi7   Cmin7

C ° = C-   Cdim   C^°7^

C ^7^~SUS~ = Csus7   C7^(ADD F)^

Chord inversions are shown by the addition of a diagonal line to the right of the basic chord symbol, followed by the letter denoting the bass note for the inversion (a, below). The diagonal line can also be used to indicate a bass note that is dissonant with the chord above (b, below).

Composers and Works

Composer	Dates	Composition	Page(s)
Babbitt, Milton	1916–	*First Composition* from *Three Compositions for Piano*	314
Bach, J. S.	1685–1750	Duet no. 2 in F Major from *Clavier-Übung,* Part III, BWV 803	53
Bach, J. S.		English Suite no. 1, BWV 806 in A Major (Gigue)	37
Bach, J. S.		Evangelist's recitativo from St. Matthew's Passion, BWV 244, no. 68	82
Bach, J. S.		Fugue no. 1, BWV 846 in C Major from *The Well-Tempered Clavier,* Book I	51
Bach, J. S.		Fugue no. 2, BWV 847 in C Minor from *The Well-Tempered Clavier,* Book I	49, 50, 54–58
Bach, J. S.		Fugue no. 8, BWV 853 in D-sharp Minor from *The Well-Tempered Clavier,* Book I	47, 51
Bach, J. S.		Fugue no. 9, BWV 878 in E Major from *The Well-Tempered Clavier,* Book II	52
Bach, J. S.		Fugue no. 16, BWV 861 in G Minor from *The Well-Tempered Clavier,* Book I	61, 64–66
Bach, J. S.		Invention no. 4, BWV 775 in D Minor from *Fifteen Two-Part Inventions*	27, 28, 29, 30–33
Bach, J. S.		Invention no. 8, BWV 779 in F Major from *Fifteen Two-Part Inventions*	39–40
Bach, J. S.		*Jesu, meine Freude* (Jesus My Joy), BWV 358	72
Bach, J. S.		Organ Fugue in C Minor, BWV 574	48
Bach, J. S.		Retrograde canon from *Musikalisches Opfer* (Musical Offering) BWV 1079	52
Bach, J. S.		*Vater unser im Himmelreich* (Our Father in Heaven), BWV 416	71
Bach, J. S.		*Wo Gott zum Haus nicht gibt sein Gunst* (If God does not give His Blessings), BWV 438	78
Bartók, Béla	1881–1945	*Chromatic Invention,* no. 91 from *Mikrokosmos,* vol. 3	284–285, 288
Bartók, Béla		*Major and Minor,* no. 59 from *Mikrokosmos,* vol. 2	263
Bartók, Béla		*Song of the Harvest,* no. 33 from *Forty-Four Violin Duets*	293–294
Beethoven, Ludwig van	1770–1827	Bagatelle, op. 119, no. 9	89
Beethoven, Ludwig van		Seven Variations on "God Save the King," WoO 78	113, 114, 115, 116
Beethoven, Ludwig van		Sonata (Moonlight), in C-sharp Minor, op. 27, no. 2, I, (Adagio Sostenuto)	80
Beethoven, Ludwig van		Sonata in F Minor, op. 2, no. 1, I	106, 149–158
Beethoven, Ludwig van		Sonata in C Minor (Pathétique), op. 13, no. 8	107
Beethoven, Ludwig van		Thirty-two Variations, WoO 80, Variation, XXX	106
Beethoven, Ludwig van		Twenty-four Variations on Righini's air *Venni Amore,* WoO 65	121–127
Berg, Alban	1885–1935	*Wozzeck,* op. 7, Act I, scene 3, "Marie's Lullaby"	266
Bloch, Ernest	1880–1959	"Chanty" from *Poems of the Sea*	229–230
Boulanger, Lili	1893–1918	*Je garde une médaille d'elle* (I Keep a Medal of Hers)	259–260
Brahms, Johannes	1833–1897	Symphony No. 3, in F Major, op. 90, II (Andante)	195, 331
Cage, John	1912–1992	*Aria*	316
Chopin, Frédéric	1810–1849	Mazurka, op. 7, no. 2	89
Chopin, Frédéric		Prelude, op. 28, no. 4	216–217
Chopin, Frédéric		Prelude, op. 28, no. 9	199–200
Chopin, Frédéric		Prelude, op. 28, no. 12	83
Chopin, Frédéric		Prelude, op. 28, no. 20	204, 206
Chopin, Frédéric		Prelude, op. 28, no. 21	207
Chopin, Frédéric		Prelude, op. 28, no. 22	98
Chopin, Frédéric		Scherzo, op. 39	88
Chopin, Frédéric		Valse, op. 64, no. 2	88

Composer	Dates	Composition	Page(s)
Davidovsky, Mario	1934–	*Synchronisms,* No. 3 for Cello and Electronic Sound	317
Debussy, Claude	1862–1918	*Ce qu'a vu le vent de l'Ouest* (What the West Wind Saw), no. 7 from Preludes, Book I	240
Debussy, Claude		*Clair de lune* (Moonlight) from *Suite Bergamasque*	237
Debussy, Claude		*La Cathédrale engloutie* (The Engulfed Cathedral) no. 10 from Preludes, Book I	235, 242–251
Debussy, Claude		*La Soirée dans Grenade* (Evening in Granada) from *Estampes* (Prints)	234, 241
Debussy, Claude		*Le vent dans la plaine* (The Wind on the Plain) no. 3, from Preludes, Book I	236
Debussy, Claude		*Six Morceaux Choisis,* no. 3, Menuet	238
Debussy, Claude		*Pelléas et Mélisande,* Act 1, scene 1	235
Debussy, Claude		*Sarabande* from *Pour le Piano* (For the Piano)	240, 257–258
Debussy, Claude		*Voiles* (Sails) no. 2 from Preludes, Book I	230, 231
Dodge, Charles	1942-	*In Celebration* (based on the poem by Mark Strand)	319
Dufay, Guillaume	1398?-1474	*Missa Sancti Jacobi,* IX *(Communio)*	239
Ellington, Duke (and Billy Strayhorn)	1899–1974	"Day Dream"	190–191
Franck, César	1822–1890	*Choral no. I pour Grand Orgue*	218
Handel, George F.	1685–1759	Suite (Partita) in G Major, G 211–217	328
Haydn, Franz Joseph	1732–1809	Sonata in E Minor, Hob. XVI:34, I (Presto)	82
Haydn, Franz Joseph		Sonata in C Major, Hob. XVI:35, III	167–170
Haydn, Franz Joseph		Sonata in G Major, Hob. XVI:G1, I	130–134
Haydn, Franz Joseph		Symphony No. 97, II	96
Hindemith, Paul	1895–1963	Piano Sonata no. 2, I	264
Ives, Charles	1874–1954	"The Cage" (no. 64 of 114 Songs)	265
Joplin, Scott	1868–1917	"Bink's Waltz"	99
Joplin, Scott		"The Augustine Club Waltz"	176, 329
Joplin, Scott		"The Cascades"	104
Joplin, Scott		"The Chrysanthemum"	104
Josquin des Prez	1440?-1521	*Missa Da pacem,* Credo	6
Josquin des Prez		*Missa l'homme armé super voces musicales* (Mass based on The Armed Man), Benedictus	5
Lang, Josephine	1815–1880	*"Fee 'n-Reigen"* (The Dance of the Fairies)	210
Lassus, Orlande de	1532–1594	*Beatus homo* (Happy is the man . . .)	3, 12, 16–18, 19
Lassus, Orlande de		*Beatus vir in sapientia* (Blessed is the man)	6
Lassus, Orlande de		*Missa ad imitationem moduli Iager (Jäger),* Benedictus	21
Lassus, Orlande de		*Qui vult venire post me* (He would follow me)	13
Lassus, Orlande de		*Serve bone* (Well done)	7
Lucier, Alvin	1931-	*I Am Sitting in a Room*	318
Mercer, Johnny (and Harold Arlen)	1890–1976	"My Shining Hour"	186
Mussorgsky, Modest	1839–1881	*Boris Godunov,* Act III, scene 1	227–228
Mozart, Wolfgang Amadeus	1756–1791	*Das Veilchen* (The Violet), K. 476	97, 330
Mozart, Wolfgang Amadeus		Fantasia, K. 397 in D Minor	81
Mozart, Wolfgang Amadeus		Sonata in C Major, K. 309, I	135–144
Mozart, Wolfgang Amadeus		Sonata in C Major, K. 545, III	161–164
Mozart, Wolfgang Amadeus		Sonata in F Major, K. 332, III	105
Mozart, Wolfgang Amadeus		Sonata in D Major, K. 284, III Variation VII	105
Palestrina, Giovanni Pierluigi da	1525?-1594	*Alleluja, tulerunt* (Hallelujah, they had borne . . .)	14, 15
Palestrina, Giovanni Pierluigi da		*Magnificat Secundi Toni: De posuit potentes*	13
Palestrina, Giovanni Pierluigi da		*Missa Jam Christus astra ascenderat,* Credo	9, 23–26
Palestrina, Giovanni Pierluigi da		*Missa Inviolata,* Credo	8
Penderecki, Krzysztof	1933-	*Threnos Den Opfern von Hiroschima* (Threnody to the Victims of Hiroshima)	320–321
Pisk, Paul	1893-?	"Nocturnal Interlude" from *New Music for the Piano*	366
Prokofiev, Sergei	1891–1953	Piano Sonata no. 8 in B-flat Major, op. 84, II	263
Prokofiev, Sergei		*The Moon Strolls in the Meadows* from *Music for Children,* op. 65, no. 12	84
Raison, André	1650?-1719	Passacaille in G Minor from *Messe du Deuxieme Ton* (Mass of the Second Tone)	112
Ravel, Maurice	1875–1937	*Pavane pour une Infante défunte* (Pavane for a Dead Princess)	182–183
Ravel, Maurice		*Sonatine,* I	98, 233, 237–238
Ravel, Maurice		*Sonatine,* II	232, 236
Ravel, Maurice		*Valses nobles et sentimentales* (Noble and Sentimental Waltzes)	175, 233
Reich, Steve	1936-	Four Organs	323
Respighi, Ottorino	1879–1936	*Trittico Botticelliano* (Botticelli Triptych)	230
Satie, Erik	1866–1925	*Gymnopedie,* no. 2	239

Composer	Dates	Composition	Page(s)
Schoenberg, Arnold	1874–1951	Variations for Orchestra, op. 31 (Theme)	309–311
Schubert, Franz	1797–1828	*Das Wirtshaus* (The Inn) from *Die Winterreise* (Winter's Journey) op. 89, no. 21, D. 911	70
Schubert, Franz		*Der Doppelgänger* (The Double) from *Schwanengesang* (Swan Song), D. 957, no. 13	83
Schubert, Franz		*Moment Musical* op. 94, no. 2, D. 780	68
Schubert, Franz		*Der Müller und der Bach* (The Miller and the Brook) from *Die schöne Müllerin* (The Miller's Beautiful Daughter), op. 25, no. 19, D. 795	80, 329
Schubert, Franz		String Quartet, op. 29, D. 804 in A Minor, I	209
Schubert, Franz		Symphony in B Minor ("Unfinished"), D. 759, I	205
Schubert, Franz		Waltz from *Original Tänze für Klavier* (Original Dances for Piano), op. 9, no. 22, D. 365	203
Schubert, Franz		*Wanderers Nachtlied* (Wanderers' Night Song). op. 96, no. 3, II, D. 768	71
Schuman, William	1910–1992	No. 2 from Three Score Set	265
Schumann, Robert	1810–1856	*Am leuchtenden Sommermorgen* (On a Shining Summer Morning) from *Dichterliebe* (Poet's Love) op. 48, no. 12	204
Schumann, Robert		*Ich kann niche fassen* (I Cannot Comprehend) from *Frauenlieben und Leben* (A Woman's Life and Loves), op. 42, no. 3	94
Schumann, Robert		*Im wunderschönen Monat Mai* (In the Wonderful Month of May) from *Dichterliebe* (Poet's Love) op. 48, no. I	206
Schumann, Robert		*Kleine Studie* (Short Study) from *Album for the Young*, op. 68, no. 14	174
Sousa, John Philip	1854–1932	*The Free Lance*	95
Sousa, John Philip		*The Liberty Bell*	95
Strauss, Richard	1864–1949	*Allerseelen* (All Souls Day), op. 10, no. 8	226
Strauss, Richard		*Zeitlose* (Meadow Saffron), op. 10, no. 7	228
Stravinsky, Igor	1882–1971	*Marche du Soldat* (Soldier's March) from *l'Histoire du Soldat* (The Soldier's Tale)	269–276
Stravinsky, Igor		Sonata for Two Pianos, II (Theme with Variations), Variation I	262
Stravinsky, Igor		Triumphal March of the Devil from *l'Histoire du Soldat* (The Soldier's Tale)	267
Tchaikovsky, Peter	1840–1893	Nutcracker Suite, op. 71a, III (*Valse des Fleurs*)	211
Tchaikovsky, Peter		Piano concerto no. 1 op. 23, in B-flat Minor, II	107
Turpin, Tom	?-?	"The St. Louis Rag"	104
Victoria, Tomás Luis de	1548–1611	*Magnificat Septimi Toni: De posuit potentes*	9
von Paradis, Maria Theresia	1759–1824	*Sicilienne*	90–92
Wagner, Richard	1813–1883	*Tristan und Isolde,* Prelude to Act I	207, 224
Wagner, Richard		*Tristan und Isolde,* Act II, scene 2	175, 219–220
Webern, Anton	1883–1945	*Des Herzens Purpurvogel fliegt durch Nacht* (The Heart's Purple Eagle Flies by Night), no. 2 from *Drei Lieder* (Three Songs), op. 25	307–308
Webern, Anton		*Wie bin ich froh!* (How Happy I Am!), no. I from *Drei Lieder* (Three Songs), op. 25	299–301
Wolf, Hugo	1860–1903	*Das verlassene Mägdlein* (The Forsaken Maiden) from *Gedichte von Eduard Mörike*, no. 7	186, 229, 330
Wolf, Hugo		*Der Knabe und das Immlein* (The Boy and the Bee) from *Gedichte von Eduard Mörike*	225
Wolf, Hugo		*Der Mond hat eine schwere Klag erhoben* (The moon hath been most grievously complaining) from *Italienisches Liederbuch*	255–257
Wolf, Hugo		*Wiegenlied* (Cradlesong)	73
Zipoli, Domenico	1688–1726	Toccata	97

Glossary

Aggregate   The total. (Example: The first six tones of a twelve-tone series form an aggregate with the second six tones.)

Aleatory (also Aleatoric)   Interchangeable with indeterminacy. See *indeterminacy*.

Altered chord   A chord that contains one or more factors that are not part of the prevailing diatonic system.

Altered dominant   A dominant triad or a 7th chord that contains a raised or lowered 5th and sometimes a lowered 3rd. (Example: G B D♯ F = altered dominant [V^{+7}] in C Major.)

Analog   An exact representation of something in a medium different from that of the original.

Answer (in a fugue)   Imitation of the fugue subject usually at the interval of a P5th higher or P4th lower.

Answer—real   See *real answer*.

Answer—tonal   See *tonal answer*.

Asymmetric meter   Meter in which the beats are not grouped into units divisible by two or three (Examples: $\frac{7}{8}$ and $\frac{5}{4}$ meters). Also known as *irregular* or *combination* meter.

Augmentation   A melody in increased (usually doubled) note values. (Example: In augmentation, a melody in quarter notes becomes a melody in half notes.)

Augmented 6th chords   A type of altered chord that contains the interval of an augmented 6th. The three most common types (up from the lowest-sounding tone): (1) *Italian*—M3rd and A6th; (2) *German*—M3rd, P5th, and A6th; and (3) *French*—M3rd, A4th, and A6th. The bass note is most frequently an M3rd below the tonic. Symbols: It^6, Gr^6, and Fr^6.

Avant-garde   Music or composers characterized primarily by unorthodox or experimental ideas. Applies as well to other art media.

Basso continuo   Same as *figured bass*. Usually performed by a cello, viola da gamba, or bassoon playing the bass line while a harpsichordist or pianist plays the bass notes and adds the chords as indicated by the figures (numbers).

Basso ostinato   See *ground*.

Best normal order   If a set of pitches contains two larger intervals of the same size, the best normal order is the arrangement that is most densely packed to the left of the set. See *normal order*.

Bitonality   See *polytonality*.

Borrowed chord   A chord borrowed from the parallel major or minor key. (Example: A C E♭ is a borrowed [from G Minor] chord in G Major.)

Bridge (in a fugue)   A short passage in the exposition of a fugue between entrances of the subject or answer. Acts as a modulatory passage for return to the tonic of the subject that ends in the dominant.

Bridge passage   Another term for "transition." Connects two themes. See *transition*.

Cadence—linear   See *linear cadence*.

Chance music   Interchangeable with indeterminacy. See *indeterminacy*.

Changing meters   Meter changes within a composition to show rhythmic patterns more clearly than could a single constant meter.

Chord cluster   A chord with three or more factors of which each is no more than a whole step from its adjacent factor. (Example: C C♯ D E when sounded together is a chord cluster.)

Chords of addition and omission   Chords with added or deleted tones. (A common example of an added tone chord: C E G A—the A is an added tone. Example of a chord of omission: C G C—the 3rd is omitted from the triad.)

Chromatic mediant chords   The altered mediant and submediant triads and 7th chords on occasion. (Example: E G♯ B = III in C Major.) Not common in any style, but found most often in the late romantic period.

Clausula vera   The most common cadence in two-voiced, sixteenth-century choral writing. The voices either expand to an octave (from a 6th) or contract to a unison (from a 3rd).

Cluster   See *chord cluster*.

Coda   Technically an expanded cadence. Occurs at the end of a composition and traditionally brings the composition to a convincing conclusion. May consist of a few measures or an entire subdivision in itself.

Combination meter   See *asymmetric meter.*

Combinatoriality   The combination of the first hexachords (first six tones) of two different set forms to produce all twelve tones. (Example: When the first six tones of a particular P^0 and the first six tones of I^9 are combined, the result is all twelve tones of the series with no duplications.) See *aggregate.*

Contrary motion   See *inversion—melodic.*

Countermotive   Counterpoint accompaniment to the motive in an invention. In some inventions the countermotive is utilized in ensuing developmental material.

Countersubject (of a fugue)   The continuation of counterpoint in the voice that has just completed the subject. In actuality, it should be called *counteranswer* because it appears with the answer. In most fugues, the countersubject is a fertile source of material for the remainder of the composition.

Derived set   A twelve-tone set different in order from another but retaining some particular characteristics of the original. (Example: Deriving a twelve-tone set from a prime with a particular trichord type, 0 1 6, as its first segment. The derived set might be manipulated to contain a series of four 0 1 6 trichords.)

Development (in a fugue)   The subject, answer, or possibly countersubject are stated in various keys connected by episodes (brief sections that contain neither the subject nor the answer) after the exposition has been completed.

Development (of a sonata form)   The middle section of a movement or composition in sonata allegro form. The function of this division is to depart from the tonality at the end of the exposition and to form a transition to the tonic of the recapitulation, thereby providing an opportunity to develop the themes of the exposition through variation, alteration, fragmentation, modification, and mutation. The development section is characterized by restless modulation, agitation, and increased tension.

Diminution   A melody in decreased (usually halved) note values. (Example: In diminution, a melody in quarter notes becomes a melody in eighth notes.)

Dodecaphonic   Term used to describe twelve-tone serial writing.

Dual modality   Simultaneous use of major and minor mode or combinations of church modes. Usually the two modes have the same tonic or final.

Duodecuple scale   See *scale—duodecuple.*

Dyad   Two pitches. Generally used when describing segments of a twelve-tone series. Has both melodic and harmonic connotations.

Eclecticism   Derives from the word *eclectic*. In music it refers to the borrowing of devices or ideas from many existing styles.

Electronic music   Music that is electronically produced and processed.

Eleventh chord   A superposition of five 3rds—one 3rd above the 9th of a 9th chord. (Example: G B D F A C = V^{11} in C Major.)

Episode   A short interlude in the development section of a fugue that does not contain the subject or answer but connects entrances of either in various keys. Most development sections contain a number of episodes.

Equivalences   A trichord or tetrachord in two or more arrangements or registrations but having the same intervallic content.

Exposition (of a fugue)   The first section of a fugue. Consists of an entrance in all voices of either the fugue subject or answer. When all voices have entered, the exposition gives way to the development.

Exposition (of a sonata form)   The first large section of sonata allegro form containing at least two contrasting key relationships and more often two or three contrasting themes set apart by transitions.

Expressionism   A reaction to impressionism. Its proponents hoped to create music that would be an expression of their inner world in contrast to the impressionists, who sought to represent their impressions of the external world.

Extended technique   Usually refers to traditional instruments that are played in unusual ways but may also include amplifiers and noninstruments such as sirens and auto horns. Examples include plucking piano strings, striking a harp with the knuckles, and singing into the piano with the damper pedal down.

Free atonality   A kind of atonal writing that allows free use of the twelve tones of the chromatic scale but does not order or prescribe the arrangement as in serial technique.

Free tonality   Term used to designate music that contains a definite tonal center but is not related to traditional major or minor keys. As opposed to chromaticism, which also utilizes a wide variety of tones but is placed in a setting of functional harmony where each scale degree (and its chromatic alterations) has a traditional role in the operation of key-centered tonality.

French augmented 6th chord   See *augmented 6th chords.*

Fugue   A contrapuntal composition in two or more voices, based on a subject (theme) that is introduced at the beginning in imitation and recurs frequently in the course of the composition. A monothematic composition, except for double or triple fugues that contain two or three subjects.

Fusion   A form of popular music beginning in the 1970s that blended elements of jazz and rock.

German augmented 6th chord   See *augmented 6th chords.*

Graphic notation   A score where musical textures and events are implied through the use of graphic analogs (analogies). A dark area on a score may imply loud sounds while a white area suggests silence.

Ground   A short melodic figure of four to eight measures maintained in the lowest voice and repeated throughout the composition. Same as basso ostinato.

Hexachord   Six pitches. In the Middle Ages and the Renaissance, it referred to a six-tone segment of the total diatonic range, or gamut. Generally used when describing segments of the twelve-tone series. Has both melodic and harmonic connotations.

Hocket (thirteenth century)   Adjacent notes and rests alternating among different voices or parts in such a way that one voice is silent while the other sings.

Hocket (sixteenth century)   The overlapping of phrases at the cadence point where one voice rests and then immediately begins the new phrase.

Imitation   The restatement in close succession of melodic figures in different voices in polyphonic textures.

Indeterminacy   Indefinite or uncertain. Refers in music to some aspect of a composition that the composer places beyond his conscious control and that is thus left to chance.

Interval class   Intervals (not including the unison) may be grouped in six interval classes by the number of half steps between the two pitch classes. In this system only the numbers 1 through 6 are used, and intervals of greater than six half steps are grouped with their inversions. (Example: Interval class 1 contains both the m2 and the M7.)

Inversion (of a twelve-tone series and pitch-class set) The reversal of the direction (up or down) of each successive tone of the prime series, starting with the first tone (symbol: I^0). Transposed up a half step, the inversion becomes I^1, another half step up I^2, and so on.

Inversion (of the vertical order of voices)   A device in counterpoint in which the vertical order of two simultaneous voices is reversed. When the counterpoint is purposely contrived to sound as well in the "upside down" order, it is known as *invertible counterpoint.* Inversion of vertical order is not to be confused with melodic inversion in which the direction (up or down) of a single melody is reversed.

Inversion—melodic   Reversal of melodic direction. Upward direction in the original becomes downward direction in the inversion, an ascending 6th becomes a descending 6th, and a descending 3rd becomes an ascending 3rd. In tonal music, the inversion is usually diatonic rather than exact. Melodic inversion is synonymous with *contrary motion.*

Invertible counterpoint   Two-voiced counterpoint that is purposely contrived to sound as well in reversed (upside down) order. Inversion may be at any interval, but the octave is most common.

Irregular meter   See *asymmetric meter.*

Italian augmented 6th chord   See *augmented 6th chords.*

Linear cadence   Melodic lines that converge or diverge at the cadence point. Oblique motion is also possible.

Linear harmony   Harmony that results from melodic motion without regard for traditional (functional) harmonic progression.

Melismatic   Describes a style of vocal writing in which several or many pitches are set to a single syllable of a text.

Melodic doubling   The doubling of melodic lines to create parallel movement. Also called *melodic parallel.*

Melodic inversion   See *inversion—melodic.*

MIDI   **M**usical **I**nstrument **D**igital **I**nterface, a communications standard for connecting synthesizers to computers and other synthesizers.

Mikropolyphonie   A contemporary musical style featuring many-voiced, rhythmically intricate, highly chromatic counterpoint.

Minimalism   The gradual process of unfolding a very limited (minimal) body of motivic material, often with a high degree of literal repetition. The material is often simple, tonal/modal, and largely diatonic. A typical minimal composition, Steve Reich's *Four Organs,* consists entirely of a single chord whose individual tones are gradually augmented.

Modal mixture   A blending of the resources of the parallel major and minor scales that often results in modal ambiguity.

Monophony   A single line of melody with no accompaniment. (Example: Gregorian chant or folk melodies that do not require a supporting accompaniment.)

Movement   A unit of a larger work that may stand by itself as a complete composition. Such divisions are usually self-contained. Most often the sequence of movements is arranged fast-slow-fast or in some other order that provides contrast.

Musique concrète   Employs "live" sounds from the environment that are recorded and processed or modified by tape techniques such as splicing and varying the speed of the tape. One of the early types of electronic music.

Musica ficta   Accidentals added to modal compositions of the sixteenth century and earlier. Such accidentals were not included by the composers but were added by singers to eliminate tritones and provide leading tones for the modes that lacked them. Now *musica ficta* accidentals are usually written above the staff.

Nationalism   The use of materials that are identifiably national or regional in character, including folk music, folk stories, myths, or literature.

Neapolitan 6th chord   A major triad based on the lowered 2nd degree of the major or minor scale. (Example: D♭ F A♭ = N in C major.) Because the chord is most often found in first inversion, it is called the Neapolitan 6th.

Neoclassicism   A reaction to the freedom and lack of order in the form and content of compositions of the romantic period. A return to discipline, form, and symmetry of the classical period. Immediately followed the post-romantic and impressionistic period. Representative composer: Paul Hindemith.

New Age music   A form of popular music in the 1980s and 1990s consisting of a blend of minimalism, jazz, and electronic music. Also called *space music*.

Ninth chord   A superposition of four 3rds—one 3rd above the 7th of the 7th chord. (Example: G B D F A = V^9 in C Major.)

Nonaccentual rhythms   Absence of dynamic accents.

Nonfunctional harmony   Harmony that is more the result of voice leading than of harmonic progression within a major or minor key. See *linear harmony*.

Normal order   In set theory, the term indicates the ascending order of intervals (from small to large) of a trichord, tetrachord, pentachord, or hexachord. (Example: A trichord in normal order = 0 1 6 as against 0 6 1.)

Nota cambiata   A common dissonant melodic device of sixteenth-century vocal music. The decoration of a descending 3rd. The figure consists of four tones: a dotted half note that descends one step to a quarter note (the nota cambiata) and then descends a 3rd to a half note and up a step to another half note.

Octatonic scale   An eight-tone scale. The traditional octatonic scale is a pattern of alternating whole and half steps.

Order number   The number that represents the position of any given tone in the twelve-tone series. (Example: The 3rd tone in a given series is *order number* 2—remember that the first tone is always 0.)

Ostinato   A short musical pattern that is repeated again and again. Ostinato is often used as an accompaniment device but may be the central element in some folk music and in twentieth-century minimalism.

Palindrome   A literary term referring to a sentence that reads the same backward as forward. (Example: "Madam, I'm Adam.") In the context of twelve-tone serial music it denotes a series with the same interval content forward and backward.

Pandiatonicism   The use of the tones of a diatonic scale in such a way that each tone is stripped of its usual function in the key.

Parallel chords   Chords in which all factors or voices move in parallel motion. Parallel chords are sometimes diatonic (Example: C E G to D F A) and sometimes chromatic (Example: C E G to B D♯ F♯).

Parameter   Variables that are independent of each other. In music the word *parameter* most often refers to such basic components as pitch, melody, rhythm, timbre, and so on. As an example, pitch is a parameter that is independent of timbre—a given pitch may have a particular timbre, but no matter what timbre is selected the pitch remains the same.

Pentachord   Five pitches. Generally used when describing segments of the twelve-tone series or pitch-class set. Has both melodic and harmonic connotations.

Pentatonic scale   A five-tone scale. (Example: C D E G A [C].)

Permutation   A term used in connection with the twelve-tone series and involving a change of the order of a set.

Pitch class   A more recent term for a pitch. Considered broader because pitch class includes octave duplications, whereas a pitch designates only a single sound.

Planing   See *parallel chords*.

Polychord   Simultaneous use of two chords. Spacing is important in the use of polychords because the chords must be spaced sufficiently apart to be heard as two distinct entities.

Polyphony   Simultaneous interacting melodies. A texture of independent but compatible melodic layers sounding at the same time. (Examples: A Bach fugue, a Bach two-part invention, a Palestrina mass.) Music of both the Renaissance and the baroque period was predominantly polyphonic. The terms *polyphony* and *counterpoint* are used interchangeably.

Polytonality   Simultaneous use of two or more tonalities.

Portamento   A common dissonance found in sixteenth-century vocal writing, resembling the anticipation of harmonic counterpoint in the eighteenth century. Most often of quarter-note value in $\frac{4}{2}$ meter. Approached by step and left by repetition.

Pre-dominant   Any chord in functional harmony that normally resolves to the dominant chord. (Examples: IV, ii, N^6, Gr^6, etc.)

Prime series (in twelve-tone technique)   The twelve-tone series as it is originally constructed (symbol: P^0). The same series transposed up a half step is P^1, another half step is P^2, and so on.

Primitivism   A reaction to the refined and fragile music of such composers as Debussy. Its proponents sought to eliminate the subtlety and gentility of previous music and emphasize the mechanistic, the violent, the animal nature, and the more earthy aspects of music.

Quartal chords   Chords constructed through a superposition of 4ths rather than the conventional 3rds as in tertian harmony. (Example: B E A or B E A D.)

Quintal chords   Chords constructed through a superposition of 5ths rather than the Conventional 3rds as in tertian harmony. (Example: D A E B or A E B.)

Real answer   An exact transposition (usually interval by interval, but in any case by diatonic interval) of a fugal or other contrapuntal subject, usually at the P5th above or P4th below.

Recapitulation   The third section of a movement or composition in sonata allegro form. Contains the return of the themes stated in the exposition. Conventionally, all themes in the recapitulation are returned to the tonic key.

Recapitulation (of a fugue)   The third and final part of the fugue containing the return of the subject and/or answer in the tonic key of the composition. Not all fugues have recapitulations, and in some the recapitulation is quite abbreviated.

Retransition   A transition at the end of the development section in sonata allegro form that leads back to the first theme of the recapitulation.

Retrograde   A melody, subject, motive, and so on, in reverse order or backward. (Example: A melody C D G E F in retrograde is F E G D C.) *Cancrizans* is another term meaning "retrograde."

Retrograde (of a twelve-tone series)   The prime series sounded in reverse order from last to first. Symbol for the retrograde set is R^0, transposed up a half step it is R^1, transposed up another half step it is R^2, and so on. It is important to remember that R^0 begins on the last pitch of P^0.

Retrograde inversion (of a twelve-tone series)   The inversion of the prime series in reverse order from last pitch to first. Symbol for the retrograde inversion is RI^0, transposed up a half step it is RI^1, transposed up another half step it is RI^2, and so on. It is important to remember that the RI form begins on the last tone of I^0.

Rock music   The primary form of popular music in the mid–twentieth century characterized by a heavy bass beat. Beginning as "rock 'n' roll" in the 1950s, rock came to mean any form of popular music in the 1970s. See *fusion.*

Romanticism   The period of musical writing from roughly 1825 to 1900. Characterized by a tendency to accentuate the impulsive, the unusual, the adventuresome, the impetuous, and the passionate attitudes toward musical composition.

Scale-duodecuple   The twelve tones of the octave each with equal status. Although the older term *chromatic scale* also denotes twelve tones, its relation to key and tonal systems makes it inappropriate for present-day purposes. The term *duodecuple* is used in connection with serial music.

Serialism   An extension of the twelve-tone technique. An example is Milton Babbitt's composition *Three Compositions for Piano,* where other parameters such as rhythm, dynamics, articulations, and timbres (as well as pitch) are given a specific order.

Set   A collection of pitch classes, usually without regard to their order. See *normal order.*

Set type   Sets are classified according to the interval between the first pitch class of the set and each successive pitch class. The lowest pitch is assigned the number 0, and the other pitches are assigned numbers indicating their distance in half steps above the lowest pitch.

Shifted tonality   Sudden tonality change without preparation or modulation in the traditional sense.

Sonata A composition usually in three or four movements for (1) piano or harpsichord solo or (2) solo instrument and accompaniment. These multimovement compositions positions developed in the seventeenth century and attained their classic form in the mid–eighteenth century.

Sonata allegro form A compositional structure used most often in the first movement of a sonata, symphony, trio, string quartet, and so on. It consists of three main sections: an exposition, a development, and a recapitulation.

Sound mass Denotes a texture of such density and complexity that the parts cannot be distinguished individually.

Space music See *New Age music.*

Stochastic music Music written according to a system based on a probability distribution. After the probabilities have been set by the composer, random selections for various musical parameters are then chosen, usually by a computer. These selections are then used to write the composition.

Stretto (in a fugue) Overlapping of subjects (or answers) in different voices. A subject in one voice is not completed before the same subject is introduced in another voice.

Subject (of a fugue) A short melody that is used as the basis for a fugue.

Syllabic Describes a style of vocal writing in which one pitch is used for each syllable of a text. It contrasts with melismatic writing, which employs many notes per syllable.

Tetrachord Modern interpretation: a four-tone scale segment. (Example: C D E F is the lower tetrachord of the C Major scale.) The term was adapted from Greek music, where it referred to a four-tone scale segment in descending order.

Third relationship Relationship of a 3rd between roots of adjacent chords. When prominent progressions employ 3rd relationship in concentration or in succession, particularly ascending, tonal emphasis is decreased.

Third relationship cadence A cadence in which the roots of the two chords lie in 3rd relationship. (Example: E G# B progresses to C E G in a cadence.)

Thirteenth chord A superposition of six 3rds—one above the 11th of an 11th chord. (Example: G B D F A C E = V^{13} in C major.)

Tonal answer The subject (of a fugue) transposed usually to the P5th above or the P4th below. However, slight modifications are made in a tonal answer so that the intervallic distance is not always the same as in the subject. The modifications generally entail replacing dominant implications with tonic. Thus, if a fugue subject begins on the dominant tone, the answer begins on the tonic.

Total serialism All (or at least most) of the elements or dimensions of a twelve-tone serial composition are serialized. (Example: Serialization of pitch, intensity, duration, and timbre.)

Transition A passage that provides a musical link between one theme and the next. The term is used most often to designate passages in the exposition and recapitulation of sonata allegro form that furnish a smooth connection between themes.

Trichord Three pitches. Generally describes segments of twelve-tone sets. Has both melodic and harmonic connotations. *Trichord* is used in place of *triad* by contemporary composers and theorists because triad has key and tonal implications.

Tritone The common name for the A4 or d5 interval. Usually avoided in earlier practice, it became an important structural element in much twentieth-century music.

Twelve-tone row Same as *12-tone series. Series, set,* and *row* are used synonymously. Authors and composers of the 1960s and 1970s prefer the term *set.*

Variation—continuous A type of composition employing variation techniques in which the variations are fused together in the continuous flow of the music. The most common type employs a ground (basso ostinato).

Variation—principle The transformation of a melody, harmony, or rhythm with changes or elaborations. A modification of a melody, harmony, or rhythm, especially using one of the techniques developing the potential of the theme or subject material.

Variation—theme and variations A genre in which a theme, usually in sectional form, is stated simply and ends with a cadence. Variations follow this theme, maintaining sufficiently the character and form of the original to identify them as variations.

Whole-tone scale The harmonic or melodic use of a six-tone scale in which each degree is a whole step from the next. (Example: C D E F♯ G♯ A♯ [C].)

Index